PRACTICE PROBLEMS
and SOLUTIONS

to accompany

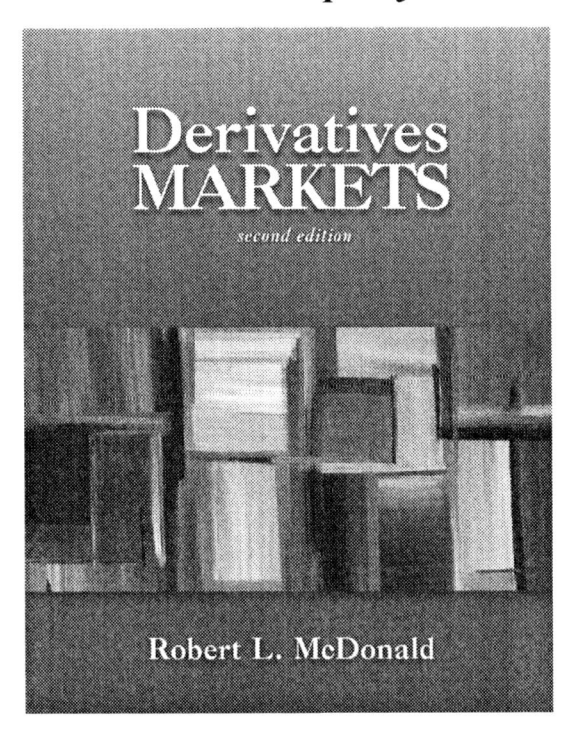

Rüdiger Fahlenbrach
The Ohio State University Fisher College of Business

PEARSON
Addison Wesley

Boston San Francisco New York
London Toronto Sydney Tokyo Singapore Madrid
Mexico City Munich Paris Cape Town Hong Kong Montreal

Practice Problems and Solutions to Accompany McDonald, *Derivatives Markets*, 2nd Edition

Copyright © 2006 Pearson Education, Inc.

All rights reserved. No part of this publication may be reproduced, stored in a retrieval system, or transmitted, in any form or by any means, electronic, mechanical, photocopying, recording, or otherwise, without the prior written permission of the publisher. Printed in the United States of America. For information on obtaining permission for use of material in this work, please submit a written request to Pearson Education, Inc., Rights and Contracts Department, 75 Arlington Street, Suite 300, Boston, MA 02116, fax your request to 617-848-7047, or e-mail at
http://www.pearsoned.com/legal/permissions.htm.

ISBN 0-321-318-12-9
1 2 3 4 5 6 7 8 9 10-OPM-09 08 07 06 05

Table of Contents

Contents		iii
Chapter 1	Introduction to Derivatives	1
Part One	**Insurance, Hedging, and Simple Strategies**	
Chapter 2	An Introduction to Forwards and Options	3
Chapter 3	Insurance, Collars, and Other Strategies	5
Chapter 4	Introduction to Risk Management	7
Part Two	**Forwards, Futures, and Swaps**	
Chapter 5	Financial Forwards and Futures	9
Chapter 6	Commodity Forwards and Futures	11
Chapter 7	Interest Rate Forwards and Futures	13
Chapter 8	Swaps	15
Part Three	**Options**	
Chapter 9	Parity and Other Option Relationships	17
Chapter 10	Binomial Option Pricing: I	19
Chapter 11	Binomial Option Pricing: II	21
Chapter 12	The Black-Scholes Formula	23
Chapter 13	Market-Making and Delta-Hedging	25
Chapter 14	Exotic Options: I	27
Part Four	**Financial Engineering and Applications**	
Chapter 15	Financial Engineering and Security Design	29
Chapter 16	Corporate Applications	32
Chapter 17	Real Options	36
Part Five	**Advanced Pricing Theory**	
Chapter 18	The Lognormal Distribution	38
Chapter 19	Monte Carlo Valuation	40
Chapter 20	Brownian Motion and Ito's Lemma	42

Chapter 21	The Black-Scholes Equation	44
Chapter 22	Exotic Options: II	47
Chapter 23	Volatility	49
Chapter 24	Interest Rate Models	51
Chapter 25	Value at Risk	53
Chapter 26	Credit Risk	55
Answer Section		57

Chapter 1
Introduction to Derivatives

1. A buyer of a crude oil futures contract makes money if the unknown future price of crude oil is higher than a price agreed to today.

    (a) Give an example of an entity that might be interested in buying such a contract.
    (b) Give an example of an entity that might be interested in selling such a contract.

2. Futures contracts on crude oil are very popular. Several years ago, a Bordeaux wine futures contract was introduced at an exchange. That contract is not traded anymore—the trading volume never reached a critical mass. Can you think of reasons why it is more difficult to establish a futures contract for wine than for another commodity such as crude oil?

3. XYZ stock has a bid price of $97.50 and an ask price of $98.20. You would like to buy 100 shares, and contact two brokers about their cost structure. Broker A has a proportional transaction cost of 0.2% and a $5 account setup fee, while broker B has a transaction cost of $30.

    Who should you buy the shares from?

4. Would your answer to Question 1.3 change if you wanted to buy 150 shares?

5. XYZ stock has an ask price of $50.25. Suppose you buy 50 shares. If there is a brokerage commission of $15, and your roundtrip transaction costs are $57.50, what is the bid price of XYZ stock?

6. Suppose that the XYZ stock has a bid price of $50.25 and an ask price of $51.37. You buy 10 shares of XYZ, and immediately after that, the bid price moves to $51.25 and the ask price moves to $52.22. What are your roundtrip transaction costs?

7. What is the profit (or loss) of the market maker who sold you the security in Question 1.6?

8. Suppose you short-sell 200 shares of MNO stock. The bid price for MNO stock is $12.32, the ask price is $12.66.

    Suppose your counterparty tells you that she is concerned about your credit risk. Therefore, she tells you that she will keep the proceeds from the short sale and asks you to provide an additional 20% of the proceeds as a haircut. How much money do you have to transfer to your counterparty?

9. Suppose you wish to short-sell 100 shares of MNO stock, which has a bid price of $44.22 and an ask price of $46.42. You cover the short position 270 days later when the bid price is $46.87 and the ask price is $49.05. Suppose that there is a 0.4% commission to engage in the short-sale and a 0.3% commission to close the short-sale. Suppose the lender keeps the entire proceeds from the short sale as collateral.

   (a) What profit did you make?
   (b) Suppose the 9-month interest rate is 6%, and that the rebate for MNO stock offered by the lender is 2%. How much interest accrues during the 9 months in which you have the short position? Does this reduce or increase your profit?

10. Do an online search of the term "hard to borrow." In the context of short-sales, what does this mean?

Chapter 2
An Introduction to Forwards and Options

1. You often enter forward contracts in everyday life. Demonstrate that your order of a home delivery pizza is a forward contract.

2. (a) Suppose you enter into a short 9-month forward position at a forward price of $1,050. What is the payoff in 9 months for prices of $950, $1,000, $1,050, $1,100 and $1,150?
   (b) Suppose you sell a 9-month call option with a strike price of $1,050. What is the payoff in 9 months at the same prices for the underlying asset?
   (c) Comparing the payoffs of parts (a) and (b), which contract should give you as the seller the higher initial premium?

3. Look up call and put S&P 500 option quotes from the *Wall Street Journal* or download them from *cboe.com*. Take an option of your choice and draw a payoff and profit diagram for a short position.

4. Suppose MNO stock pays no dividends and has a current price of $150. The forward price for delivery in one year is $157.50. Suppose the one-year effective annual interest rate is 5%.
   (a) Graph the payoff and profit diagrams for a short forward contract on MNO stock with a forward price of $157.50.
   (b) Is there any advantage to short selling the stock or selling the forward contract?
   (c) Suppose MNO paid a dividend of $3 per year and everything else stayed the same. Is there any advantage to selling the forward contract?

5. Suppose the 6-month $1,200-strike S&R index call option has an ask price of $130.12 and a bid price of $128.22. Suppose you can enter into an S&R index forward contract for $1,260. The 6-month effective interest rate is 5%.
   (a) Draw, in the same diagram, the profit for a long call and a long forward position.
   (b) Above what price is the profit of the call option smaller than the profit of the forward contract?

6. Suppose the 6-month $1,200-strike S&R index put option trades at a bid of $72.97 and at an ask of $74.44. Suppose you can enter into an S&R index forward contract for $1,260. The 6-month effective interest rate is 5%.
   (a) Draw, in the same diagram, the profit for a short put and a long forward position.
   (b) At what price is the profit of the put option the same as the profit of the forward contract? If the index level is higher than the threshold you calculated, which instrument (put or forward) makes more money?

7. Why is the seller of a put option a buyer of the underlying? What about the seller of a call option?

8. The S&R index is currently trading at $1,200. Which of the following option(s) is (are) in the money?

   (a) 1,300-strike put option
   (b) 1,000-strike put option
   (c) 1,200-strike call option
   (d) 1,100-strike call option

9. Figure 2.13 depicts the risk of a home owner's insurance contract without considering the risk of the insured asset—the house. Redraw Figure 2.13, but include the value of the house, and also an aggregate position of the house and the insurance. Can you see now why you have bought insurance, and not a speculative instrument?

10. You have bought a new car for $15,000. You are shopping for collision & damage waiver car insurance policies. Policy A has a deductible of $250, policy B has a deductible of $1,000. Both policies cover $15,000, less the deductible. Draw the **payoff** diagrams of both contracts. Based on the diagram, which policy is more expensive? Why?

Chapter 3
Insurance, Collars, and Other Strategies

For the following problems assume the effective 9-month interest rate is 4%, and the FTSE100 forward price is 4,446. We assume for simplicity that the FTSE100 index does not pay dividends. You should use these premiums for FTSE100 index options with 9 months to expiration:

Strike	Call	Put
3,925	713.07	
4,025	653.62	248.81
4,275	520.47	356.04
4,325	496.46	
4,425	450.98	430.79
4,725	333.96	
4,775	317.11	633.46
5,025	243.19	799.92

1. Suppose that you buy the FTSE100 index for £4,275, buy a £4,275 put, and borrow £4,110.58. Perform a payoff and profit calculation mimicking Table 3.1. Graph the resulting payoff and profit diagrams for the combined position, using 9 different index values from £4,075 to £4,975.

2. Suppose you short the FTSE100 index for £4,275 and sell a £4,275-strike put. Construct payoff and profit diagrams for this position. Verify that you obtain the same payoff and profit diagram by borrowing £4,110.58 and selling a £4,275-strike call.

3. Suppose you short the FTSE100 index for £4,275, buy a £4,025-strike call, and sell a £4,025-strike put. Construct payoff and profit diagrams for this position. Verify that you obtain the same payoff and profit diagram by borrowing £3,870.19.

4. Verify that you earn the same profit and payoff by (a) buying the FTSE100 index for £4,275 and buying a £4,775-strike put and (b) buying a 4,775-strike call and lending £4,591.35.

5. Verify that you earn the same profit and payoff by (a) shorting the FTSE100 index for £4,275 and (b) selling a £5,025-strike call, buying a £5,025-strike put, and lending £4,831.73

6. (a) Calculate the price of a long butterfly spread using the following call options: £3,925-strike call, £4,325-strike call, and £4,725-strike call.

   (b) Use the put-call parity to derive the price of the corresponding butterfly spread using put options.

7. LIFFE (the London International Financial Futures and Options Exchange) allows investors to trade many particular FTSE100 index option strategies. One such strategy is called "Guts." It is defined as buying a call and buying a put at a higher strike.

   Draw the payoff and profit diagram of a guts using the £4,275-strike call and £4,425-strike put. Can you see why the strategy is called guts?

8. LIFFE allows investors to trade many particular FTSE100 index option strategies. One such strategy is called "Call Ladder." It is defined as buying a call, selling a call at higher strike, and selling a call at an equally higher strike. Draw the payoff and profit diagram of a call ladder using the £3,925-strike call, the £4,325-strike call, and £4,725-strike call. Can you see why the strategy is called a call ladder?

9. LIFFE allows investors to trade many particular FTSE100 index option strategies. One such strategy is called "Iron Condor." It is defined as selling a put, buying a put at a higher strike, buying a call at an even higher strike, and selling a call at even higher strike.

   Draw the payoff and profit diagram of an Iron Condor using the £4,025-strike put, the £4,275-strike put, the £4,425-strike call and £4,775-strike call. For which kind of market view is the long iron condor the appropriate strategy?

10. LIFFE also allows so-called volatility strategy trades. One such strategy is called a "Call Spread versus Underlying." It is defined as buying the call, selling a call at a higher strike, and selling the FTSE100 index.

    Draw the payoff and profit diagram of this volatility strategy trade using the £4,025-strike call and the £4,275-strike call.

    Why is the strategy a volatility strategy? Which direction of price movements are you hoping for?

Chapter 4
Introduction to Risk Management

For the problems of Chapter 4, consider the following two firms:

S.O. extracts oil, with fixed costs of $20/barrel and variable costs of $8/barrel.

Plastics Corp. produces PET resin. It buys oil and manufactures the resin. One barrel of oil can be used to produce two units of resin. One unit of resin sells for 0.4 times the price of one barrel of oil, plus $15. The fixed cost per unit of resin is $7 and the non-oil variable cost is $3.30 per unit of resin.

The one-year forward price of oil is $42/barrel. The one-year continuously compounded interest rate is 4%. One year oil option prices are shown in the table below:

Strike	Call Price	Put Price
35	$8.085	$1.359
40	$5.106	$3.185
42	$4.174	$4.174
45	$3.032	$5.915
50	$1.711	$9.397

1. If S.O. does nothing to manage oil price risk, what is its profit one year from now per barrel of oil? If, on the other hand, S.O. sells forward **half** of its expected oil production, what is its estimated profit one year from now? Contruct graphs illustrating both the unhedged and the partially hedged profit.

2. Compute the estimated profit in one year if S.O. buys a put option with a strike of $40($50). Draw profit diagrams for both options, and include the unhedged profit. Describe the difference in the profit diagrams of the $40-strike hedged and the $50-strike hedged position.

3. If Plastics Corp. does nothing to manage oil price risk, what is its profit one year from now, per barrel of oil? If it wants to hedge the price of oil, should Plastics Corp. buy or sell oil forwards?

4. If Plastics Corp. chooses to hedge their oil price exposure with futures so that they are completely immune to changes in the oil price, how many oil futures should they buy per unit of resin produced? What is its estimated profit one year from now? Construct graphs illustrating both unhedged and hedged positions.

5. Compute the estimated profit in one year if Plastics Corp. buys one call option per ten units of resin with a strike of $35($45). Draw a graph of profit in each case.

6. Compute the estimated profit in one year if Plastics Corp. sells a $40-strike put, $50-strike call collar per ten units of resin. Draw the profit diagram.

7. Suppose that Plastic Corp. insures against a price increase by purchasing a $45-strike call on oil. Find the strike price for an oil put that would generate a zero-cost collar for Plastics Corp. Use a continuously compounded interest rate of 4%, a volatility of 26%, and a time-to-expiration of one year. The oil forward price is $42.

8. Derive the intermediary steps leading to the following equations:
    (a) Equation 4.4 (Variance of the return on the hedged position)
    (b) Equation 4.5 (Variance-minimizing hedge position)
    (c) Equation 4.6 (Minimum variance)

    Use the following Table for Questions 4.9 and 4.10:

Oil Price ($)	Extraction Schedule (Millions of Barrels)		
	Scenario A	Scenario B	Scenario C
35	1	0.5	1.2
35	1.2	0.8	1.1
45	1.2	1.1	1.1
45	1.0	1.4	1.04
50	1.0	1.2	0.95
50	1.2	1.6	0.88

9. (a) Suppose that the fixed cost for S.O. is constant at $20 million per year. If the variable costs are $12/barrel, what is the standard deviation of S.O.'s revenues in Scenario B?
    (b) What is the correlation coefficient between oil price and the extraction schedule in Scenario C? What about the correlation coefficient between oil price and revenues in Scenario C? Explain the difference, if any.

10. Compute the variance-minimizing hedge ratio for S.O.'s revenues for Scenario C. What is the reduction in the standard deviation of S.O.'s revenue?

Chapter 5
Financial Forwards and Futures

1. Describe four alternative ways to buy a pizza, using the terminology in Chapter 5.1 (outright purchase, fully leveraged purchase, prepaid forward contract, and forward contract).

2. A $74 stock pays a $0.75 dividend every three months, with the first dividend coming one month from today. The continuously compounded risk-free rate is 5%.
   (a) What is the price of a prepaid forward contract that expires one year from today?
   (b) What is the price of a forward contract that expires on the same date?

3. A $74 stock pays a 5% continuous dividend. The continuously compounded risk-free rate is 5%.
   (a) What is the price of a prepaid forward contract that expires one year from today?
   (b) What is the price of a forward contact that expires on the same date? Compare the forward price to the stock price and explain your result.

4. Suppose the stock price is $74, and the continuously compounded interest rate is 5%.
   (a) What is the 9-month forward price, assuming dividends are zero?
   (b) If the 9-month forward price is $77, what is the annualized forward premium?
   (c) If the 9-month forward price is $75.309, and the stock pays constant quarterly dividends, with the first dividend coming three months from today, and the last one coming immediately before the expiration of the forward contract, what is the quarterly dividend payment the stock makes?

5. The MNO stock trades at $66, the risk-free rate is 5%, and the MNO stock pays constant quarterly dividends of $0.45. Assume that the first dividend is coming three months from today, and the last one coming immediately before the expiration of the forward contract. You can trade MNO single stock futures with an expiration of nine months.
   (a) Suppose you observe a 9-month forward price of $67.50. What arbitrage would you undertake?
   (b) Suppose you observe a 6-month forward price of $66.75. What arbitrage would you undertake?

6. The ABC spot price is $44.25 and the continuously compounded risk-free interest rate is 5%. MNO stock pays constant quarterly dividends. Assume that the first dividend is coming three months from today, and the last one coming immediately before the expiration of the forward contract. You can trade MNO single stock futures with an expiration of six months. You observe a 6-month forward price of $44.162.
   (a) What constant quarterly dividend payment is implied by this forward price?
   (b) Suppose you believe that the company will pay a $1.00 quarterly dividend at the next two dividend dates. What arbitrage would you undertake?
   (c) Suppose you believe that the company will pay a $0.25 quarterly dividend at the next two dividend dates. What arbitrage would you undertake?

7. The Chicago Mercantile Exchange (CME) allows trading S&P 500 e-mini futures. Retrieve the current contract specifications for this contract. Why do you think this contract was introduced in 1997?

8. Suppose the S&P 500 index futures price is currently 900. You wish to sell three mini futures contracts on margin.
   (a) What is the notional value of your position?
   (b) Does it hurt you if the index moves up or down? What is your exposure to the smallest possible index move against you?
   (c) Assuming a 15% initial margin, what is the value of the initial margin?
   (d) Suppose you earn a continuously compounded rate of 3% on your margin balance, your position is marked to market weekly, and the maintenance margin is 85% of the initial margin. What is the lowest S&P index futures price, one week from today, at which you will receive a margin call?

9. Suppose the S&P 500 currently has a level of 900. The continuously compounded return on a one-year T-bill is 5%. You wish to hedge a $135,000 thousand portfolio that has a beta of 0.75 and a correlation of 1.0 with the S&P 500. You cannot trade fractions of contracts.
   (a) What is the one-year futures price for the S&P 500, assuming a dividend yield of 3%?
   (b) How many S&P 500 E-mini futures contracts should you short to hedge your portfolio?

10. Suppose that the Euro-denominated interest rate is 4.5%, the dollar-denominated interest rate is 3%, and the current exchange rate is 0.84 dollars per Euro.
    (a) What is the 6-month forward rate in New York?
    (b) What is the 6-month forward rate in Frankfurt?

Chapter 6
Commodity Forwards and Futures

1. The Chicago Board of Trade trades mini-sized silver futures.
   (a) Find the contract specifications for this particular contract.
   (b) The contract specifications have details on the deliverable grades for the silver futures. In particular, they specify:

   "The contract grades for delivery shall be refined silver in a bar cast in a basic weight of either 1,000 troy ounces or eleven hundred troy ounces (the bar may vary no more than 10 percent more or less); assaying not less than 999 fineness; and made up of one of the brands and markings officially listed by the Exchange."

   In your opinion, why are the deliverable grades specified so detailed? After all, silver is a commodity; wouldn't it be enough to write "you need to deliver one 1000 troy ounce bar of silver"?

2. Suppose that the spot price for silver is $7.3 per troy ounce. Assuming a 3.5% continuously compounded annual risk-free rate and a lease rate of 2%, what are the forward prices for 1, 3, 5, 7, 13, 25, and 37 months? Is this an example of contango or backwardation?

3. The Chicago Mercantile Exchange introduced trading of futures on frozen pork bellies in 1961.
   (a) Without looking at the contract specifications, try to think of how you would specify delivery.
   (b) Now look up the contract specifications.
   (c) Why is the position limit so much smaller in the expiring contract?

4. The current price for frozen pork bellies is 91.90 cents per lb. Forward prices for 3, 4, 6, and 8 months are 92.80, 92.80, 94.20, and 97.20. The 3, 4, 6, and 8 months continuously compounded annual risk-free rates are 2%, 2.25%, 2.75%, and 2.75%. What is the annualized lease rate for each maturity? Is this an example of contango or backwardation?

5. Your grandmother would like to buy gold for investment purposes. She has received a brochure for gold coins, in particular for South African Krugerrand (The coin depicts Paul Kruger, President of the original South African Republic from 1883 to 1902).

   The catalogue states that:

   "The ever popular Krugerrand gives the average person convenient access to gold and is a good example of gold as an economic asset, a store of value and a form of money all combined together in one coin."

   In words your grandmother could understand, explain why you do not necessarily agree with the above statement. Show your grandmother that she should not buy Krugerrand if she can create a synthetic position in gold.

6. Suppose the platinum spot price is $825 per ounce. Suppose further that platinum cannot be loaned. Five hundred ounces of platinum can be stored for $250/quarter. Storage costs are paid at the end of each quarter in storage. The continuously compounded annual risk-free rate is 4%.

   (a) What is the minimum price of a 9-month platinum forward contract for storage to occur?
   (b) Do you think platinum is stored?

7. The spot price of platinum is $825 per troy ounce. Suppose that the continuously compounded annual risk-free rate is 5%, and that the one-year forward price is $850.125. Ignore storage costs.

   (a) Suppose platinum cannot be loaned. What is the return on a cash and carry arbitrage strategy?
   (b) Now suppose platinum can be loaned. What is the return on a cash and carry arbitrage strategy?

8. Suppose the price of corn is $320.34 per bushel, the 6-month forward price is $326.811, the continuously compounded annualized storage rate is 2%, and the continuously compounded annual interest rate is 5%.

   Is there a convenience yield priced in the forward price? If so, how large is it?

9. Using the data of Question 6.8, demonstrate that the lower bound for the long forward price is indeed $326.811, based on a reverse cash and carry arbitrage, if the only entities you could borrow corn from receive a convenience yield from corn.

10. Suppose again the price of corn is $320.34 per bushel, the continuously compounded annualized storage rate is 2%, the continuously compounded convenience yield is the one you calculated in question 6.8, and the continuously compounded annual interest rate is 5%.

    (a) Suppose you are the average investor in the corn market. What is the minimum price at which you will agree to enter a short 6-month forward corn contract?
    (b) Using the results and scenarios described in Questions 6.9 and 6.10, evaluate whether arbitrage is possible at the following 6-month corn forward prices:

       1) $327.44

       2) $333.56

       3) $326.82

Chapter 7
Interest Rate Forwards and Futures

1. Suppose you observe the following zero-coupon prices per $1 of maturity payment: 0.98039 (1-year), 0.96117(2-year), 0.92860(3-year), 0.89717(4-year), 0.86261(5-year). For each maturity year, compute the zero-coupon bond yields (effective annual and continuously compounded), the par coupon rate, and the one-year implied forward rate.

2. Suppose you observe the following one-year implied forward rates: 0.04(1-year), 0.05(2-year), 0.0425 (3-year), 0.03(4-year), 0.06(5-year). For each maturity year, compute the zero-coupon bond prices, effective annual and continuously compounded zero-coupon bond yields, and the par coupon rate.

3. Suppose you observe the following par coupon bond yields: 0.05(1-year), 0.055(2-year), 0.055 (3-year), 0.0675(4-year), 0.09(5-year). For each maturity year, compute the zero-coupon bond prices, effective annual and continuously compounded zero-coupon bond yields, and the one-year implied forward rate.

4. Suppose that to hedge interest rate risk on your lending, you enter into a forward rate agreement (FRA) that will guarantee a 4.25% effective annual interest rate for one year on $225,000.00. On the date you lend the $225,000.00, the actual interest rate is 4.5%. Determine the dollar settlement on the FRA assuming:

   (a) Settlement occurs on the date the loan is initiated.
   (b) Settlement occurs on the date the loan is repaid.

Use the following zero-coupon bond prices to answer the next five questions:

Days to Maturity	Zero Coupon Bond Prices
90	0.98965
180	0.97706
270	0.96579
360	0.95012
720	0.89421
1,080	0.86384
1,440	0.82270
1,800	0.79292086

5. What is the rate on a synthetic FRA for a 90-day loan commencing on day 270? A 450-day loan commencing on day 270?

6. What is the rate on a synthetic FRA for a 270-day loan commencing on day 90? Suppose you have decided to distrust your house bank and to create the FRA on your own. What positions in zero-coupon bonds would you use to create a "homemade" FRA to secure a 270-day loan of $50 million, starting at day 90?

7. Use the 1,080 days to maturity zero bond above and determine its PVBP. What is its modified duration? What is its Macaulay duration?

8. We will use the 1,800 days-to-maturity zero bond with a face value of $1,000 from the above table.
   (a) Calculate its Macaulay duration.
   (b) Calculate the approximate bond price change for a 40 basis point increase in the yield.
   (c) Calculate the exact new bond price based on the new yield to maturity.
   (d) Calculate the convexity of the zero-coupon bond.
   (e) Now use the formula that takes into account both duration and convexity to approximate the new bond price. Compare your result to the results of (b) and (c).

9. Use the 3-year and 5-year zero coupon bonds of the above table to calculate an implied forward rate between year 3 and year 5.
   (a) What is the annualized implied forward rate?
   (b) Suppose that the interest rate you can obtain in the market is $r_0(3, 5) = 5\%$. If you think that there is an arbitrage opportunity, create an arbitrage portfolio to exploit the mispricing. If you think there is no arbitrage opportunity, please explain why.

10. Compute the derivative of the bond price with respect to the yield, $dB(y)/dy$, and derive the equation for the price value of a basis point.

Chapter 8
Swaps

1. Suppose the 1-year, 2-year, and 3-year oil forward prices are 50.85, 45.94, and 42.97, respectively. The 1-year, 2-year, and 3-year interest rates are 3%, 3.5%, and 3.75%, respectively. What is the 2-year swap price?

2. Suppose the 1-year, 2-year, and 3-year oil forward prices are 50.85, 45.94, and 42.97, respectively. The 1-year, 2-year, and 3-year interest rates are 3%, 3.5%, and 3.75%, respectively.
   (a) What is the three-year swap price?
   (b) What is the "uneven-year" swap price? (That is, the first swap settlement will be in one-year and the second and final settlement will be in three years.)

3. Consider the three-year swap of Question 8.2, part (a). Suppose you are the fixed-rate payer in the swap. Have you over- or underpaid in the first period? Have you over- or underpaid in the second period? What is the cumulative overpayment (or underpayment) after the second swap settlement? Verify that the cumulative overpayment (or underpayment) is zero after the third payment.

4. Suppose the annualized continuously compounded Euro-denominated interest rate is 4% and the annualized continuously compounded dollar-denominated interest rate is 3.25%. The spot exchange rate is $1.27/Euro. Europia, a Paris-based firm conducting business in Euros has issued a 3-year 3.25% dollar-denominated bond at par in the amount of $250 million. The firm wishes to guarantee the Euro value of the payments.
   (a) Construct the Euro/dollar forward curve for the next three years (be careful about using the right currency in the numerator).
   (b) What should Europia do to guarantee a Euro value of its payments?
   (c) What is the present value of the hedged Euro cash flow?

5. RF Asset Management has $5 billion in investment grade bonds under management. The fund's managers are convinced that the Dow Jones Index will outperform bonds over the next four years, and would therefore like to create exposure to stocks for half of their assets under management by entering in a total return swap. Suppose for simplicity that the fund has hedged the interest rate risk of its bond portfolio so that the $5 billion bond portfolio returns 4.25% each year over the next four years. What are the annual payments RF Asset Management receives if the Dow Jones total returns (i.e., dividends plus capital gains) over the next four years are +12, +8, 0, and –13%?

   Suppose you observe the following quarterly oil forward prices:

Quarter	1	2	3	4	5	6	7	8
Oil forward price	46.88	46.44	45.94	44.97	43.25	42.80	41.40	40.87

6. Using the information about oil forward prices in the above table, construct the set of swap prices for oil for one through eight quarters. Assume that the interest rate for the first quarter is 0.7%, and that the rate increases by 0.7% each quarter.

7. Suppose the oil forward prices are as in the above table. Suppose further that the interest rate for the first quarter is 0.7%, and that the rate increases by 0.7% each quarter. What are the total costs of prepaid 4- and 8-quarter oil swaps?

8. Using the information in the table above, and given the 8-quarter oil swap price you calculated in Question 8.6, construct the implicit loan balance for each quarter over the life of the swap. What is the balance at the end of the eighth quarter?

9. Use the oil forward prices of the table above, and assume that the interest rate for the first quarter is 0.7%, and that the rate increases by 0.7% each quarter. What is the price of an eight-period swap for which one barrel of oil is delivered during the first four quarters and two barrels of oil are delivered during the last four quarters? What is the price of an eight-period swap for which two barrels of oil are delivered during the first four quarters and one barrel of oil is delivered during the last four quarters? Which swap price is higher? Why?

10. If the zero-coupon bond prices for the next eight quarters are 0.9891, 0.9775, 0.9653, 0.9515, 0.9506, 0.9452, 0.9390, and 0.9346 respectively, what is the fixed rate in a four-quarter interest rate swap with the first settlement in quarter three?

Chapter 9
Parity and Other Option Relationships

1. A stock currently sells for $12.00. A 9-month European put option with a strike of $15.00 has a premium of $3.1422. Assuming a 4% continuously compounded risk-free rate and a 2% continuous dividend yield, what is the price of the associated call option?

2. A stock currently sells for $86.00. A 10-month European call option with a strike of $95.00 has a premium of $5.7405. Assuming a 4% continuous dividend yield and a European put premium of $14.6371, what is the continuously compounded risk-free rate?

3. Suppose the exchange rate is €0.79/$, the Euro-denominated continuously compounded interest rate is 3.75%, the dollar-denominated continuously compounded interest rate is 2%, and the price of a one-year 0.85-strike European put on the dollar is €0.0587. What is the price of a one-year 0.93-strike European call?

4. Suppose the continuously compounded Canadian dollar-denominated interest rate is 2%, the continuously compounded Euro-denominated interest rate is 3%, the spot exchange rate is 1.541 Can$/Euro, and the price of a Euro-denominated European put to buy one Canadian dollar with 6 months to expiration and a strike price of €0.6667 is €0.0352.

    (a) What is the spot exchange rate Euro/Can$?
    (b) What is the Can$-denominated European Euro put price for which there is no arbitrage opportunity?

    For the next four problems, consider the following American put prices for Smith & Sons, Inc, a non-dividend paying stock currently trading at $54.00/share. Assume that the annual, continuously compounded risk-free interest rate is 13%.

Strike Price	1 Month	2 Months	3 Months
50	2	3	5
55	4	?	8
60	8	10	12

    Time to Maturity

5. Determine the maximum and minimum option price for the 55-strike American put option maturing two months from today.

6. Determine the time-to-expiration boundaries for the 2-month 55-strike American put option.

7. Determine the strike-price boundaries for the 2-month 55-strike American put option.

8. Now put together all boundaries from Questions 9.5, 9.6, and 9.7.

   (a) Is there an arbitrage opportunity at a price of $4.25? If so, how would you exploit the arbitrage opportunity?

   (b) Is there an arbitrage opportunity at a price of $6.25? If so, how would you exploit the arbitrage opportunity?

   (c) Is there an arbitrage opportunity at a price of $8.25? If so, how would you exploit the arbitrage opportunity?

9. Your friend Peter, who is enrolled in the same program as you, is good in marketing, while you are a financial expert. To motivate both of you to study hard for the midterm in your respective weaker area, Peter tells you:

   If my percentage score on the finance midterm exam is higher than your percentage score on the marketing midterm exam, you will have to pay me the percentage point difference in dollars. Otherwise, you don't need to pay me anything.

   If the underlying asset is your marketing percentage score, and you agree to Peter's suggestion, what have you bought or sold? What if the underlying asset is Peter's finance percentage score?

10. A financial expert makes the following statement:

    It is rarely optimal to exercise an American call option on a non-dividend paying stock early. However, when the underlying stock hits a 52-week high, early exercise is optimal because the probability of the stock moving up even more is so low. In such a situation, you can do nothing but lose by not exercising.

    Do you agree or disagree? Why?

Chapter 10
Binomial Option Pricing: I

1. Assume today's stock price is $15, the option's strike price is $15, the continuously compounded risk-free interest rate is 6%, the time to expiration is nine months, and the continuously compounded dividend yield is 2%. u = 1.46, d = 0.73.

    (a) What are the premium, Δ, and B for a European call?
    (b) What are the premium, Δ, and B for a European put?

2. Assume today's stock price is $15, the option's strike price is $17, the continuously compounded risk-free interest rate is 6%, the time to expiration is nine months, and the continuously compounded dividend yield is 2%. u = 1.46, d = 0.73.

    (a) Verify that the price of a European put is $3.403.
    (b) Suppose you observe a put price of $4. What is the arbitrage?

3. Assume today's stock price is $15, the option's strike price is $15, the continuously compounded risk-free interest rate is 6%, the time to expiration is 10 months, and the continuously compounded dividend yield is 2%. u = 1.32, d = 0.79. Construct a two-period binomial tree for a call option. At each node, provide the premium, Δ, and B.

4. Repeat the option price calculation in the previous question for stock prices of $10, $12, $17, and $25. For a stock price of $25, can you explain the three values for delta?

5. Assume today's stock price is $35, the option's strike price is $45, the continuously compounded risk-free interest rate is 6%, the time to expiration is nine months, the continuously compounded dividend yield is 2%, and the stock's annualized standard deviation is 30%.

    (a) Construct the three-period binomial tree for the stock price.
    (b) Calculate the value of an American put option. Is the option early exercised? If so, at which node(s) do you exercise early?

6. Let S = $28, K = 22, r = 0.06, sigma = 0.30, δ = 0.04, T = 8 months, and the number of binomial periods n = 2.

    (a) What are u and d?
    (b) Construct the binomial tree for the stock.
    (c) Calculate the price of a European and American call.
    (d) Is there a difference in the premium of the European and American call? Why (or why not)?

7. Suppose that the exchange rate is 0.79 €/$. Let r($) = 3%, r(€) = 5%, u = 1.1850, d = 0.8581, T = 15 months, n = 3, and K = 0.8 €.

    (a) What is the price of a 15-month European call?
    (b) What is the price of a 15-month European put?

8. Suppose that the exchange rate is 0.79 €/$. Let r($) = 3%, r(€) = 5%, u = 1.1850, d = 0.8581, T = 15 months, n = 3, and K = 0.8 €.

   (a) What is the price of a 15-month American call?
   (b) What is the price of a 15-month American put?

9. Let S = 63, K_1 = 55, K_2 = 65, r = 6%, sigma = 0.35, δ = 0, T = 1 year, and the number of binomial periods n = 2. Determine the price of a (European) call bull spread.

10. Let S = 63, K = 60, r = 6%, sigma = 0.35, delta = 0, T = 1, and the number of binomial periods n = 2. A chooser option is an option that lets you choose after a certain period whether an option is a European call or a European put. Suppose that the time at which you need to choose is equal to t = T/2. What is the price of the chooser option?

Chapter 11
Binomial Option Pricing: II

1. Consider a one-period binomial model with h = 1, where S = $100, r = 6%, sigma = 35%, and δ = 4%.

   (a) Compute the value of a European call with a strike of K = 0.
   (b) Compute the value of an American call with a strike of K = 0.
   (c) Explain the difference.

2. Repeat Question 11.1, only assume that

   (a) r = 0%. What happens? Why?
   (b) δ = 0%. What happens? Why?

3. Consider a one-period binomial model with h = 1, where S = $100, r = 6%, sigma = 0%, and δ = 4%. Should you early-exercise an American call with a strike price of $90? Why?

4. The textbook states that:

   [...] the option is equivalent to a leveraged investment in the stock and, hence, is riskier than the stock.

   Consider a one-period binomial model, where T = 1, S = $100, r = 5%, sigma = 25%, and δ = 0%. K = 90.

   (a) Calculate the call option price.
   (b) What does "the option is equivalent to a leveraged investment" mean?
   (c) If the stock moves up (down), what is the return on the stock (in the risk-neutral world)?
   (d) If the stock moves up (down), what is the return on the option (in the risk-neutral world)?
   (e) Is an investment in the option riskier than an investment in the stock? Why?

5. The main text calculates a one-period example of how to value an option using true probabilities. Furthermore, the text states that:

   "Any consistent pair of α and γ will give the same option price."

   Recalculate the example for α = 12% and α = 22%. What is γ in each of the cases?

6. If we set $\alpha = r$, the risk-free rate (i.e., we use risk-neutral pricing), what is γ in that case?

The following closing prices of the Dow Jones Industrial Index are used by the next two questions:

6-Jan-03	8784.89
13-Jan-03	8586.74
21-Jan-03	8131.01
27-Jan-03	8053.81
3-Feb-03	7864.23
10-Feb-03	7908.80
18-Feb-03	8018.11
24-Feb-03	7891.08
3-Mar-03	7740.03
10-Mar-03	7859.71
17-Mar-03	8521.97
24-Mar-03	8145.77
31-Mar-03	8277.15
7-Apr-03	8203.41

7. Compute the average monthly continuously compounded return for the above series from 06-Jan-03 to 07-Apr-03. What is the average annualized continuously compounded return?

8. Compute the monthly standard deviation of continuously compounded returns for the above series from 06-Jan-03 to 07-Apr-03. What is the annualized standard deviation of the continuously compounded returns?

9. Let $S = \$50$, sigma $= 0.4$, $r = 0.06$, $t = 1$, and $\delta = 0.03$. Using Equation 11.17 to compute the probability of reaching a terminal node and $Su^i d^{n-i}$ to compute the price at that node, plot the risk-neutral distribution of year-one stock prices as in Figures 11.8 and 11.9 for $n = 50$ and $n = 100$.

10. Suppose $S = \$45$, $K = \$53$, $r = 0.06$, $T = 0.5$ years, sigma $= 0.25$, and $\delta = 0$. Explicitly construct an eight-period binomial tree using the Cox-Ross-Rubinstein expressions for u and d.

Chapter 12
The Black-Scholes Formula

1. Suppose S = 25, K = 23, sigma = 32%, r = 4%, delta = 2%, and T = 0.5. Use a spreadsheet to verify that the Black-Scholes price of a European call option is $3.4114, and that the Black-Scholes price of a European put option is $1.2048.

2. Let S = 47, K = 45, sigma = 35%, r = 0, and delta = 0.04.

   (a) Compute the Black-Scholes put price for one year to maturity and for a variety of very long times to maturity. What happens to the option price as $T \to \infty$?
   (b) Set r equal to the dividend yield. Now what happens? Why?

3. Suppose S = $25, sigma = 30%, $\delta = 0$, r = 0.07, and T = 0.5.

   (a) What is the price of a 22-strike put option with six months to expiration?
   (b) What is the six-month forward price for the stock?
   (c) What is the price of a one-year 22-strike put option, where the underlying asset is a futures contract maturing at the same time as the option?

4. Let S = $100, K = 100, sigma = 0, r = 0.05, delta = 0, and T = 1. Use the Black-Scholes formula to derive the price of a European call option. Hint: $N(-\infty) = 1$, $N(-\infty) = 0$, and $\ln(1) = 0$.

5. Let S = $100, K = 100, sigma = 0, r = 0.05, delta = 0, and T = 1.

   (a) Use the Black-Scholes formula to derive the price of a European put option. Hint: $N(+\infty) = 1$, $N(-\infty) = 0$, and $\ln(1) = 0$.
   (b) Use put-call-parity to verify your results for 12.4 and 12.5, part (a).

6. Let S = $100, K = 100, sigma = 0, r = 0.05, delta = 0.07, and T = 1.

   (a) Use the Black-Scholes formula to derive the price of a European call option. Hint: $N(+\infty) = 1$, $N(-\infty) = 0$, and $\ln(1) = 0$.
   (b) Use the Black-Scholes formula to derive the price of a European put option. Hint: $N(+\infty) = 1$, $N(-\infty) = 0$, and $\ln(1) = 0$.
   (c) Use put-call-parity to check your results against those obtained in (a) and (b).
   (d) Can you explain the difference between your results and the results obtained in Exercises 12.4 and 12.5?

7. Consider a bear spread where you sell a 20-strike put and buy a 25-strike put. Suppose sigma = 0.30, r = 0.04, delta = 0.02, and T = 1. Draw a graph with stock prices ranging from 0 to 50 depicting the profit on the bear spread for 1 day, 6 months, and 9 months prior to the date of expiration.

8. Consider a bear spread where you sell a 20-strike put and buy a 25-strike put. Suppose sigma = 0.30, r = 0.04, delta = 0.02, and T = 1.

   (a) Suppose S = 5. What are delta, gamma, vega, theta, and rho?
   (b) Suppose S = 50. What are delta, gamma, vega, theta, and rho?

9. Assume S = 975, sigma = 0.3, r = 0.05, δ = 0.02, T = 0.5, K_1 = 950, and K_2 = 1,050.

   (a) Draw the profit diagram of a 2 to 3 ratio spread (i.e., you buy two 950-strike calls and sell three 1,050-strike calls).
   (b) Draw the delta diagram of the ratio spread for a range of stock prices from 800 to 1,400.
   (c) Draw the vega, theta, rho, and gamma of the ratio spread for a range of stock prices from 800 to 1,400.

10. Suppose S = 100, sigma = 0.30, δ = 0.05, and T = 1. Evaluate the following statement:

    Given the numbers above, the value of an in-the-money call (i.e. a call for which S > K) is always higher than the value of the corresponding out-of-the-money put with the same strike price.

    Is the statement true? If yes, why? If not, why not?

Chapter 13
Market-Making and Delta-Hedging

1. Suppose S = 25, sigma = 32%, r = 4%, δ = 0%, and T = 182 days. Suppose you buy a 23-strike call. What is delta? If the option is on 100 shares, what investment is required for a delta-hedged portfolio? What is your overnight profit if the stock price tomorrow is S = 24.55? What if the stock price is $26.25?

2. Suppose S = 25, sigma = 32%, r = 4%, δ = 0%, and T = 182 days. Suppose you buy a 23-strike put. What is delta? If the option is on 100 shares, what investment is required for a delta-hedged portfolio? What is your overnight profit if the stock price tomorrow is S = 24.55? What if the stock price is $26.25?

3. Suppose S = 25, sigma = 32%, r = 4%, δ = 0%, and T = 182 days. Suppose you buy a 23-25-bear strike using put options. If you delta-hedge this position, what investment is required? What is your overnight profit if the stock price tomorrow is $24.55? What if the stock price is 26.25?

4. The textbook states that *"gamma measures the change in delta."* This exercise demonstrates the statement. Suppose S = 25, sigma = 32%, r = 4%, δ = 0%, and T = 0.5.

    (a) Suppose you buy a 23-strike call. Draw delta for a stock price ranging from 0 to 50.
    (b) Use a ruler and follow tangentially the figure of delta that you drew to determine the shape of gamma.
    (c) Now calculate and draw a figure of gamma.
    (d) Use a 30-strike call option to create a delta-gamma neutral hedge. What is your overnight profit if the stock price tomorrow is S = $24.55? What if the stock price is $26.25?

5. The textbook states that:

    "if the market maker were able to buy a put with the same strike price and maturity as the written call [...], then by buying 100 shares to offset the risk of the position, the market-maker would have used put-call parity to create a hedge that is both gamma- and delta-neutral for the life of the options."

    (a) Suppose sigma = 32%, r = 4%, δ = 0%, and T = 182 days. Suppose you buy a 30-strike put and sell a 30-strike call. Show that the above statement is correct by calculating delta and gamma for the aggregate position for stock prices of 20, 25, 30, 35, and 40.
    (b) Now use the put-call-parity formula to algebraically show the above statement is always true. Is a position as the above vega-neutral? Theta-neutral? Rho-neutral?

6. Reproduce the analysis of Table 13.3 assuming that the stock price moves as follows: down the first day, down the second day, up the third, fourth, and fifth day. Use sigma = 30%, r = 8%, and δ = 0.

7. Suppose S = $25, sigma = 32%, r = 4%, δ = 0%, and T = 182 days. Consider a 25-strike call. Compute a delta-gamma-theta approximation for the value of the call after 15 days. Consider stock prices of 23 to 25 in $0.10 increments and compare the actual option premium at each stock price with the predicted premium.

8. Suppose S = $25, sigma = 32%, r = 4%, δ = 0%, and T = 365 days. Consider a 25-strike call. For stock prices from $10 to $40, in $0.50 intervals:

    (a) Compute the actual price with 50 days to expiration.
    (b) Compute the estimated price with 50 days to expiration using a delta approximation.
    (c) Compute the estimated price with 50 days to expiration using a delta-gamma approximation.
    (d) Compute the estimated price with 50 days to expiration using a delta-gamma-theta approximation.
    (e) Graph the results from the above calculations, using stock prices from $10 to $40. Also graph the differences between the actual price and the approximations.
    (f) What do you conclude?

9. Suppose S = 25, r = 4%, sigma = 0.32, δ = 0%, and T = 182 days. Suppose you buy a 30-strike put. You are concerned about changes in volatility.

    (a) Draw a diagram of the option price on the y-axis and sigma on the x-axis for values of sigma from 0.2 to 0.5, using 0.005 increments. Do you earn or lose money if volatility increases?
    (b) Suppose you can use a 25-strike put to vega-hedge this position. How many units of the 25-strike put should you buy/sell?
    (c) Suppose you want to delta-vega hedge your position. How many shares do you need to buy (or sell)?
    (d) Suppose you want to delta-gamma-vega hedge your position of one long 30-strike put. Suppose you can use a 25-strike put and a 20-strike call to hedge your position. Do you need both the put and the call to construct your gamma-vega neutral position? Show the necessary fractions of all instruments you need to buy.

10. Suppose S = 25, sigma = 32%, r = 4%, δ = 0%, and T = 182 days. Suppose you buy a 30-strike put. You are concerned about changes in interest rate risk.

    (a) Draw a diagram of the option price on the y-axis and the interest rate on the x-axis for values of sigma from 0.01 to 0.10, using 0.002 increments. Do you earn or lose money if the interest rate increases?
    (b) Suppose you can use a 25-strike put to rho-hedge this position. How many units of the 25-strike put should you buy/sell?

Chapter 14
Exotic Options: I

1. The textbook states that:

    In addition to cases where the firm cares about the average exchange rate, averaging is also used when a single price at a point in time might be subject to manipulation or price swings induced by thin markets.

    Do a "Google" search of the terms "corner the market" and "silver". Do you think it is easy to manipulate prices in a market?

2. Footnote 2 of the main textbook states that you can think of path dependence in the context of a binomial pricing model. Assume today's stock price is $35, the continuously compounded risk-free interest rate is 6%, the time to expiration is 9 months, the continuously compounded dividend yield is 2%, and the stock's annualized standard deviation is 30%.

    (a) Construct the three-period binomial tree for the stock price.
    (b) Demonstrate the path dependence of an Asian **geometric** average strike call with one year to maturity in a three-period binomial tree.
    (c) Calculate the price of the geometric average strike call.

3. Assume today's stock price is $35, the continuously compounded risk-free interest rate is 6%, the time to expiration is 9 months, the continuously compounded dividend yield is 2%, and the stock's annualized standard deviation is 30%.

    (a) Demonstrate the path dependence of an Asian **arithmetic** average strike call with one year to maturity in a three-period binomial tree.
    (b) Calculate the price of the arithmetic average strike call.
    (c) How does your answer compare to the answer to Question 14.2 (c)?

4. Assume today's stock price is $35, the continuously compounded risk-free interest rate is 6%, the time to expiration is 9 months, the continuously compounded dividend yield is 2%, and the stock's annualized standard deviation is 30%.

    (a) Compute the price of an Asian arithmetic average price call with a strike of $37.
    (b) Compute the price of an Asian geometric average price call with a strike of $37.
    (c) Which of the two is higher? Why?

5. Equation 14.10 of the textbook states that a "knock-in" option plus a "knock-out" option is equal to an ordinary option. Use a standard arbitrage tableau to demonstrate this relationship.

6. Let S = $27, K = $28, sigma = 0.30, r = 0.06, δ = 0, and T = 0.5.
   (a) Compute the price of a knock-in call with a barrier of $30.
   (b) Compute the price of a knock-in put with a barrier of $30.
   (c) Compute the price of ordinary call and put options with a strike of $28. Calculate the price difference between the knock-in options calculated in (a) and (b) and the ordinary options. Explain the considerable differences between the two numbers.

7. Suppose S = $27, K = $28, sigma = 0.30, r = 0.06, δ = 0, and T = 1.
   (a) What is the price of a standard European call?
   (b) Suppose you have a compound call giving you the right to pay $1 three months from today to buy the option in part (a). For what stock price in three months will you exercise this option?
   (c) What is the price of this compound call?
   (d) What happens to the critical boundary if the time of exercise of the compound call approaches the time of the exercise of the underlying option? Why?

8. Suppose S = $27, K = $28, sigma = 0.30, r = 0.06, δ = 0, and T = 1.
   (a) What is the price of a standard European put?
   (b) Suppose you have a compound call giving you the right to buy the option in part (a) for $X three months from today. If the critical stock price below which you will exercise the option is $25.69701, what is the strike price X for the compound call on the put option?
   (c) What is the price of this compound option?

9. Suppose S = $27, K = $25, sigma = 0.30, r = 0.06, δ = 0, and T = 0.5.
   (a) What is the price of a European gap call, paying S – K whenever S is larger than $30?
   (b) What is the price of a European gap call, paying S – K whenever S is larger than $15?
   (c) Although the call in part (b) pays out more often—the barrier for S is lower—the price you calculated is lower than that of the option in part (a). Why?

10. Suppose S = $27, sigma = 0.30, r = 0.06, δ = 0, and T = 1. Suppose further that Q = $35, $sigma_Q$ = 0.25, $δ_Q$ = 0, and ρ = –0.3. What is the price of an exchange call option with S as the underlying asset and 0.8 * Q as the strike price? What is the price of an exchange put option with 0.8 * Q as the underlying asset and S as the strike price?

Chapter 15
Financial Engineering and Security Design

1. Suppose the price of CDE stock today is $46.22, the quarterly dividend is $0.53, and the annual continuously compounded interest rate is 4.6%.

   What is the price of a zero-coupon equity-linked bond promising to pay one share of CDE in five years?

2. Suppose the price of CDE stock today is $46.22, the first quarterly dividend is $0.53, and the annual continuously compounded interest rate is 4.6%. Suppose further that the dividend grows by 15% for quarters 2–7, and by 5% for quarters 8–16.

   What is the price of a zero-coupon equity-linked bond promising to pay one share of CDE in five years?

3. Assume that the issuer of the bond of Questions 15.1 and 15.2 would like the equity-linked bond to be issued at par.

   (a) If the dividends are constant at $0.53, as in Question 15.1, what is the quarterly coupon payment so that the bond is issued at par?

   (b) If the dividends are growing as in Question 15.2, what is the constant quarterly coupon payment so that the bond is issued at par?

4. Suppose a gold note pays one unit of gold in the future, with annual cash coupons. Suppose the spot price of gold is $350/oz, the 3-year forward price is $347.385/oz, the 1-year continuously compounded interest rate is 1.25%, the 2-year rate is 1.5%, and the 3-year rate is 1.75%.

   (a) What is the annual coupon if the note is issued at par?
   (b) What is the annual coupon as a fraction of the spot price?
   (c) Is the coupon rate on gold higher or lower than the interest rate? Why?

5. Consider a 2-year currency-linked note that pays $1,000 at maturity. Suppose the 1-year continuously compounded dollar interest rate is 5.5%, and the 2-year dollar rate is 6%. Furthermore, the 1-year continuously compounded Euro interest rate is 4%, and the 2-year Euro interest rate is 5%. The current exchange rate x(0), denominated as $/Euro, is 0.85. What is the coupon that makes this a par bond?

6. The main textbook derives the value of a CD when the underlying option is an Asian option. In that context, values of a geometric price Asian call of $240.97 and of an arithmetic price Asian call of $273.12 are mentioned. Use the software accompanying the book to confirm these two prices.

7. A financial consulting firm offers you an S&P 500 boosted CD (SPBCD). The equity-linked instrument is structured with a four-year maturity that earns the depositor 90% of the appreciation of the S&P 500 Index over the last 16 quarters' geometric average closing price, and returns at least the original investment.

   Suppose the continuously compounded four-year interest rate is 4%, the 4-year index volatility is 30%, the S&P 500 index today is 1,200, and the continuously compounded dividend yield is 1.5%.

   What is the commission the financial consulting firm earns?

8. The following text stems from a communication of McKesson, a health-care company, to their shareholders. It discusses convertible preferred securities the company had issued.

   In February 1997, a wholly-owned subsidiary trust of the Company issued 4 million shares of preferred securities to the public and 123,720 common securities to the Company, which are convertible at the holder's option into McKesson HBOC common stock. The proceeds of such issuances were invested by the trust in $206,186,000 aggregate principal amount of the Company's 5% Convertible Junior Subordinated Debentures due 2027 (the "Debentures"). The Debentures represent the sole assets of the trust. The Debentures mature on June 1, 2027, bear interest at the rate of 5%, payable quarterly, and are redeemable by the Company at 103.0% of the principal amount.

   Holders of the securities are entitled to cumulative cash distributions at an annual rate of 5% of the liquidation amount of $50 per security.[...] The preferred securities will be redeemed upon repayment of the Debentures and are callable by the Company at 103.0% of the liquidation amount.

   Explain, to the best of your ability, the structure of these securities. You should revise the Marshall & Ilsley example of the main textbook before doing so.

9. Liquid Yield Option Notes (LYONs) are an equity-linked financial instrument that was originally developed by Merrill Lynch.

   Do an Internet search and find out what a LYON is and how it works.

10. The following text stems from a communication of Lowe's to their shareholders. It discusses Liquid Yield Option Notes (LYONs) that the company had issued.

    In February 2001, the Company issued $1.005 billion principal of Liquid Yield Option (TM) Notes (LYONs) at an issue price of $608.41 per LYON. Interest will not be paid on the LYONs prior to maturity. On February 16, 2021, the maturity date, the holders will receive $1,000 per LYON, representing a yield to maturity of 2.5%. Holders may convert their LYONs at any time on or before the maturity date, unless the LYONs have been purchased or redeemed previously, into 8.224 shares of the Company's common stock per LYON. The Company may redeem for cash all or a portion of the LYONs at any time on or after February 16, 2004 at a price equal to the sum of the issue price and accrued original issue discount on the redemption date. Holders of the LYONs may require the Company to purchase all or a portion of their LYONs on February 16, 2004 at a price of $655.49 per LYON or on February 16, 2011 at a price of $780.01 per LYON. The Company may choose to pay the purchase price of the LYONs in cash or common stock, or a combination of cash and common stock. [...]

    When answering the following questions, assume for simplicity that Lowe's issued the LYONs on February 16th, 2001.

(a) Draw a timeline of critical events and explain the rights and obligations to the investor and to Lowe's. When would an investor like to exercise his right to convert? When would Lowe's like to buy back the LYONs?
(b) Why is the yield to maturity 2.5%?
(c) Can Lowe's buy back the LYONs on February 16th, 2003? If so, at what price?
(d) Can Lowe's buy back the LYONs on February 16th, 2005? If so, at what price?
(e) Can Lowe's buy back the LYONs on August 16th, 2005? If so, at what price?
(f) If the investor decides to ask Lowe's to buy back his LYONs on February 16th, 2011, what return would he have achieved?

Chapter 16
Corporate Applications

1. The following information stems from a pricing supplement of one recent debt issue of the World Bank:

    EUR 100,000,000
    Callable Fixed Rate Step-up Notes
    due September 4, 2008

   Here is an incomplete list of the terms and conditions:

   - Aggregate Principal Amount: EUR 100,000,000
   - Issue Price: 100.00 per cent of the Aggregate Principal Amount
   - Issue (Settlement) Date: September 4, 2002
   - Form of Notes: Bearer Notes
   - Authorized Denomination: EUR1,000
   - Maturity Date: September 4, 2008
   - Interest Basis (Condition 5): Fixed Interest Rate
   - Fixed Interest Rate:
     (a) Interest Rate:
     - 4.00 per cent per annum in respect of the Interest Period beginning on (and including) the Issue Date and ending on (but excluding) September 4, 2003
     - 4.00 per cent per annum in respect of the Interest Period beginning on (and including) September 4, 2003 and ending on (but excluding) September 4, 2004
     - 4.250 per cent per annum in respect of the Interest Period beginning on (and including) September 4, 2004 and ending on (but excluding) September 4, 2005
     - 4.375 per cent per annum in respect of the Interest Period beginning on (and including) September 4, 2005 and ending on (but excluding) September 4, 2006
     - 4.500 per cent per annum in respect of the Interest Period beginning on (and including) September 4, 2006 and ending on (but excluding) September 4, 2007
     - 5.000 per cent per annum in respect of the Interest Period beginning on (and including) September 4, 2007 and ending on (but excluding) the Maturity Date
     (b) Fixed Rate Interest Payment Dates: September 4 of each year commencing on September 4, 2003
   - Bank's Optional Redemption: Yes
     (a) Notice Period: Not less than 10 relevant business days
     (b) Amount: All and not less than all
     (c) Date(s): September 4 of each year commencing on September 4, 2003 and ending on September 4, 2007
     (d) Early Redemption Amount (Bank): 100 per cent of the Principal Amount of the Notes

Answer the following:

(a) What is a bearer bond? (You might want to do an online search if you don't know.)
(b) Why do you think this is called a fixed interest rate note? After all, the interest payments change almost every year.
(c) What is the call feature of this bond? When can bonds be called?
(d) Do you think this bond was priced higher or lower than a comparable non-callable step-up note? Why?
(e) Do investors have a conversion provision? If so, what is it?

2. Suppose that $\bar{B} = \$150$, $A_0 = \$150$, $r = 6\%$, $\sigma = 32\%$, $\delta = 0$, and $T = 10$ years.

   (a) Calculate the value of the debt using a put option.
   (b) Compare the value of the debt of the company with the value of a similar 6%, 10-year zero-coupon bond issued by the government. What do you conclude?
   (c) Calculate the yield of the firm's debt, and compare your answer to part (b)
   (d) How do your answers to (a) – (c) change if the volatility of the assets is 15%?

3. Suppose that $\bar{B} = \$150$, $A_0 = \$150$, $r = 6\%$, $\sigma = 32\%$, $\delta = 0$, and $T = 10$ years. Suppose further that the expected return on assets is 12%.

   (a) Calculate the expected return on equity.
   (b) Calculate the expected return on debt. Why is this different from your answer in Question 16.2 (c)?
   (c) Calculate the return on equity using the Modigliani-Miller formula. Why does using the Modigliani-Miller equation for the expected return on equity yield a different result?

4. Calculate the yields and expected returns of the senior bonds and intermediate bonds in Table 16.1, and confirm the given results.

5. Suppose that $A_0 = \$150$, $r = 6\%$, $\sigma = 32\%$, $\delta = 0$, and $T = 10$ years. Suppose the firm has three debt issues, with maturity values of $50, $50, and $50, ranked in seniority from highest to lowest. Calculate the value of the three tranches of debt, plus the value of equity, and state their yields and expected returns.

6. A bond covenant is an agreement between investors and the issuer of bonds that protects the bond investors. One common covenant is that the firm is not allowed to issue more debt that is senior to the existing senior debt. Use the data given in Question 16.5 to answer the following questions:

   (a) Calculate the yields, values, and expected returns for the four tranches of debt if the company issues an additional $20-face value zero-coupon bond of subordinated debt that has less seniority than the junior tranche.
   (b) Calculate the yields, values, and expected returns for the four tranches of debt if the company issues a $20-face value zero-coupon bond of debt that has a higher seniority than the current senior debt.
   (c) Calculate the value of the equity and the expected return of equity for both cases.
   (d) What do you conclude?

7. Suppose a firm has assets of $200 million with a single debt issue consisting of 30,000 zero-coupon bonds, each with a maturity value of $5,000 and T = 6 years to maturity. The asset volatility is 25% and the continuously compounded risk-free rate is 5%. Assume that the dividend yield is zero. The firm has 4 million shares outstanding. Each of the 30,000 zero-coupon bonds is convertible into 80 shares. Conversion is not allowed prior to maturity.

   (a) What is the price of the convertible zero-coupon bond with a principal of $5,000? How does this price compare to a simple non-convertible zero-coupon bond?
   (b) What is the conversion premium?

8. Suppose S = 54.25, K = 54.25, sigma = 0.32, r = 0.05, divyield = 0, and T = 3 years. Suppose that a company has issued a three-year at-the-money executive stock option that vests immediately, and for which recipients can exercise the option in year 1, 2, or 3.

   Construct a three-period binomial tree and calculate the annual expenses based on the Bulow-Shoven scheme.

9. The Ralph E. Price corporation used to compensate executives with 5-year European call options, granted at the money, with the implicit understanding of repricing the option if the underlying share price fell dramatically. If there was a drop of 50% from the initial share price, the company's board would reset the strike price of the options to equal the new share price. The maturity of the repriced option would equal the remaining maturity of the original option. In recent years, the repricing of executive stock options got some bad press, so the board decided to change its policy and give executives regular Black-Scholes options plus an upfront additional bonus payment that is equivalent to the value of the repricing promise. How much bonus payment does the board have to pay per option?

10. On October 1, 1997, WorldCom Inc. offered to buy MCI Communications Corporation. Below is a paraphrased statement of the offer, as communicated in a letter from Bernard Ebbers, President and CEO of WorldCom, to Bert Roberts, Chairman and CEO of MCI:

    "I am writing to inform you that this morning WorldCom is publicly announcing that it will be commencing an offer to acquire all the outstanding shares of MCI for $41.50 of WorldCom common stock per MCI share. The actual number of shares of WorldCom to be exchanged for each MCI share in the exchange offer will be determined by the stock price of WorldCom on the closing day of the offer, but will be no less than 1.0375 shares (if WorldCom's average stock price exceeds $40) or more than 1.2206 shares (if WorldCom's average stock price is less than $34)."

    Two weeks later, on October 15th, GTE bid for MCI, offering $40 in cash. On that day, WorldCom stock closed at $ 35.4375. Suppose that, if approved on October 15, the WorldCom offer would have taken exactly four months to close (since WorldCom needed to obtain antitrust approval), while the GTE offer could have been closed immediately. Finally, assume that on October 15, 1997, the continuously compounded 4-month risk-free rate was 5.5%, the volatility (annual standard deviation) of WorldCom was 0.38, and WorldCom was not expected to pay any dividends over the following four months.

(a) Letting S_T denote the closing price of WorldCom on February 15th, 1998, complete the following final payoff table of the WorldCom offer (i.e, the payoff to an MCI shareholder as of February 15th, 1998), carefully translating the text of the above offer into numbers.

WorldCom Price	Final Payoff in Terms of S_T
$S_T <$	
$\leq S_T <$	
$\leq S_T$	

(b) Draw the final payoff of the WorldCom offer. (Hint: calculate 34 * 1.2206).

(c) Show that you can replicate the payoff of the WorldCom offer with a portfolio holding only bonds, put and call options.

(d) Given the information in the exercise, use the Black-Scholes formula to find the value of a 40-strike European call option on WorldCom with 4 months to expiration.

(e) Use the portfolio you constructed in part (c) of the exercise to evaluate the WorldCom offer as of October 15th.

(f) If you were a shareholder of MCI, would you have accepted the WorldCom or the GTE offer? Why?

Chapter 17
Real Options

1. Suppose we can invest in a machine, costing $15, that will produce three widgets a year forever. In addition, the cost of each widget is $1.20. The price of one widget is $0.80 next year and will increase by 5% each year. Assume an effective annual risk-free interest rate of 7% per year. We can invest at any time in one such machine. Using the static NPV, what is the most you would pay to acquire the rights of that machine?

2. Use the effective annual risk-free interest rate and growth rate and all other inputs from Question 17.1.

    (a) Calculate the maximum NPV we can attain by waiting an appropriate time before we invest.

    (b) Now suppose that the investment cost decreases each year by 3% due to technological advancements in the widget production process. All other parameters remain unchanged. Do you invest before or after the optimal investment time of part (a)? Why?

3. Use the perpetual call option formula and appropriate inputs to calculate the investment trigger price and the NPV option price for the project described in Question 17.2 (a). What is the exact time period after which the trigger price is reached?

4. The vice president of Widgets Incorporated makes the following statement:

    The calculations we have made in Exercises 17.1 to 17.3 have assumed that there is no risk involved in the production and sale of widgets. Ignoring this risk is dangerous as we will overestimate the value of the investment option. For example, any volatility of revenues will lead to weaker cash flows in some instances, and therefore we should revise our NPV calculations downward.

    (a) Carefully evaluate the statement of the vice president.

    (b) Demonstrate your case by using the inputs of Exercise 17.3 and values for sigma of 0.10 and 0.20.

5. Consider a project that costs $100 today and that pays $400 in one year if the economy performs well (the stock market goes up) and $120 if the economy performs badly (the stock market goes down). The probability of the economy performing well is 40%, the effective annual risk-free interest rate is 4%, the expected return on the market is 10%, and the beta of the project is 2.3. Compute the risk-neutral probability of the economy performing well, and calculate the value of the project.

6. Repeat the binomial pricing of the project with a two-year horizon in section 17.2 using a forward tree.

7. Suppose a project costs $200 and begins producing an infinite stream of cash flows one year after investment. Expected annual cash flows for the first year are $12, and are expected to grow annually at a rate of 2%. Suppose further that the effective annual risk-free interest rate is 7%, the risk premium on the market is 6%, and the beta of the project is –0.1.

    (a) What is the value of the project using a standard static discounted cash flow calculation?

    (b) Suppose we have two years during which to decide whether to accept the project; at the end of that time, we either invest in the project, or lose it. Suppose further that cash flows are lognormally distributed with 40% volatility. Construct a two-period binomial forward tree for the evolution of cash flows and price the project using the two-period binomial tree. Indicate at which nodes you exercise your option to undertake the project.

8. Now suppose that we have a longer time period to decide whether to undertake the project or not.

    (a) Repeat Problem 17.7, but now assume that we have the investment rights for five years. Draw a five-period binomial tree. How does your answer compare to the result in 17.7 (b)?

    (b) Now assume that we can exercise the project whenever we want. Is the option price higher or lower than what you calculated in part (a)? Why?

9. A mine costing $755 will produce three ounces of gold on the day the cost is paid. Assume that the spot price of gold is $325/oz, the effective annual lease rate is 4%, and the effective annual risk-free rate is 5%.

    (a) What is the value of the mine if gold volatility is zero?

    (b) What is the value of the mine if gold volatility is 20%?

10. A mine costing $12,000 will produce five ounces of gold per year forever at a marginal extraction cost of $250 per ounce, with production beginning one year after the mine opens. Assume that the spot price of gold is $325/oz, the effective annual lease rate is 4%, and the effective annual risk-free rate is 5%.

    (a) What is the value of the mine if gold volatility is zero? At which gold price per ounce do you start extraction?

    (b) What is the value of the mine if gold volatility is 25%? At which gold price per ounce do you start extraction?

Chapter 18
The Lognormal Distribution

1. Graph the normal densities of a normally distributed variable with a mean of 4 and both a standard deviation of 3 and a standard deviation of 5 in the same graph. Use values for x between −20 and 20, and use 0.25 increments.

2. Graph the cumulative normal distributions of a normally distributed variable with a mean of 4 and both a standard deviation of 3 and a standard deviation of 5 in the same graph. Use values for x between −20 and 20, and use 0.25 increments.

3. Draw these five numbers randomly from a standard normal distribution: {0.32, 0.01, −1.2, −0.33, 0.42}. What are the equivalent draws from a normal distribution with mean −5 and variance 32?

4. Suppose $x_1 \sim N(3, 1)$ and $x_2 \sim N(2, 0.64)$. The correlation between x_1 and x_2 is +0.2. What is the distribution of $x_1 - 2x_2$?

5. Suppose $x \sim N(0, 1)$
   (a) What is $E(e^x)$?
   (b) What is $Var(e^x)$?

6. Assume that S(0) = $35, a = 0.06, sigma = 0.2, and delta = 0.02. What is the expected value of the continuously compounded three-year return if the stock is lognormally distributed?
   (a) Calculate an expression for the stock price after three periods, using Formula 18.20.
   (b) Calculate the expected value of the stock price after three years.
   (c) Calculate the median of the stock price after three years.

7. Assume that S(0) = $35, a = 0.06, sigma = 0.2, and delta = 0.02. What is prob[S(t) < 28] for t = 2?

8. Assume that S(0) = $35, a = 0.06, sigma = 0.2, and delta = 0.02. What is prob[S(t) > 45] for t = 4?

9. Assume that S(0) = $35, a = 0.06, sigma = 0.2, and delta = 0.02. What is E[S(t)|S(t) > 45] for t = 4?

10. Find a series of daily prices for General Electric from January 1, 1999 to December 31, 2004.
    (a) Calculate continuously compounded daily returns for GE.
    (b) Calculate the mean and standard deviation of the daily returns.
    (c) Calculate 1,507 random numbers generated by a normal distribution with the same mean and standard deviation as the daily returns of GE (one way to do so is to use "random number generation" in Excel's Tools, Data Analysis add-on).
    (d) Draw a histogram of all GE returns and superimpose the histogram of your normal random numbers.
    (e) How does the GE histogram compare to the normal distribution histogram?

Chapter 19
Monte Carlo Valuation

1. Let $u_i \sim U(0, 1)$. Compute $\sum_{i=1}^{12} u_i - 6$, 100, 200, 500, and 1,000 times. Use the Random Number Generator of the Data Analysis add-on of Excel to draw 100, 200, 500, and 1,000 standard-normal observations. Construct a histogram of both for each of the 100, 200, and 500 observations and compare the results. What do you conclude?

2. Suppose that $x_1 \sim N(-0.5, 2.25)$. Compute 5,000 random draws of e^{x_1}.

    (a) What are the theoretical mean and variance of e^{x_1}?
    (b) What are the mean and variance of your random sample?
    (c) Create a histogram of the 5,000 draws. What do you conclude?

3. Suppose we wish to draw random stock prices for 3 years from today. Use Equation 19.3, and set $S(0) = 45$, $a = 0.08$ and sigma = 0.30. Calculate the theoretical mean and standard deviation as well as the mean and standard deviation from a sample of 5,000 random draws.

4. Use the inputs of Question 19.3 and simulate a sequence of stock prices. To do so, divide the three years into 36 intervals of one month each. Construct a dynamic Excel diagram that varies with each draw of the simulated stock price.

5. The Black-Scholes price for a European call option with S = $28, K = $35, sigma = 0.4, r = 0.05, delta = 0, and t = 0.5 is 1.241211. Use a Monte Carlo simulation to compute this price. Compute the standard deviation of your estimates. What happens to the standard deviation of your estimates if you increase the life of the option?

6. The Black-Scholes price for a European put option with S = $28, K = $35, sigma = 0.4, r = 0.05, delta = 0, and t = 0.50 is 7.377058. Use a Monte Carlo simulation to compute this price. Compute the standard deviation of your estimates. How many trials do you need to achieve a standard deviation of $0.01 for your estimates?

7. Suppose $S(0) = 28$, $r = 0.05$, sigma = 0.4 and delta = 0, and t = 0.5. Use a Monte Carlo simulation to compute prices for claims that pay the following:

    (a) $S_1^{1/4}$
    (b) S_1^4

8. Suppose the probability of a market crash is $\lambda = 4\%$ per year.

   (a) Calculate the probability of at least one market crash in any given year.
   (b) Calculate the probability of seeing two or more crashes over a period of 20 years.
   (c) Let $t = 30$. Use the uniform distribution and an appropriate table to create 1,000 random draws from a Poisson distribution.

The following two problems ask you to use the Longstaff/Schwartz method to value an American put option with a strike price of $K = 1.15$:

9. Assume that $S(0) = 1$, $K = 1.15$, and the continuously compounded risk-free interest rate $r = 6\%$.

   (a) Create a table similar to Figure 19.1 indicating at which nodes early exercise might be optimal.
   (b) Conduct an early exercise analysis at $t = 2$.
   (c) Conduct an early exercise analysis at $t = 1$.

10. Use your results of Question 19.9 to answer the following two problems:

    (a) Verify that the price of an American put option is $0.1513. Be sure to allow for the possibility of early exercise at $t = 0$.
    (b) Calculate the price of a European put option and compare it to the result you obtained in part (a).

Chapter 20
Brownian Motion and Ito's Lemma

1. Suppose that $\alpha = 0.08$, sigma = 0.3. Suppose further that returns are normally distributed. What is the probability of having a one-hour return of less than –100%? Assume 365 days per year and 24 hours a day.

2. Let $t_0 = 0$, T = 0.25 and h = 1 month. Suppose further that $\alpha = 0.1$ and sigma = 0.3.
   (a) Demonstrate how you get from Equation 20.3 to Equation 20.4.
   (b) Demonstrate how you get from $X(t+h) - X(t) = \alpha h + \sigma Y(t+h)\sqrt{h}$ to Equation 20.7.

3. True or False?
   (a) The arithmetic Brownian motion does not allow a non-random drift.
   (b) Under geometric Brownian motion, the percentage change in the asset value is normally distributed.
   (c) In a stochastic process that incorporates mean reversion, the parameter lambda measures the mean of the process.
   (d) For a very small time interval, you can draw a Brownian motion using a fine pencil.
   (e) Arithmetic Brownian motion is a good process to model stock prices, because the very small time intervals used prevent the stock price from becoming negative.
   (f) Over a short interval of time, the random component of a geometric Brownian motion dominates the impact of the drift term.
   (g) A pure Brownian motion is not a stochastic process, because the standard deviation is 1 and it does not have a drift.

4. Suppose $\alpha = 8\%$, and sigma = 0.3. Construct a table similar to Table 20.1. At what time does the contribution of the mean to the movement of a discrete version of the Brownian motion become more important than the contribution of the random component?

5. Use Ito's Lemma to determine the process followed by dS^4, assuming that S(t) follows a geometric Brownian motion, and that sigma = 0.3, alpha = 0.08, and delta = 0.04.

6. Use Ito's Lemma to determine the process followed by $dS^{1/4}$, assuming that S(t) follows a geometric Brownian motion, and that sigma = 0.3, alpha = 0.08, and delta = 0.04. Interpret the drift term you calculate.

7. Use Ito's Lemma to determine:
   (a) the process followed by dS^a, assuming that S(t) follows an arithmetic Brownian motion as specified in Equation 20.8.
   (b) the process followed by dS^4, assuming that S(t) follows an arithmetic Brownian motion, and that sigma = 0.3 and alpha = 0.08.
   (c) the process followed by $dS^{1/4}$, assuming that S(t) follows an arithmetic Brownian motion, and that sigma = 0.3 and alpha = 0.08.

8. Suppose that S follows Equation 20.36 and Q follows Equation 20.37. Use Ito's Lemma to find the process followed by S/Q^2.

9. Let $dX = \alpha dt + \beta dZ_x$ and $dY = \lambda dt + v dZ_y$, where Z_x and Z_y are correlated Brownian motions with a correlation coefficient of ρ. Please note that the two processes follow arithmetic Brownian motions which means that you cannot use Formula 20.38—you have to derive a formula yourself, using the multivariate Ito's Lemma.
   (a) Use Ito's Lemma to find $d(XY)$.
   (b) Use Ito's Lemma to find $d(X/Y)$.

10. Stock prices and interest rates are oftentimes modeled as correlated stochastic processes. A common specification is the following:

    $dS = \mu S dt + \sigma_S S dZ_S$ and $dr = \lambda(\alpha - r)dt + \sigma_r \sqrt{r} dZ_r$

    where dZ_r and dZ_S are correlated so that $E[dZ_r dZ_S] = \rho dt$

    Using Ito's Lemma, derive the general price process for a claim that depends on S, r, and t.

Chapter 21
The Black-Scholes Equation

The following five exercises walk you through an explicit calculation of the Black-Scholes formula, using the solution techniques outlined in Section 21.3, in particular the subsection "Derivative Prices as Discounted Expected Cash Flows."

1. If we assume that the stock earns the risk-free rate of return (i.e., we perform risk-neutral valuation), the stock price follows the following stochastic process:

$$dS = (r - \delta)Sdt + \sigma S dZ^*$$

   Derive an expression for $d\{\ln[S(t)]\}$.

2. (a) How is $\ln[S(t)]$ distributed?

   (b) Use your answer to part (a) to write down a function for $S(T)$, given that the price today is $S(t)$. Hint: You should review Chapter 20.4.

3. The section "Derivative Prices as Discounted Expected Cash Flows" describes how the call option can be evaluated as

$$C[S(t), K, \sigma, r, T-t, \delta] = e^{-r(T-t)} \int_K^\infty [S(T) - K] f^*[S(T), \sigma, r, \delta; S(t)] dS(T)$$

   (a) Why do we integrate from K onwards, and not from minus infinity to plus infinity?
   (b) Separate the above integral into the difference of two integrals, the first integral involving $S(T)$, and the second involving K.

4. Let us first look at the second integral of your result for Question 21.3.
   (a) Factor out K, and rewrite this integral as a probability.
   (b) Use the definition of $S(T)$ you derived in Exercise 21.2 to solve the expression $S(T) > K$ in terms of the standard normally distributed variable (i.e., you want to end with an expression such as: prob(y > [...]), where y ~ N(0, 1).
   (c) What is the probability of the standard normal variable being larger than the value you calculated in part (d)? Compare your result to Equation 12.2(b).
   (d) Put your result of part (c) together with the terms you factored out in part (a) and compare it to the second part of the Black-Scholes formula. What do you conclude?

5. We will now tackle the first integral we separated in Question 21.3 (b).

    (a) Replace S(T) in the integral using the equation you derived in Question 21.2.

    (b) You showed in Question 21.4 that S(T) > K implied that y > -d_2. Therefore, you can replace the lower limit of integration K with -d_2, and change f*[S(T)] to f*(y), where y is the standard normal distributed variable. Write out the integral with these changes and replace f*(y) by the probability density function of the standard normal distribution. Verify that you get the formula:

    $$S(t)e^{(-\delta-0.5\sigma^2)\times(T-t)} \times \frac{1}{\sqrt{2\pi}} \int_{-d_2}^{\infty} e^{\sigma\sqrt{T-t}y-\frac{1}{2}y^2} dy$$

    (c) In order to complete the argument, we need some calculus results. Verify that you can rewrite the expression

    $$S(t)e^{(-\delta-0.5\sigma^2)\times(T-t)} \times \frac{1}{\sqrt{2\pi}} \int_{-d_2}^{\infty} e^{\sigma\sqrt{T-t}y-\frac{1}{2}y^2} dy$$

    as

    $$S(t)e^{(-\delta-0.5\sigma^2)\times(T-t)} \times \frac{1}{\sqrt{2\pi}} \int_{-d_2}^{\infty} e^{-\frac{1}{2}(y-\sigma\sqrt{T-t})^2 + \frac{1}{2}\sigma^2(T-t)} dy$$

    (d) Our ultimate goal is to rewrite the equation we derived in part (c) so that we can reformulate it as a standard normal distribution. The first step is to factor out all terms that do not depend on y to simplify the expression. Verify that the equation

    $$S(t)e^{(-\delta-0.5\sigma^2)\times(T-t)} \times \frac{1}{\sqrt{2\pi}} \int_{-d_2}^{\infty} e^{-\frac{1}{2}(y-\sigma\sqrt{T-t})^2 + \frac{1}{2}\sigma^2(T-t)} dy$$

    is equivalent to

    $$S(t)e^{(-\delta)\times(T-t)} \times \frac{1}{\sqrt{2\pi}} \int_{-d_2}^{\infty} e^{-\frac{1}{2}(y-\sigma\sqrt{T-t})^2} dy$$

    (e) Carefully study the equation above. If we could change $y - \sigma\sqrt{T-t}$ to a simple variable, say b, we would have again a standard normal variable in the later expression. There is a mathematical technique called change of variable that does precisely that. Define $b = y - \sigma\sqrt{T-t}$. Be very careful to apply the same transformation to the lower limit of integration, -d_2. Verify that the formula of part (d) can be changed to

    $$S(t)e^{(-\delta)\times(T-t)} \times \frac{1}{\sqrt{2\pi}} \int_{-\infty}^{d_1} e^{-\frac{1}{2}(b)^2} db$$

    Hint: Use the fact that $d_1 = d_2 + \sigma\sqrt{T-t}$ and that $b \geq -d_1 \Leftrightarrow b < d_1$ for a standard normal distributed variable.

    (f) Compare the last expression you derived in part (e) to the first part of the Black-Scholes formula. Take this result, combine it with Exercise 21.4 and conclude.

6. Verify that the Black-Scholes formula for a European put option satisfies the boundary condition $V[S(T), T] = \max[0, K - S(T)]$.

For the following three problems assume that S follows Equation 21.5 and Q follows Equation 21.33. Suppose $S(0) = 100$, $Q(0) = 80$, $T = 1$, $r = 0.08$, delta $= 0.04$, delta$_Q = 0.01$, sigma $= 0.3$, sigma$_Q = 0.5$ and $\rho = 0.4$. Use Proposition 21.1 to find solutions to the problems:

7. What is the value of a claim paying $Q(T)^{0.5} \times S(T)$? Verify your answer using Proposition 20.4.

8. What is the value of a claim paying $Q(T)^{-2} \times S(T)$? Verify your answer using Proposition 20.4.

9. What is the price of a claim paying $Q(T) \times \max(S(T) - 105, 0)$?

10. Verify that the Black-Scholes European put option formula satisfies Equation 21.11.

Chapter 22
Exotic Options: II

1. Suppose $S = \$72$, $K = \$70$, $\sigma = 0.4$, $r = 0.05$, $T - t = 4$ months, and $\sigma = 0.02$.

    (a) What is the value of a claim that pays \$5 if $S > K$ in 4 months?
    (b) What is the value of a claim that pays \$5 if $S < K$ in 4 months?
    (c) What is the value of a portfolio of the two claims described in (a) and (b)? What security does your portfolio resemble?

2. Suppose $S = \$72$, $K = \$70$, $\sigma = 0.4$, $r = 0.05$, $T - t = 4$ months, and $\delta = 0.02$.

    (a) What is the value of a claim that pays five shares if $S > K$ in 4 months?
    (b) What is the value of a claim that pays five shares if $S < K$ in 4 months?
    (c) What is the value of a portfolio of the two claims in (a) and (b)?
    (d) Why is the value of that portfolio not equal to $5 \times S(0)$?

3. Suppose $S = \$72$, $K = \$70$, $\sigma = 0.4$, $r = 0.05$, $T - t = 4$ months, and $\delta = 0.02$.

    (a) Suppose $H = 65$. What is the price of a cash down and in call?
    (b) Without using the software, evaluate the following claim:
    Suppose $S(0) > H$. If the barrier H is equal to the strike price K, the cash down and in option is equivalent to the normal Black-Scholes option.
    Is this statement correct? Why? Why not?

4. Evaluate the following claim:
    A rebate option is sometimes worth less than the deferred rebate option, because the stochastic nature of the discount factor can have a negative impact on the price of the rebate option.

5. Consider the following option. Suppose $S = \$72$, $K = \$70$, $\sigma = 0.4$, $r = 0.05$, $T - t = 1$ year, and $\delta = 0.02$.

    (a) Calculate the Black-Scholes price of the above option.
    (b) An investment bank offers you a price of \$10.884 for the above option if you agree to the following modification: Your payoff is limited to $S - K$ whenever the stock price reaches $1.5 \times K$. The payoff is immediate should that barrier be reached. Should you accept the investment bank's offer?

6. Consider the following hypothetical example: Microsoft seeks to hire a new VP as head of creative services. Steve Jobs is approached. After some consideration, Steve Jobs agrees to a one-year contract if the following conditions are met: $1,000,000 base salary, and a "worry-free package" of either $1,500,000 in cash, or 75,000 Microsoft or 75,000 Apple options, whichever is larger. Assume that the current price of Microsoft is $28, the current price of Apple is $29, the correlation between Apple and Microsoft is 0.4, the volatility of Microsoft is 30%, the volatility of Apple is 35%, and the risk-free interest rate is 5%. Further assume that neither Apple nor Microsoft pay a dividend.

   (a) What is the value of the compensation package?
   (b) Suppose that the correlation coefficient is instead –0.4. Is the value of the compensation package higher or lower than in part (a)? Why?

7. One of the footnotes of the main text claims that $BSCall(s, K, \sigma r, T, \delta) = BSCall(Se^{-\delta T}, Ke^{-rT}, \sigma, 0, T, 0)$. Demonstrate this using the Black-Scholes formula.

8. On Monday, February 1st your boss walks over to your desk to tell you that one of her clients is interested in a quanto forward contract on the Nikkei 225 Index. Having recently read Chapter 22 of the McDonald textbook, you tell your boss that the price of such a quanto forward is:

$$V_{t,T}(Y_t, x_t; T) = Q_t \times e^{(r_f - \delta_Q - \rho s \sigma_Q)(T-t)},$$

with all variables as defined in the textbook. Your boss looks suspiciously at the equation and asks you why there are no exchange rates, but a correlation coefficient in the equation. You briefly consider telling her that this is the consequence of applying Itô's Lemma to a product of two correlated stochastic processes that model the exchange rate and the index level, but then, after some thoughts, you decide to go another way.

You decide to demonstrate that the above pricing equation yields the same result as a two period binomial model that prices a quanto forward contract on the Nikkei 225 with an expiration date exactly one year from now.

Since you would like the binomial tree to be as accurate as possible, you decide to look up and construct the relevant input variables from Bloomberg or another financial data source of your choice.

9. Your boss was pleased with your above answer to Question 22.8 and takes you to her next client meeting on February 2nd. After half an hour of discussion, you realize that the client really wants to buy a quanto option and not a quanto forward contract. In fact, the client is interested in a quanto put option on the Nikkei 225 Index with a strike that is currently 10% out of the money and with an expiration date of April 14th so that he does not have to report an open derivatives position in the annual report's balance sheet on April 16th. The client would like the size of the contract to be $10,000 times the difference between the strike price and the index level at expiration.

   (a) Your boss instructs you to price such an option using an appropriate version of the Black-Scholes formula.
   (b) Furthermore, your boss would like you to qualitatively describe the necessary hedging portfolio.

10. Your boss is concerned that there might be fluctuations in the correlation between the Nikkei Index and the exchange rate. In particular, she thinks that the correlation is not exactly the one that you used in Question 22.9, but could rather be the correlation you used in Question 22.9 + 0.2 or –0.2.

    What consequences does this have for the Black-Scholes price you calculated? Explain the differences.

Chapter 23
Volatility

1. Suppose you observe the following yields and volatilities:

Period	Yield to Maturity	1-Year Forward Price Volatility
1	0.05	—
2	0.055	0.12
3	0.06	0.12
4	0.07	0.128

   (a) What is the two-year forward price for a one-year bond?
   (b) What is the price of a call option that expires in two years, giving you the right to pay $0.92 to buy a bond expiring in one year?
   (c) What is the price of an otherwise identical put?

2. Using the yields and volatilities of Question 23.1, what is the price of a three-year interest rate cap with a 7.2% effective annual cap rate?

3. Suppose you observe the following yields and volatilities:

Period	Yield to Maturity	1-Year Forward Price Volatility
1	0.06	—
2	0.065	0.14
3	0.072	0.13
4	0.075	0.12
5	0.08	0.11

   (a) What is the four-year forward price for a one-year bond?
   (b) What is the price of a call option that expires in four years, giving you the right to pay $0.85 to buy a bond expiring in one year?
   (c) What is the price of an otherwise identical put?

4. Consider two zero-coupon bonds with 5 years and 10 years to maturity, respectively. Let a = 0.25, b = 0.15, r = 0.06, $\sigma_{Vasicek}$ = 12%, and $\sigma_{CIR} = \sigma_{Vasicek}/\sqrt{r}$. We assume that the interest rate risk premium is 0 for both bonds. Assume that both bonds have a par value of $1,000.

   Compute the prices, deltas, and gammas of the bonds using the CIR and Vasicek models.

5. Consider a five-year coupon bond that pays a 7% coupon annually. Let a = 0.25, b = 0.08, r = 0.06, $\sigma_{Vasicek} = 12\%$, and $\sigma_{CIR} = \sigma_{Vasicek}/\sqrt{r}$. Assume that the interest rate risk premium is zero, and that the bond has a par value of $1,000.
    (a) What is the price of the bond using the Vasicek model?
    (b) What is the price of the bond using the CIR model?

6. Develop a three-period Black-Derman-Toy interest rate and zero-coupon tree for the following input parameters:

Period	Yield to Maturity	Volatility in One Year
1	0.10	—
2	0.11	0.19
3	0.12	0.18

    Hint: You will need to use Equations 23.50–23.53 of the main text and the Microsoft Excel solver tool. Define five cells for each time t: two cells with the Formulas 23.50 and 23.51(23.52 and 23.53), two cells with the corresponding target values from the table above, and a cell in which Excel's solver can minimize the squared deviations of the equations above from the target values.

7. Equations 23.52 and 23.53 solve for R_2 and σ_2. Develop a similar set of equations for R_3 and σ_3.

8. Extend the BDT trees you constructed in Question 23.6 by one year, using the following values:

Period	Yield to Maturity	Volatility in One Year
4	0.125	0.17

9. We will now value a three-period coupon-bond using the interest rate tree we developed in Question 23.6. Assume we have a treasury bond with a 10 percent coupon (interest is paid annually), a face value of $100, and three years left to maturity.

    (a) Using the Black-Derman-Toy interest rate tree you developed, determine the value of this coupon bond at t = 0. Produce a figure showing the coupon-bond tree including the coupon payments at each node.
    (b) Produce the tree for the coupon bond less accrued interest (=less coupon payment).

10. Consider a two-year European call and put option on the three-year Treasury bond whose value you calculated in Question 23.9. We will value this option using our standard binomial tree approach.

    (a) Should you use the bond price tree with or without the coupon payments to value the option? Why?
    (b) What is the value of a two-year 95-strike European call option on the three-year treasury bond with an annual coupon of 10%?
    (c) What is the value of a two-year 95-strike European put option on the three-year treasury bond with an annual coupon of 10%?
    (d) Now suppose instead that both the call and put option are American-style options. Recalculate their prices.

    Therefore, the value of the American put option is equal to $1.668.

Chapter 24
Interest Rate Models

1. Consider the expression in Equation 24.6. What is the exact probability that, over a one-month horizon, stock A will have a loss of 15%?

   For the following questions, assume that the initial stock prices of stocks A, B, C, and D are $50. The three stocks have the following properties:

	Alpha	Sigma	Dividend Yield	Correlation with B	Correlation with C
Stock A	0.12	0.24	0.03	0.32	0.11
Stock B	0.22	0.42	0	1	0.4
Stock C	0.16	0.33	0	0.4	1
Stock D	0.219	0.418	0	0.99	0.4

2. Assuming a $5 million investment in one stock, compute the 90% and 97.5% VaR for stocks A and B over 1-day, 1-week, and 1-month horizons.

3. Assume a $5 million investment that is 50% in stock B and 50% in stock D.

   (a) Compute the 97.5% VaR for the position over a 1-week horizon.

   (b) Compare your answer to the calculations of Question 24.2 (relating to stock B). What do you conclude?

4. What are the 93% and 97.5% 1-week, and 1-month VaRs for a portfolio that has $2 million invested in stock A and $4 million invested in stock B?

5. Using the delta-approximation method and assuming a $5 million investment in stock A, compute the 93% and 97.5% 1-week VaR for a position consisting of stock A plus 0.5 sold 45-strike call options for each share. Assume a risk-free rate of 8% and a time to expiration of 0.5 years of the option.

6. Repeat the previous problem, but calculate the exact value of the portfolio. What do you conclude?

7. Confirm that the mean and standard deviation of Example 24.5 of the main textbook are indeed 8.392% and 16.617%, respectively.

8. Compute the 97.5% 1-week VaR for a written call ratio spread on stock A (buy 100,000 50-strike call and sell 200,000 60-strike calls) using delta-approximation. Assume a risk-free rate of 8% and a time to expiration of 0.5 years of the option.

   Draw a payoff diagram of the short call ratio spread. Do you think this is a good approximation? Why?

9. Recalculate the 97.5% 1-week VaR for the written call ratio spread using Monte-Carlo simulation. Use at least 10,000 simulations. What accounts for the difference in the results compared to question 7, if any?

10. Complete Example 24.10 of the main textbook and calculate the 95%, 1-week VaR for the hypothetical 12-year $1 bond. Assume that you have $1 million invested in the hypothetical 12-year bond.

Chapter 25
Value at Risk

1. Using weekly price data, compute historical annual volatilities for the Dow Jones Industrial, Microsoft, and Boeing for 1991 through 2004. Also compute the volatility for the entire period. What do you conclude by comparing the fourteen annual volatilities with the overall volatility?

2. Compute daily volatilities for 1991 through 2004 for the Dow Jones Industrial Index, Microsoft, and Boeing. Annualize the daily volatilities by multiplying by $\sqrt{252}$.

3. Compute an EWMA estimate, with b = 0.94, of Boeing's volatility, using daily data from January 1999 to December 2004. Plot the time-series of volatility.

4. Estimate a Garch(1, 1) model for Boeing, using data from January 1999 to December 2004.
   (a) Calculate B1, B2, and B3.
   (b) Calculate the unconditional volatility.
   (c) Repeat part (a) and (b), but exclude all observations which have an absolute daily return above 10%. Which days do you exclude? Can you see a particular problem for your time period? Compare your results to the results of part (a) and (b).

5. In the same figure, plot the time-series of EWMA estimates from Question 25.3, and the conditional volatilities of the Garch (1, 1) model with and without the excluded days of extreme returns from Question 25.4. Assume that for the days you excluded in the Garch(1, 1) estimation of Question 25.4(c), the volatility is the same as the previous day's volatility.

   Compare the graphs and describe the differences. What do you conclude?

6. Suppose S = $100, r = 8%, sigma = 30%, T = 0.25, and delta = 0. Use the Black-Scholes formula to generate call and put prices with strike prices ranging from $40 to $250, with increments of $5. Compute the implied volatility from these prices by using the formula for the VIX.

7. Compute January 12th bid and ask volatilities (using the Black-Scholes implied volatility function) for S&P 500 options expiring March 20th. Plot the implied volatility curves for both puts and calls. Be careful and include the dividend yield. Do you observe a volatility smile?

8. Compute January 12th implied volatilities using the average of the bid and ask prices for S&P 500 options expiring June18, 2005. Do you observe a volatility smile?

9. Assume S = $72, r = 5%, sigma = 40%, T = 0.5, delta = 0. Further assume that $\lambda = 0.04$, $\alpha_j = -0.5$, and $\sigma_j = 0.35$.

   (a) Use the Merton jump formula to generate an implied volatility plot for the following strike prices: K = 42, 48, 51, ..., 102.
   (b) Now assume that $\alpha_j = +0.5$. Use the Merton jump formula to generate an implied volatility plot for K = 45, 48, 51, ..., 99.
   (c) Plot both implied volatility curves in the same graph.
   (d) Evaluate the following statement:

   "Whenever we incorporate jump risk into option prices, implied volatilities calculated by inverting the Black-Scholes model are higher for in-the-money call options, and thus fit the observed volatility smirk of index options very well."

10. Assume S = $75, r = 6%, sigma = 40%, T = 1, and delta = 0. For strike prices from 45 to 105, in increments of 5, use beta values of –4, –2, 0, 2, and 4 to create CEV call option prices. Plot the implied volatility curves.

Chapter 26
Credit Risk

For the first six problems, assume that a firm has assets of $150, with $\sigma = 0.35$, $\alpha = 12\%$, and $\delta = 0$. The risk-free interest rate is 5%.

1. The firm has a single outstanding debt issue with a promised maturity payment of $200 in 10 years. What are the true and risk-neutral probabilities of bankruptcy? What is the credit spread?

2. Suppose the firm issues a single zero-coupon bond with maturity value of $180. Compute the yield, probability of default, and expected loss given default for times to maturity of 1, 2, 5, 10, 100, and 500 years. Explain your results.

3. Suppose the firm issues a single zero-coupon bond with time to maturity of 2 years and a maturity value of $300.

    (a) Compute the price, yield to maturity, default probability, and expected recovery for this bond.
    (b) Why is the yield so high?

4. Suppose the firm issues a single zero-coupon bond with a time to maturity of 5 years.

    (a) Suppose the maturity value of the bond is $100. Compute the yield and default probability for standard deviations of 0.01, 0.05, 0.10, 0.20, 0.40, 0.60, and 0.90.
    (b) Suppose the maturity value of the bond is $200. Compute the yield and default probability for standard deviations of 0.01, 0.05, 0.10, 0.20, 0.40, 0.60, and 0.90.
    (c) Explain your results.

5. Suppose that there is a 5% chance per year that the firm's asset value can jump to zero. Assume that the firm issues 10-year zero coupon debt with a promised payment of $175. Using the Merton jump model, compute the debt price and yield, and compare the results you obtain to a scenario where the jump probability is zero.

6. Suppose the firm has a single outstanding debt issue with a promised maturity payment of $175 in 5 years. Assume that bankruptcy is triggered by assets (which are observable) falling below $75 in value at any time over the life of the bond—in which case, the bondholder receives $75 at that time—or by assets being worth less than $175 at maturity, in which case, the bondholder receives the asset value. What is the price of the bond, and what is its yield? What is probability of bankruptcy over the life of the bond? What is the credit spread?

7. Use the information from the rating example of the main textbook to calculate a five-year transition matrix.

8. Suppose you create a CDO by using three bonds with a maturity value of $1,000, a default probability of 20%, a recovery value of $520, and a time-to-maturity of one year. The risk-free interest rate is 5%.

   The promised payoffs to the three tranches of the CDO are:

   Senior: 1,500

   Mezzanine: 800

   Subordinated: 700

   (a) Produce a table similar to Table 26.7 of the main textbook, assuming that the bond defaults are uncorrelated.
   (b) Explain yield and default probability of the senior tranche.

9. Repeat the previous problem, but assume that the three defaults are perfectly correlated.

10. Using the three $1,000 maturity value bonds and all assumptions given in Question 26.8, produce a table similar to Tables 26.9 and 26.10 (Nth to default bonds). Use Monte-Carlo simulation to price the 1st, 2nd, and 3rd to default bonds. Assume a default correlation of 0.4.

Answer Section

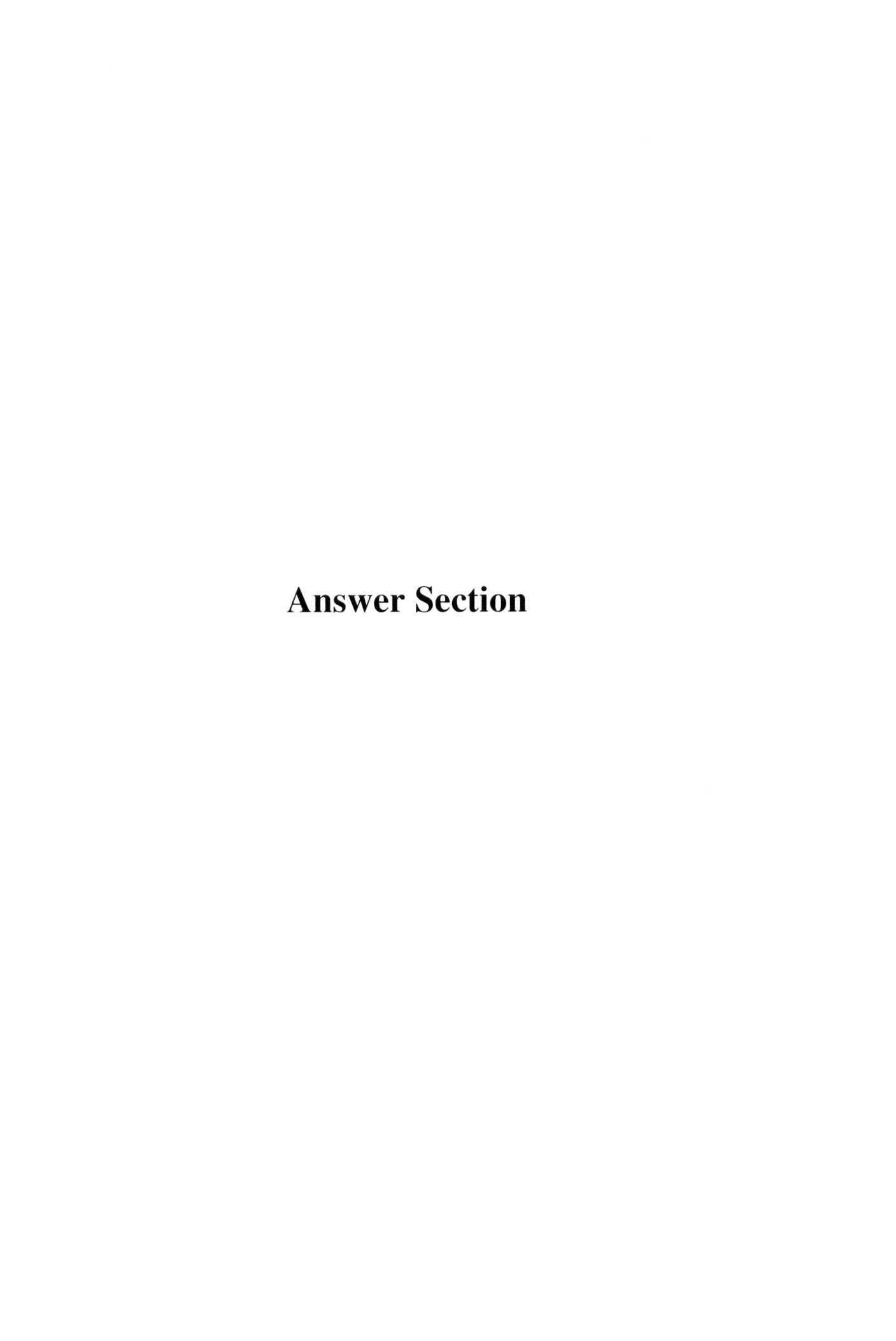

Chapter 1   Introduction to Derivatives

1. (a) The airline industry is a very good example. The profit of an airline company is severely affected when the price of oil is rising. Passengers oftentimes buy tickets in advance, and sudden price increases for kerosene cannot be passed on to the passengers. If a contract pays off in times of higher crude oil prices, airline companies can hedge their exposure to the oil price risk.

   (b) An example would be countries whose principal revenues stem from oil export. Their revenues are severely hit if the price of oil declines. Any contract that pays off in times of declining oil prices would be attractive to them.

   Note that speculators are also very active in the crude oil market. The drastic increase in crude oil prices that we witnessed in July 2004 was rumored to be partially driven by speculators hoping for ruptures in supply of crude oil.

2. One of the problems with wine is that it is much less standardized. You can set exact quality standards for crude oil, and market participants know and respect these standards. The wine futures contract traded at the exchange promised to deliver at the end of the contract five cases of wine that the seller could choose from a wide list of estates that were classified based on the French classification system of 1855. However, there could be large differences in the development of prices for different estates. This made trading complicated, because it was not absolutely clear what would eventually be delivered.

   The concept of standardization is very important. In later chapters, the book will deal more detail with the problem of standardization and delivery.

3. Broker A:
$$(\$98.20 \times 100) + (\$98.20 \times 100) \times 0.002 + \$5 = \$9,844.64$$

   Broker B:
$$(\$98.20 \times 100) + \$30 = \$9,850.00$$

   You should buy the shares from broker A, because your total out-of-pocket expenses are smaller.

4. Broker A:
$$(\$98.20 \times 150) + (\$98.20 \times 150) \times 0.002 + \$5 = \$14,764.46$$

   Broker B:
$$(\$98.20 \times 100) + \$30 = \$14,760$$

   Yes, your answer would change. Now you should buy from broker B. Proportional transaction costs are cheaper for small quantities. That is why you often see advertisements such as "We charge 0.5%, with a minimum charge of $15."

5. Remember that the terminology bid and ask is formulated from the market makers perspective. Therefore, the price at which you can buy is called the ask price. You pay:
$$(\$50.25 \times 50) + \$15 = \$2,527.50$$

   You can sell at the market maker's bid price. You will have to pay a commission, and your broker will deduct the commission from the sales price of the shares. You receive:
$$(\text{bid} \times 50) - \$15$$

Your round-trip transaction costs amount to:

$$57.50 = \$2{,}527.50 - (\text{bid} \times 50 - \$15)$$
$$\Rightarrow \text{bid} = \$49.70$$

6. We need to take into account the increase in the quotes after our trade was executed. This has an influence on the roundtrip transaction costs. Why should the bid and ask increase after we buy the stock? If the stock is very illiquid (i.e., it is rarely traded), our purchase might signal that we have good news about the development of company XYZ, and the market maker raises the price to take into account this conjecture.

$$\text{TAC} = \$51.37 \times 10 + \$10 - (\$51.25 \times 10 - \$10)$$
$$= \$21.20$$

Our transaction costs are smaller than without an increase in the quotes.

7. Remember that the market maker can buy at the bid and sell at the ask—that is how he makes a profit for the provision of liquidity. Therefore,

$$\text{Profit of Market Maker} = \$51.37 \times 10 - \$51.25 \times 10$$
$$= \$1.20$$

Despite the increase in quotes against him, the market maker is able to make a profit.

8. A short sale of MNO entails borrowing shares of MNO and then selling them at the bid. Therefore, initially, we will receive

$$200 \times (\$12.32) = \$2{,}464$$

The counterparty will keep that amount, but requires an additional 20% as a haircut. Therefore, we will have to transfer $0.20 \times \$2{,}464 = \$492.80$ to her.

9. (a) A short sale of MNO stock entails borrowing shares of MNO and then selling them, receiving cash, and we learned that we sell assets at the bid price. Therefore, initially, we will receive the proceeds from the sale of the asset at the bid (ignoring the commissions and interest). After 270 days, we cover the short position by buying the MNO stock, and we saw that we will always buy at the ask. Therefore, we earn the following profit:

$$100 \times (\$44.22) - 100 \times (\$44.22) \times 0.004 - (100 \times (\$49.05) \times 0.003 + 100 \times (\$49.05)) =$$
$$\$4{,}422 \times 0.996 - \$4{,}905 \times 1.003 = \$4{,}404.31 - \$5{,}052.15 = -\$647.84$$

Therefore, we actually made a loss of $647.84. The stock price rose during the life of the short sale, and with rising stock prices, a short position loses money.

(b) The proceeds from short sales, less the commission charge are $4,404.31. Since the 9-month interest rate is 6%, but the lender only offers 2% on our collateral, we lose an additional $\$4{,}404.31 \times 0.04 = \$176.17$. Our short sale turned out not to be profitable!

10. Sometimes, a particular stock is scarce and difficult to borrow. Very few investors are willing to lend the stock, and the demand for borrowing that particular stock exceeds by far the supply. Oftentimes, shares right after an IPO or shares of companies that are speculated to be involved in a merger are hard to borrow. IPO stocks can be hard to borrow, because there exists empirical evidence that after the high return on the initial day of the listing, there is a gradual decline in the stock price. Since a short seller benefits from declining prices, she is very interested in such stocks. Furthermore, in an initial public offering, usually only a small number of shares is sold, so the supply of shares is scarce.

NASD® (the National Association of Securities Dealers) has implemented a hard to borrow list via Rule 3370, which is designed to prevent abusive short selling and ensures that short sellers make sure they can return the shares they borrowed.

Chapter 2 An Introduction to Forwards and Options

1. Page 21 of the book defines a futures contract. A futures contract:

    1. Specifies the quantity and exact type of the asset or commodity the seller must deliver.
    2. Specifies delivery logistics, such as time, date, and place.
    3. Specifies the price the buyer will pay at the time of delivery.
    4. Obligates the seller to sell and the buyer to buy, subject to the above specifications.

    In the context of the delivery pizza,

    1. You specify the quantity (= number of pizzas) and the exact type of the commodity (one medium pepperoni, sausage, and extra cheese).
    2. Please deliver to my home address today. You might also ask: "When will you approximately deliver—will it be within the next twenty minutes?"
    3. You know how much the pizza will cost—you usually have a delivery menu at home.
    4. The pizza store often calls you back to verify you indeed ordered, and if ever you decide you do not want to have the pizza, makes sure that you are blacklisted!

2. (a) The payoff to a short forward at expiration is equal to:

    Payoff to short forward = Forward price − Spot price at expiration

    Therefore, we can construct the following table:

Price of Asset in 6 Months	Agreed Forward Price	Payoff to the Short Forward
950	1,050	100
1,000	1,050	50
1,050	1,050	0
1,100	1,050	−50
1,150	1,050	−100

    (b) The payoff to a sold call option at expiration is:

    Payoff to sold call option = − max[0, spot price at expiration − strike price]

The strike is given: It is $1,050. Therefore, we can construct the following table:

Price of Asset in 6 Months	Strike Price	Payoff to the Call Option
950	1,050	0
1,000	1,050	0
1,050	1,050	0
1,100	1,050	−50
1,150	1,050	−100

(c) If we compare the two contracts, we immediately see that the call option leaves the seller worse off. While the forward contract has some upside potential (for all prices below $1,050), the payoff of the sold call option is less or equal than zero. Therefore, the proceeds from selling the call option should be higher. As a seller, we have granted somebody the option to walk away, and we would like to be compensated for that.

3. On August 20th, 2004, the ask and bid price for the September 2004 995-strike S&P 500 call index option (SPX) were $103.90 and &105.90, respectively. The S&P 500 index closed at 1,098.35.

If we sell the call option, we can sell at the bid price of $103.90. This is our initial proceeds. The payoff and profit diagrams look as follows:

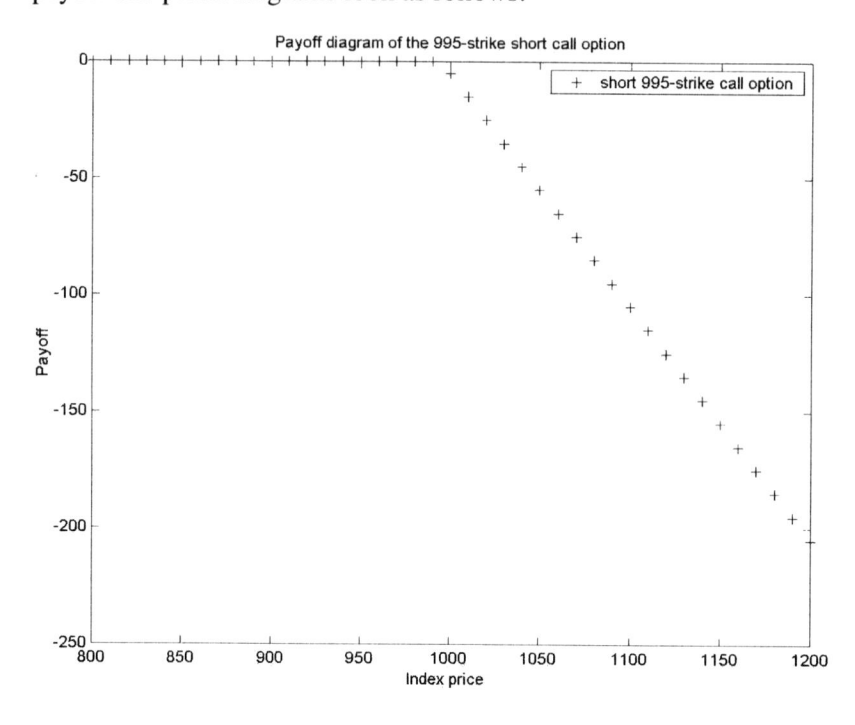

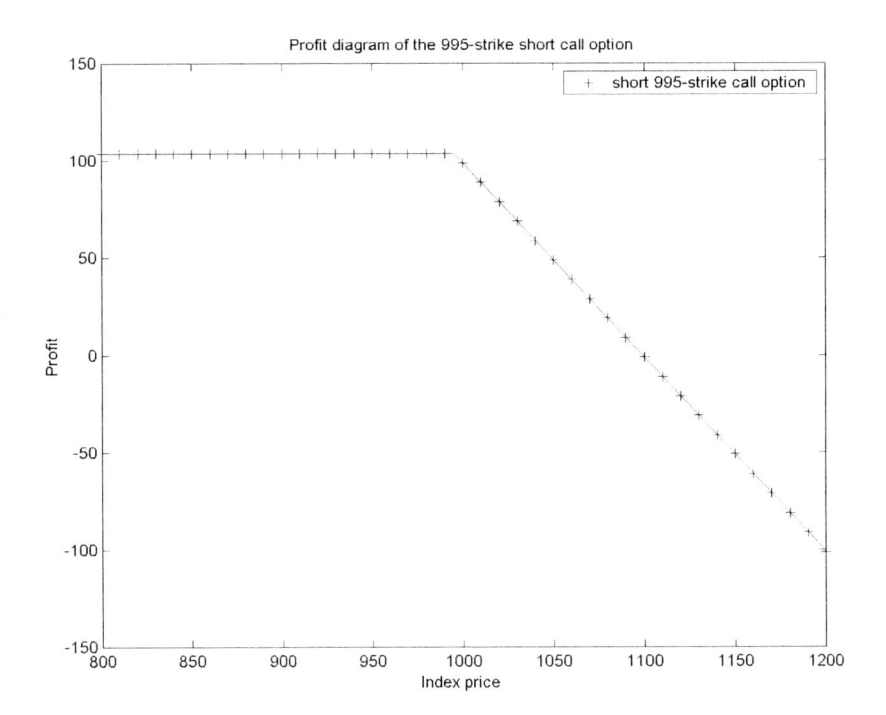

Profit diagram of the 995-strike short call option

4. (a) It does not cost anything to enter into a forward contract—as a seller, we do not receive a premium. Therefore, the payoff diagram of a forward contract coincides with the profit diagram. The graphs have the following shape:

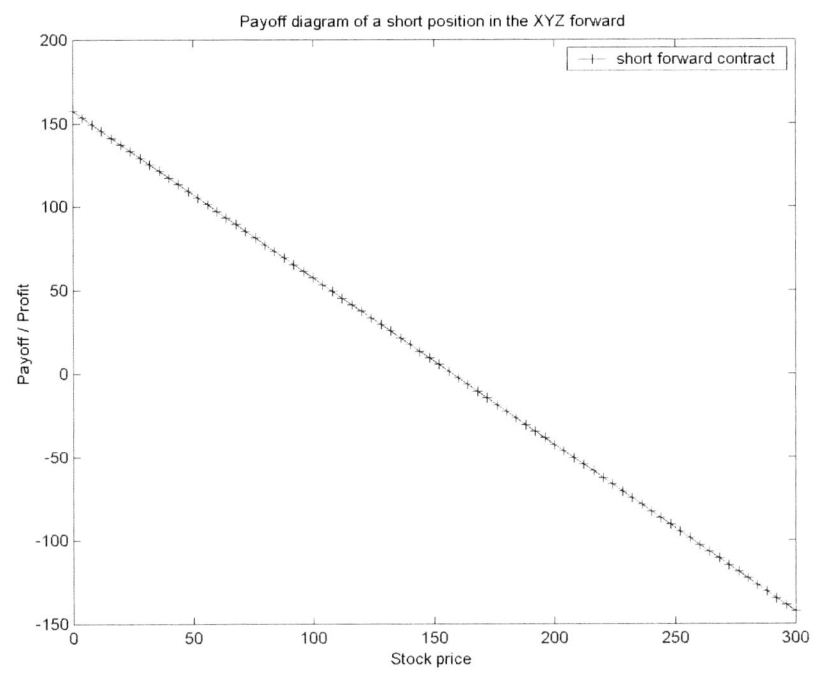

Payoff diagram of a short position in the XYZ forward

(b) We can invest the proceeds from the initial short-sale. We do so by lending $150. After one year we receive: $150 \times (1 + 0.05) = \$157.50$. Therefore, our total profit at expiration from the short sale of a stock that was financed by a loan was: $\$157.50 - S_1$, where S_1 is the value of one share of MNO at expiration. But this profit from selling the stock and lending the proceeds is the same as the profit from our short forward contract, and none of the positions requires any initial cash—but then, there is no advantage in investing in either instrument.

(c) The owner of the stock is entitled to the dividend. If we borrow an asset from a lender, we have the obligation to make any payments to the lender that she is entitled to as a stockholder. Therefore, as a short seller, we have to pay the dividend. As the seller of a forward contract, we do not have to pay the dividend to our counterparty, because she only has a claim to buy the stock in the future for a given price from us, but she does not own it yet. Therefore, it does matter now whether we short-sell the stock or the sell the forward contract. Because everything else is the same as in part (a) and (b), it is now beneficial to sell the forward contract.

5. (a)

Profit diagram of a long forward, long call

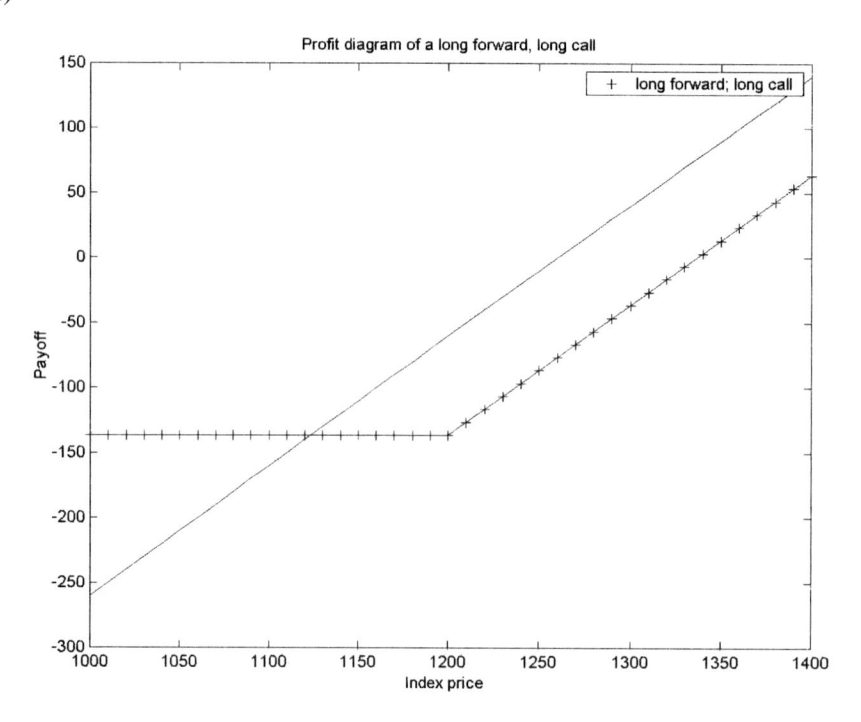

(b) From the figure in part (a), we see that the relevant intersection is in the flat part of the payoff function of the call. In solving the equation, we have to calculate the call premium at the end of the expiration, i.e., we have to take into account the accrual of interest. We therefore have to solve:

$$-\$130.12 \times (1+0.05) = S_T - \$1,260$$
$$\Leftrightarrow \quad S_T = \$1,123.37$$

6. (a)

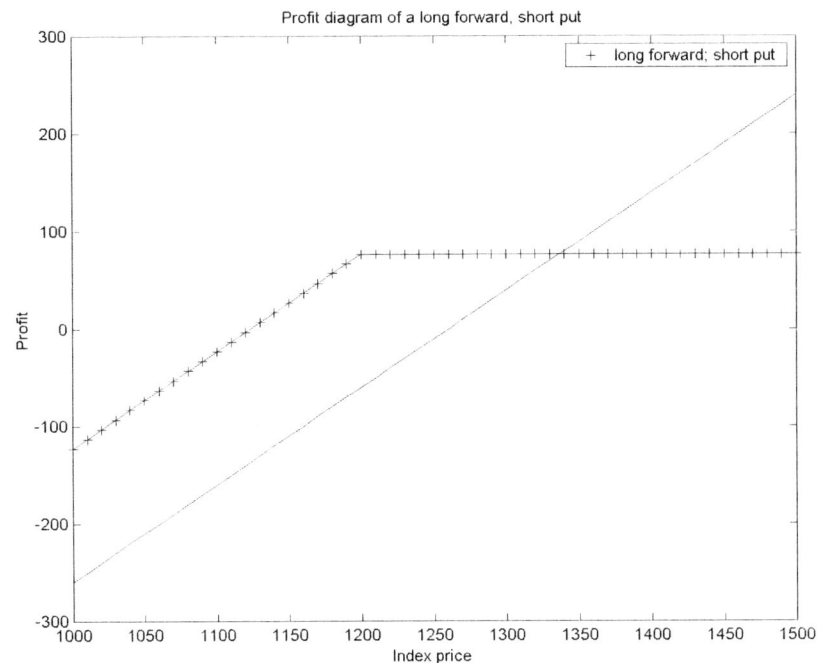

    [Profit diagram of a long forward, short put — plotted from Index price 1000 to 1500; long forward line is diagonal, short put combined position (+) rises then flattens near profit ≈ 75 beyond index ≈ 1260]

    (b) We need to solve (remember that we receive the proceeds from the sale of the put option, and can earn interest on them):

    $$\$72.97 \times (1+0.05) = S_T - \$1{,}260$$
    $$\Leftrightarrow \quad S_T = \$1{,}336.62$$

    Our profit from the sold put option is capped at the initial premium, plus interest, that we receive. Therefore, to the right of the threshold, we earn more profit with the long forward contract.

7. The buyer of the put owns a contract giving him the right to sell the index at a set price. Therefore, the buyer of the put is potentially a seller of the index.

    On the other hand, the buyer of a call option has obtained the right, but not the obligation to buy the underlying at a fixed price at some future time. Therefore, the seller of a call option is (potentially) a seller of the index.

8. The textbook defines an option as being in-the-money if it had a positive payoff if exercised immediately. Therefore,

    (a) the immediate payoff to this put option is 1,300 − 1,200 = 100. The option is in-the-money.
    (b) the immediate payoff to this put option is 1,000 − 1,200 = −200. The option is out-of-the-money.
    (c) the immediate payoff to this call option is 1,200 − 1,200 = 0. The option is at-the-money.
    (d) the immediate payoff to this call option is 1,200 − 1,000 = 200. The option is in-the-money.

    Therefore, (a) and (d) are in-the-money options.

9. Here is the profit diagram:

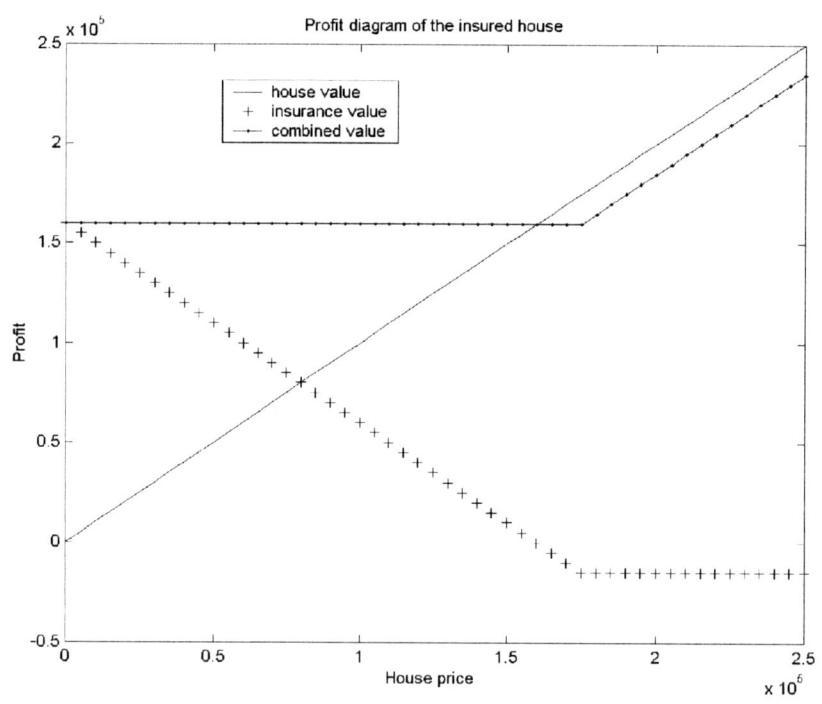

Profit diagram of the insured house (house value, insurance value, combined value vs House price)

You can see that the purchase of the insurance has guaranteed you that the value of your house, less deductible and insurance premium, cannot fall below $160,000. Please note that you do, of course, pay for this insurance. For high house prices, you see that the profit of the value of your house alone strictly dominates the value with insurance!

10. The payoff of the two policies looks as follows:

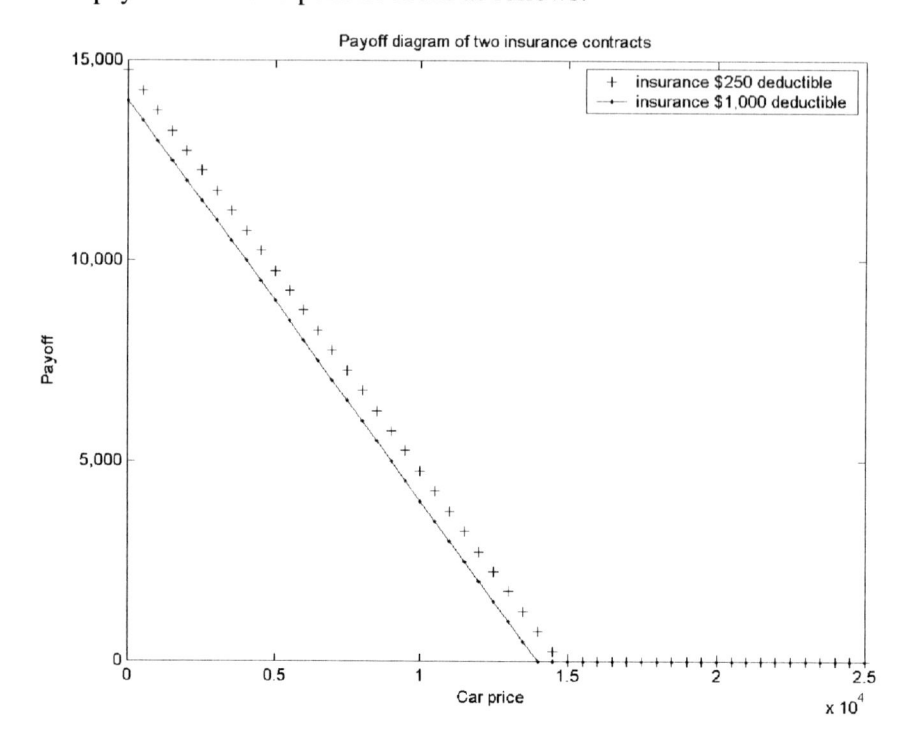

Payoff diagram of two insurance contracts (insurance $250 deductible, insurance $1,000 deductible vs Car price)

It is clear from the picture that the insurance contract with the smaller deductible pays at least the same as the contract with the $1,000 deductible, but for some future values of the car, it pays more. Therefore, the insurance contract with the smaller deductible must be worth more.

Chapter 3   Insurance, Collars, and Other Strategies

1. Initially, we have a cash flow of £4,110.58 − £4,275 − £356.04 = −£520.46. This grows to −£520,46 × 1.04 = −£541.28.

S&R Index	S&R Put	Loan	Payoff	−(Cost + Interest)	Profit
4,075.00	200.00	−4,275.00	0.00	−541.28	−541.28
4,175.00	100.00	−4,275.00	0.00	−541.28	−541.28
4,275.00	0.00	−4,275.00	0.00	−541.28	−541.28
4,375.00	0.00	−4,275.00	100.00	−541.28	−441.28
4,475.00	0.00	−4,275.00	200.00	−541.28	−341.28
4,575.00	0.00	−4,275.00	300.00	−541.28	−241.28
4,675.00	0.00	−4,275.00	400.00	−541.28	−141.28
4,775.00	0.00	−4,275.00	500.00	−541.28	−41.28
4,875.00	0.00	−4,275.00	600.00	−541.28	58.72
4,975.00	0.00	−4,275.00	700.00	−541.28	158.72

The payoff diagram looks as follows:

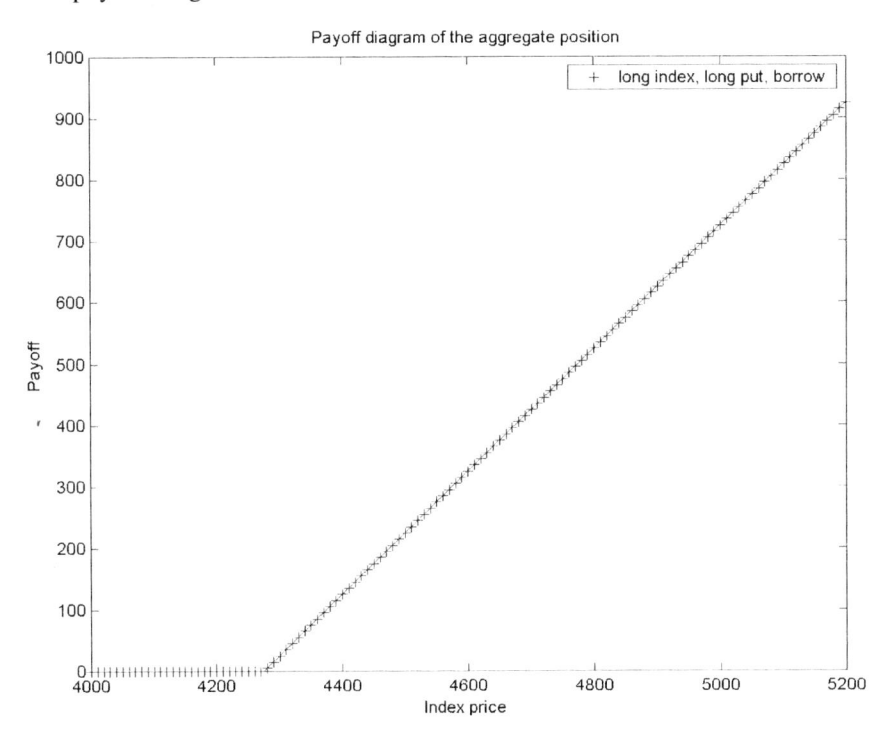

We can see from the table and from the payoff diagram that we have in fact reproduced a call with the instruments given in the exercise. The profit diagram on the next page confirms this hypothesis.

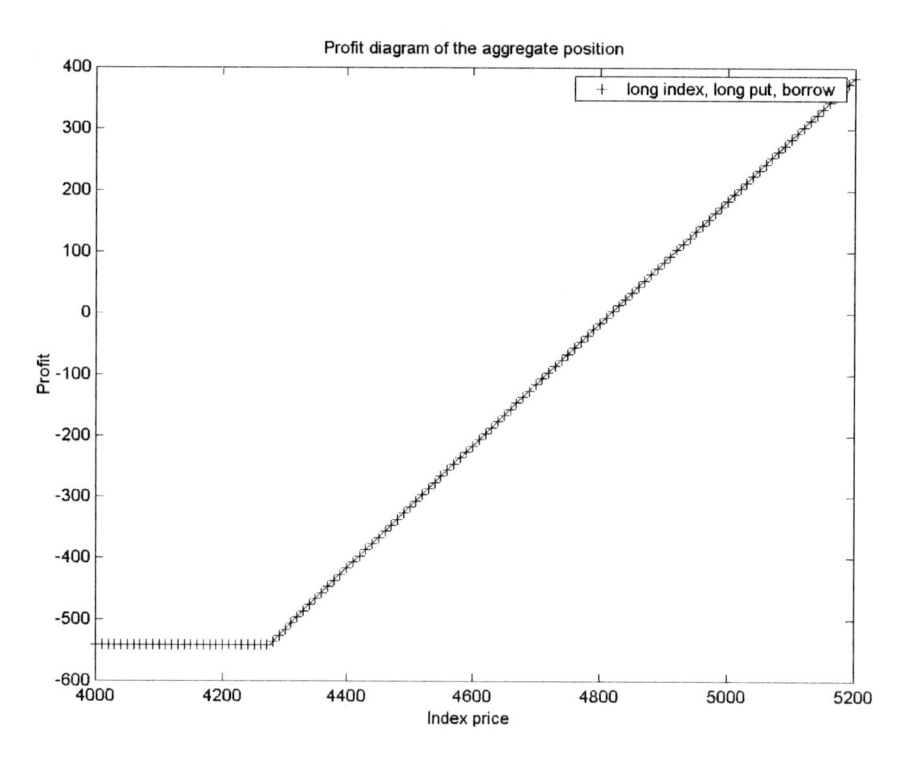

2. In order to be able to draw profit diagrams, we need to find the future value of the put premium, the call premium and the investment in zero-coupon bonds. We have for:

the put premium: £356.04 × (1 + 0.04) = £370.28,
the call premium: £520.47 × (1 + 0.04) = £541.29 and
the zero-coupon bond: £4,110.58 × (1 + 0.04) = £4,275.00

Now, we can construct the payoff and profit diagrams of the aggregate position:

Payoff diagram:

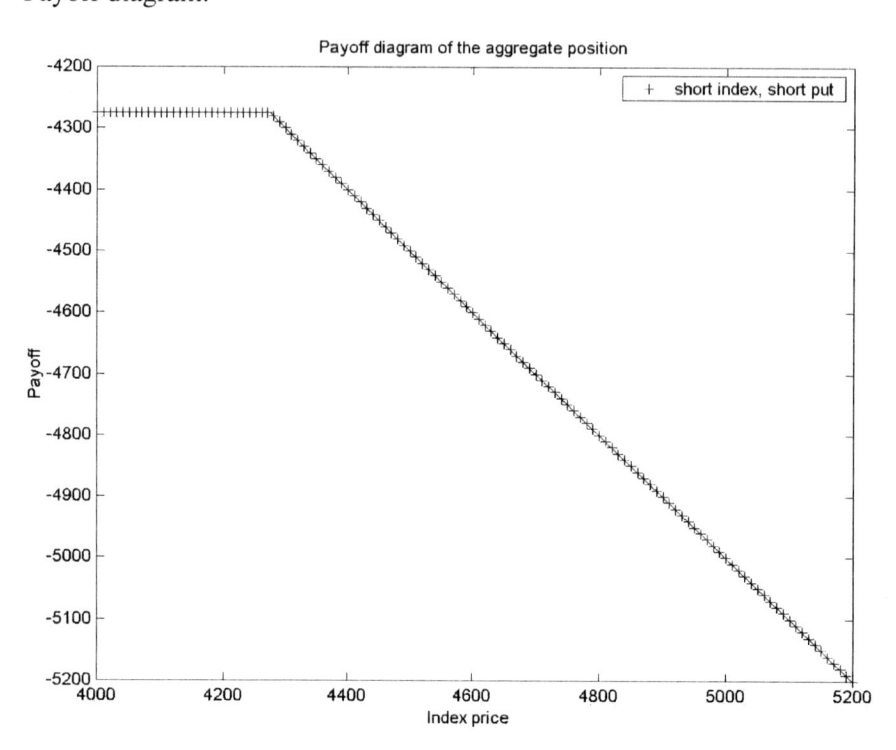

From this figure, we can already see that the combination of a short put and the short index looks exactly like a certain payout of −£4,275, minus a call with a strike price of £4,275. But this is the alternative given to us in the question. We have thus confirmed the equivalence of the two combined positions for the payoff diagrams. The profit diagrams on the next page confirm the equivalence of the two positions.

Profit Diagram for a short 4,275-strike put and a short index combined:

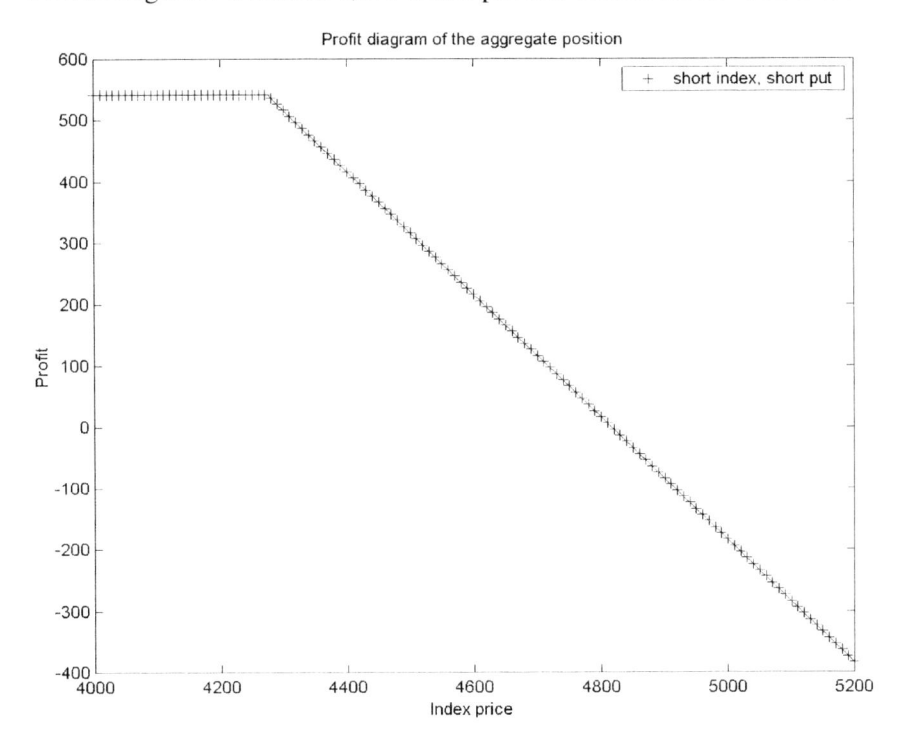

3. This question is another application of Put-Call-Parity. Initially, we have the following cost to enter into the combined position: We receive £4,275 from the short sale of the index, we have to pay the call premium, and receive the put premium. Therefore, the future value of our cost is: (653.62 − 4,275 − 248.81) × (1 + 0.04) = −4025. Note that a negative cost means that we initially have an inflow of money.

Now, we can directly proceed to draw the payoff diagram:

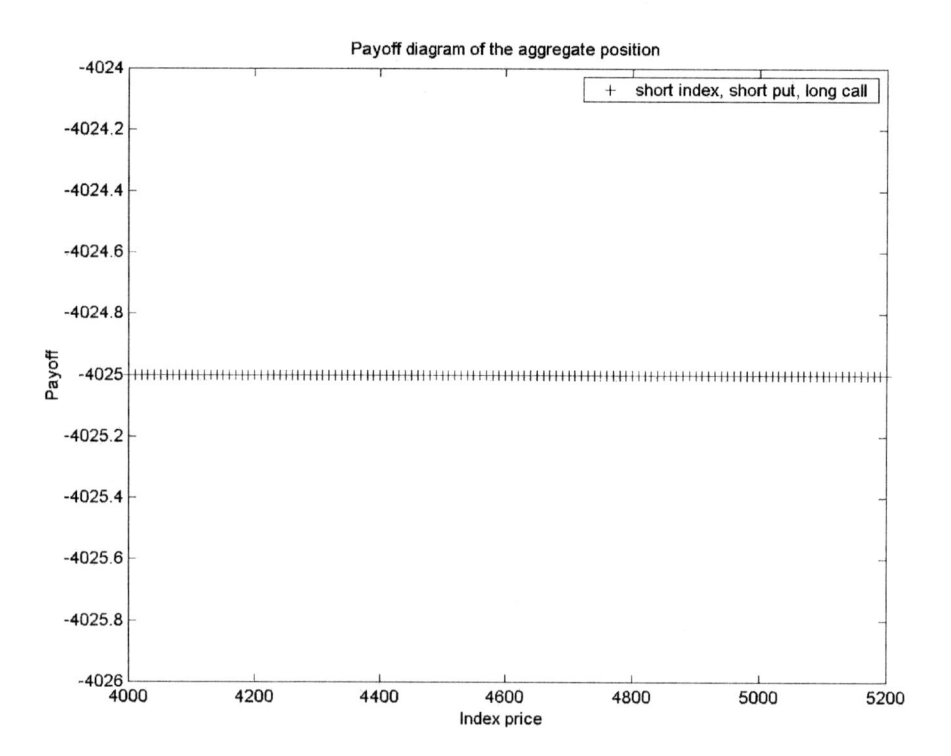

We can clearly see from the figure that the payoff graph of the short index, long call and short put looks like a fixed obligation of £4,025. Our initial cost was the present value of £4,025, so that the profit diagram is exactly zero. Note that this is what we should have hoped for. We have created a sure payoff, and the cost for that position should grow to the payoff at maturity.

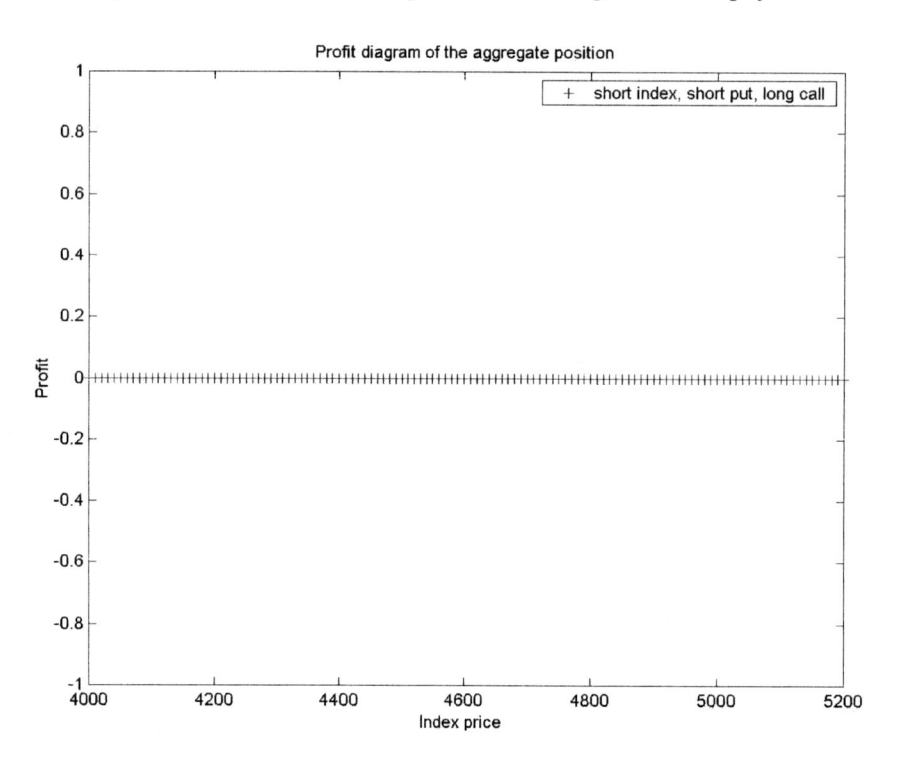

4. We now move from a graphical representation and verification of the Put-Call-Parity to a mathematical representation. Let us first consider the payoff of (a). If we buy the index (let us name it S), we receive at the time of expiration T of the options simply S_T. If we deal with options and the maximum function, it is convenient to split the future values of the index into two regions: one where $S_T < K$ and another one where $S_T \geq K$. We then look at each region separately, and hope to be able to draw a conclusion when we look at the aggregate position.

We have for the payoffs in (a) and (b):

Instrument	$S_T < K = 4775$	$S_T \geq K = 4775$
Payoff part (a)		
buy index	S_T	S_T
Long Put Option	$\max(4775 - S_T, 0)$ $= 4775 - S_T$	0
Total part (a)	4775	S_T
Payoff part (b)		
Long Call Option	$\max(S_T - 4775, 0) = 0$	$S_T - 4775$
Get repayment of loan	$4591.35 \times 1.04 = 4775$	$4591.35 \times 1.04 = 4775$
Total part (b)	4775	S_T

We now see that the total aggregate position of (a) and (b) are identical. We have proof of the payoff equivalence.

Now let us turn to the profits. If we buy the index and put option today, we need to finance it. Therefore, we borrow (£4275 + £633.46) = £4908.46, and have to repay £5,104.80 after one year.

For position (b), we have initially lent £4,591.35, and have bought the call option for £317.11. Our total cash outflow was thus (£4,591.35 + £317.11) = £4,908.46. This is exactly the same cost as in part (a). The profits of the aggregate position in part (a) and part (b) must therefore be the same.

5. Let us first consider the payoff of (a). If we short the index (let us name it S), we have to pay at the time of expiration T of the options: $-S_T$.

We have for the payoffs in (b):

Instrument	$S_T < K = 5,025$	$S_T \geq K = 5,025$
Make repayment of loan	$-4831.73 \times 1.04 = -5,025$	$-4831.73 \times 1.04 = -5,025$
Short Call Option	$-\max(S_T - 5025, 0) = 0$	$-\max(S_T - 5025, 0)$ $= 5025 - S_T$
Long Put Option	$\max(5025 - S_T, 0)$ $= 5025 - S_T$	0
Total	$-S_T$	$-S_T$

We see that the total aggregate position gives us $-S_T$, no matter what the final index value is—but this is the same payoff as in part (a). Our proof for the payoff equivalence is complete.

Now let us turn to the profits. If we sell the index today, we receive money that we can lend out. Therefore, we can lend £4,275.00, and be repaid £4,446.00 after nine months. The profit for part (a) is thus: £4446.00 − S_T.

The profits of the aggregate position in part (b) are the payoffs, less the future value of the put premium plus the future value of the call premium (because we sold the call), and less the future value of the loan we gave initially. Note that a risk-less bond is canceling out of the profit calculations. We can again tabulate:

Instrument	$S_T < K$	$S_T \geq K$
Make repayment of loan	$-4831.73 \times 1.04 = -5,025$	$-4831.73 \times 1.04 = -5,025$
Future value of borrowed money	5,025	5,025
Short Call Option	$-\max(S_T - 5025, 0) = 0$	$-\max(S_T - 5025, 0)$ $= 5025 - S_T$
Future value of premium	$243.19 \times 1.04 = 252.92$	$243.19 \times 1.04 = 252.92$
Long Put Option	$\max(5025 - S_T, 0)$ $= 5025 - S_T$	0
Future value of premium	$-799.92 \times 1.04 = -831.92$	$-799.92 \times 1.04 = -831.92$
Total	$4,446.00 - S_T$	$4,446.00 - S_T$

Indeed, we see that the profits for part (a) and part (b) are identical as well.

6. (a) The price of the butterfly-spread is $713.07 - 2 \times 496.46 + 333.96 = 54.11$.

    (b) This question is a direct application of three times Put-Call-Parity. We will use equation (3.1) in the following, and input the given variables:

    $$\text{Call}(K, t) - \text{Put}(K, t) = PV(F_{0,t} - K)$$
    $$\Leftrightarrow \text{Call}(K, t) = \text{Put}(K, t) + PV(F_{0,t}) - PV(K)$$

    $\text{Call}(3,925, t) - 2 \times \text{Call}(4,325, t) + \text{Call}(4,725, t) = \text{Put}(3,925, t) + PV(F_{0,t}) - PV(3,925)$
    $\qquad -2 \times \text{Put}(4,325, t) - 2 \times PV(F_{0,t}) + 2 \times PV(4,325)$
    $\qquad + \text{Put}(4,725, t) + PV(F_{0,t}) - PV(4,725)$

    $\Leftrightarrow \text{Call}(3,925, t) - 2 \times \text{Call}(4,325, t) + \text{Call}(4,725, t) = \text{Put}(3,925, t) - 2 \times \text{Put}(4,325, t) + \text{Put}(4,725, t)$
    $\qquad -PV(3,925 - 2 \times 4,325 + 4,725)$

    $\Leftrightarrow \text{Call}(3,925, t) - 2 \times \text{Call}(4,325, t) + \text{Call}(4,725, t) = \text{Put}(3,925, t) - 2 \times \text{Put}(4,325, t) + \text{Put}(4,725, t) - PV(0)$

    Therefore, the value of the butterfly spread using put options must be the same, £54.11.

7. The payoff diagram is as follows:

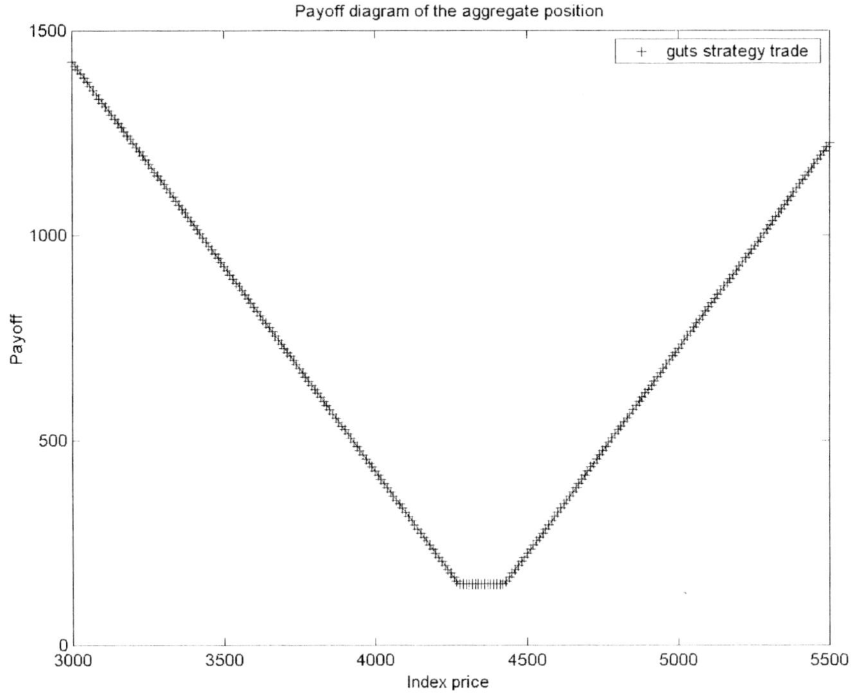
Payoff diagram of the aggregate position
guts strategy trade
Payoff
Index price
1500
1000
500
0
3000
3500
4000
4500
5000
5500

The payoff of the position is always positive. We should have learnt by now that such a position must have a big cost—there is no such thing as a free lunch! Indeed, when we look at the payoff diagram:

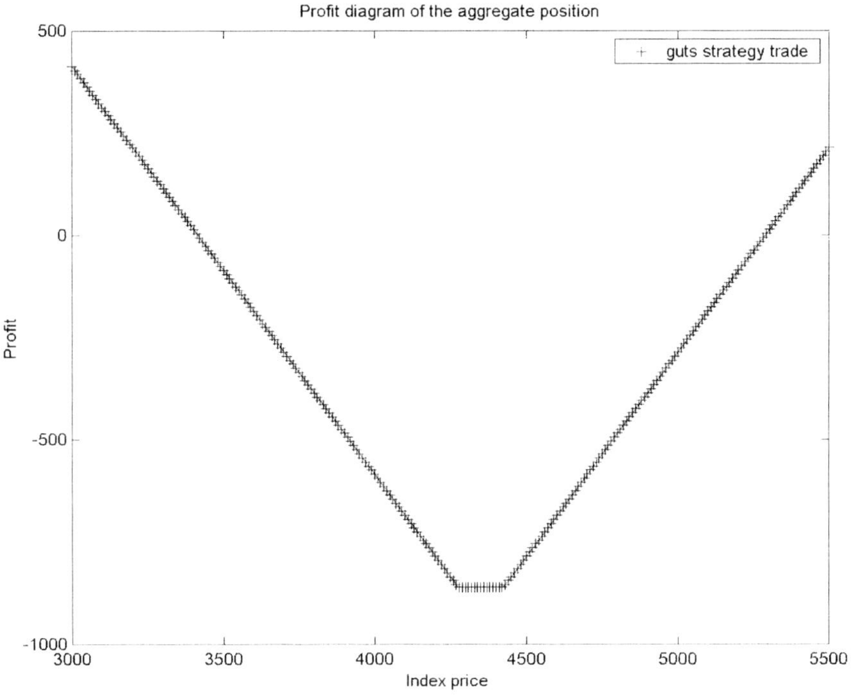
Profit diagram of the aggregate position
guts strategy trade
Profit
Index price
500
0
-500
-1000
3000
3500
4000
4500
5000
5500

The strategy is called guts, because it only pays after very wide swings in the market—hence it "takes guts" to enter in such a position.

8. The payoff figure looks as follows:

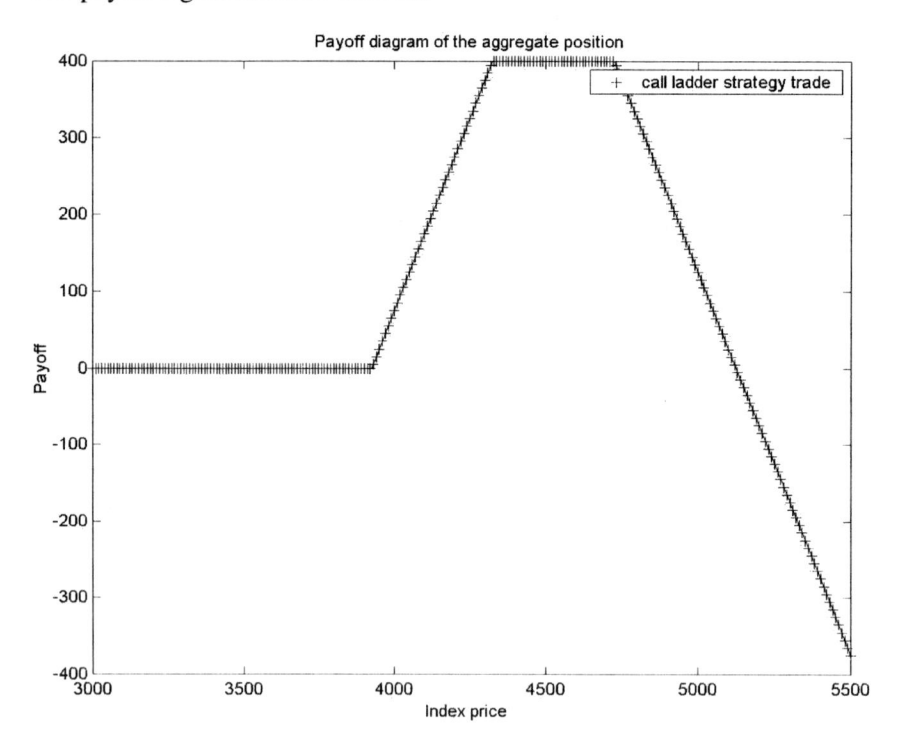

Payoff diagram of the aggregate position

The profit figure looks as follows:

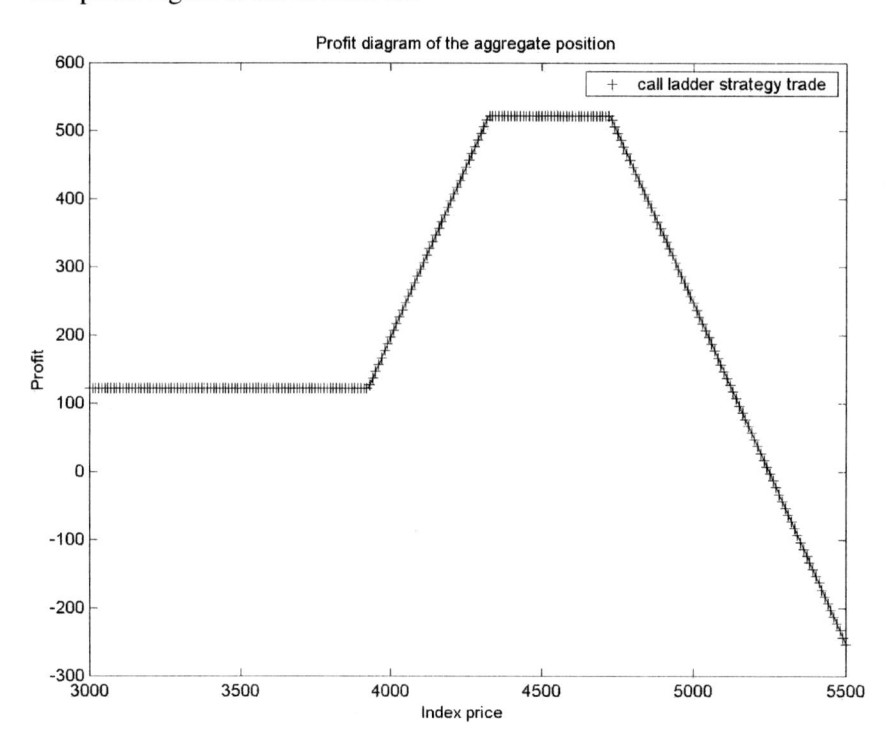

Profit diagram of the aggregate position

If you drew the pictures correctly, both payoff and profit diagram should look like a ladder. The positive profit for lower values of the index reflects the potentially unlimited downside risk the position has if the index grows a lot.

9. Payoff diagram:

[Payoff diagram of the aggregate position — iron condor strategy trade]

Profit Diagram:

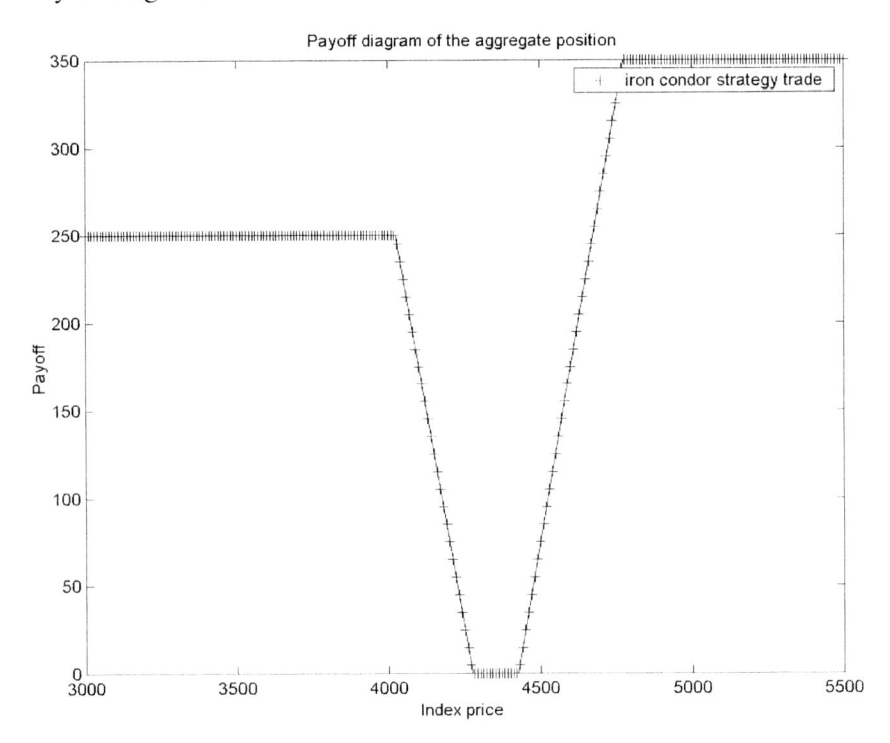

[Profit diagram of the aggregate position — iron condor strategy trade]

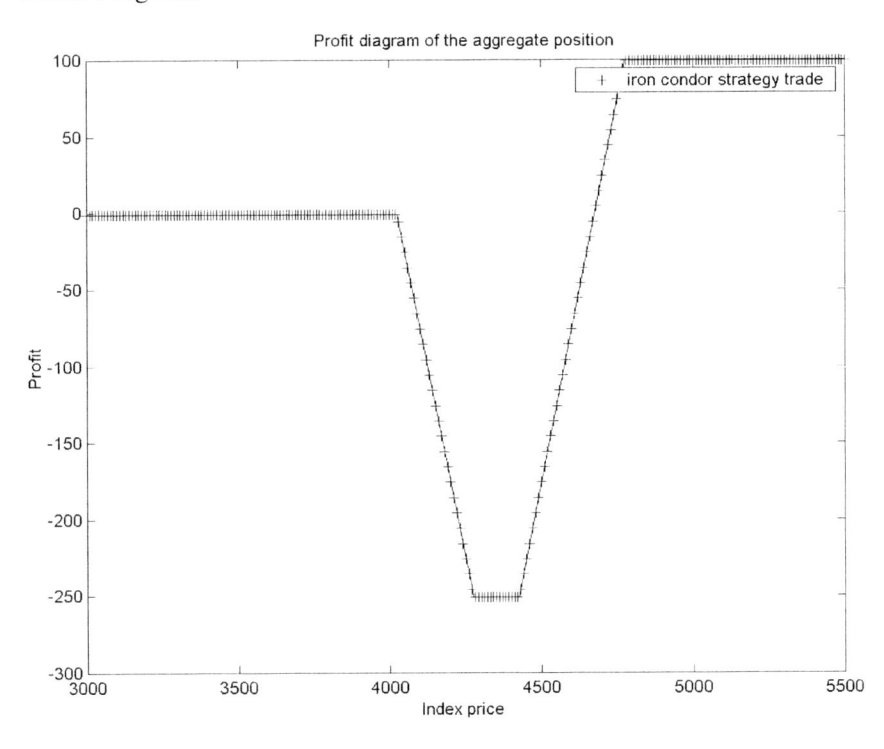

An iron condor is right for you if you expect the stock market to move significantly, but you are unsure of the direction of the market movement.

10. Payoff diagram:

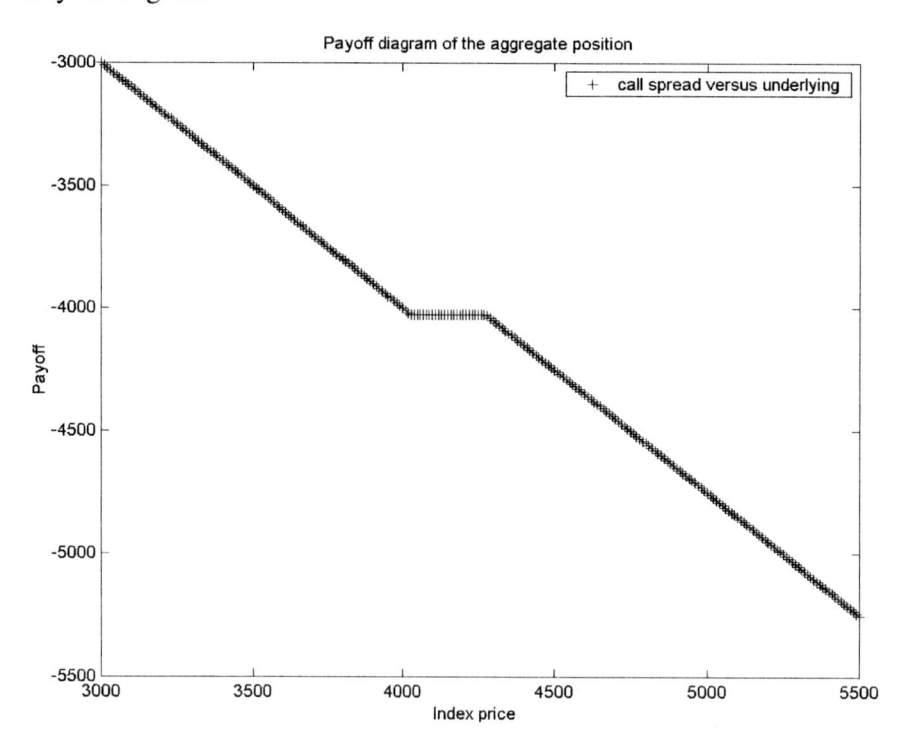

Profit Diagram:

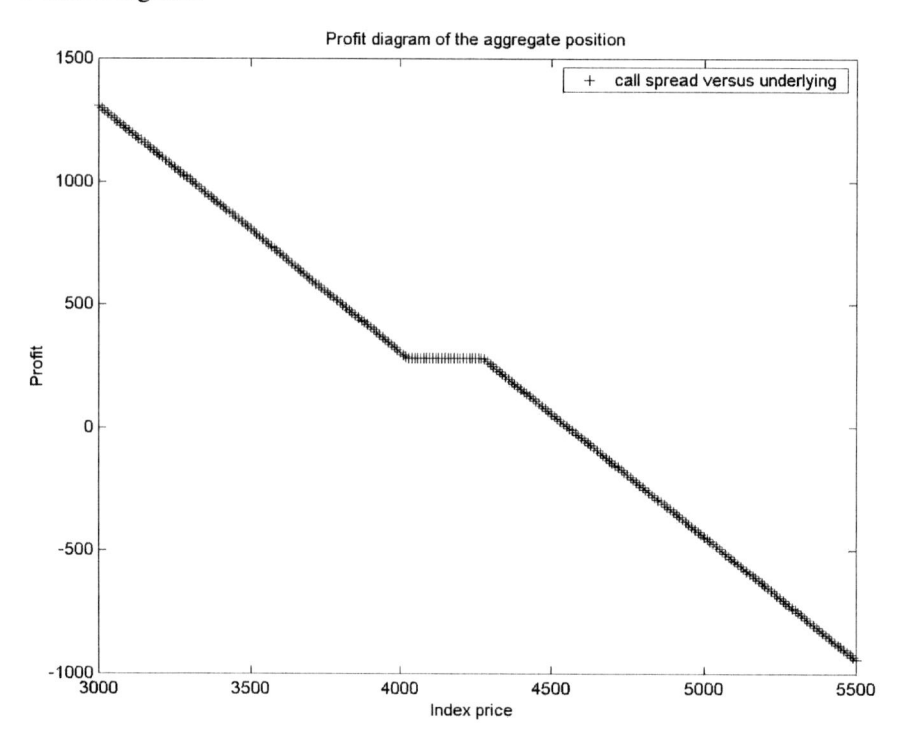

You are betting on falling markets. Your losses are potentially unlimited if the market increases towards very large numbers. You have bought some additional protection for index values between 4,025 and 4,275. Of course, you have paid for that protection (a price of 653.62 − 520.47).

Chapter 4 Introduction to Risk Management

1. The following table summarizes the unhedged and hedged profit calculations:

Oil Price per Barrel in One Year	Total Cost	Unhedged Profit	Profit on ½ Short Forward Contract	Net Income on Hedged Profit
$25	$28	−$3	$8.50	$5.50
$30	$28	+$2	$6	$8
$35	$28	+$7	$3.50	$10.50
$40	$28	+$12	$1	$13.00
$45	$28	+$17	−$1.50	$15.50
$50	$28	+$22	−$4	$18.00

We obtain the following profit diagram:

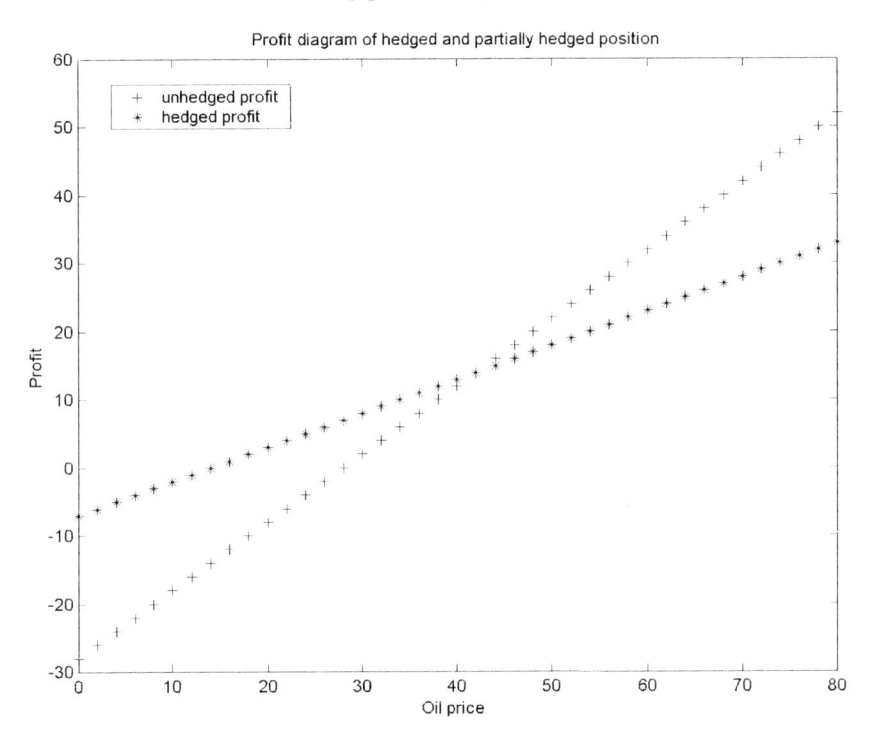

2. Please note that the continuously compounded rate of interest is given: it is 4%. Therefore, the effective annual interest rate is exp(0.04) −1 = 0.0408. In this exercise, to calculate overall profits, we need to find the future value of the put premia. For the $40-strike put, it is: $3.185 × 1.0408 = $3.315. The following table shows the profit calculations for the $40.00-strike put. The calculation for the other put is similar. The figure on the next page compares the profit diagrams for both hedging strategies.

Oil Price in One Year	Total Cost	Unhedged Profit	Profit on Long $40.00-Strike Put Option	Put Premium	Net Income on Hedged Profit
$25	$28	−$3	$15	$3.315	$8.685
$30	$28	+$2	$10	$3.315	$8.685
$35	$28	+$7	$5	$3.315	$8.685
$40	$28	+$12	0	$3.315	$8.685
$45	$28	+$17	0	$3.315	$13.685
$50	$28	+$22	0	$3.315	$18.685

Here are the profit diagrams for the different put strategies:

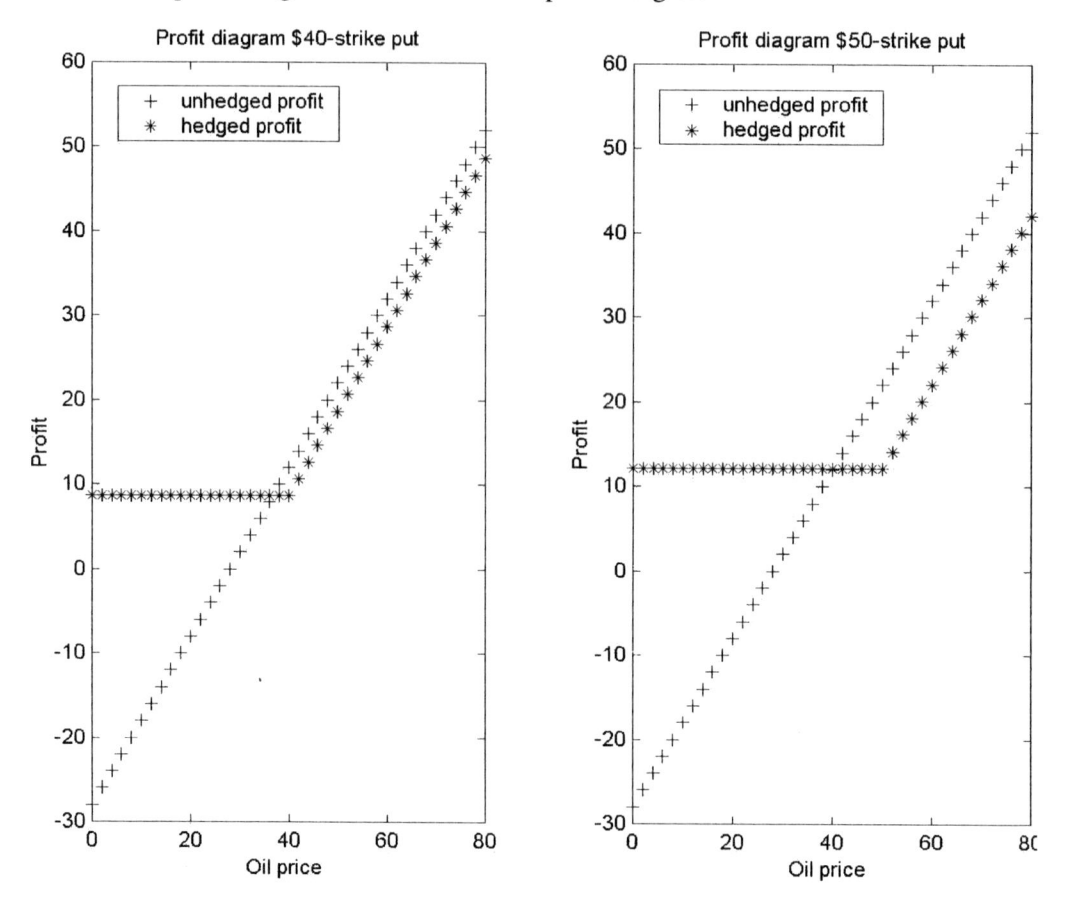

We can see from the diagrams that if oil prices increase, the unhedged position yields less profit than the hedged positions. This is the price we pay for the protection on the downside. Also note that the difference in profits between the unhedged position and the 50-strike hedged position is larger for higher oil prices than the difference for the $40 strike. We receive in return a higher profit in the low oil price region with the $50 oil price.

3. Plastics uses one barrel of oil to produce two units of resin. The variable oil costs per unit of resin are thus $0.5 \times p_{oil}$. We can write out the profits as revenue minus fixed costs, minus oil-variable costs, and minus non-oil variable cost:

$$P_{Plastics} = 0.4 \times p_{oil} + \$15 - \$7 - \$3.30 - 0.5 \times p_{oil}$$
$$= \$4.70 - 0.1 \times p_{oil}$$

The following graph shows how the profit per unit of resin of Plastics Corp. depends on the oil price.

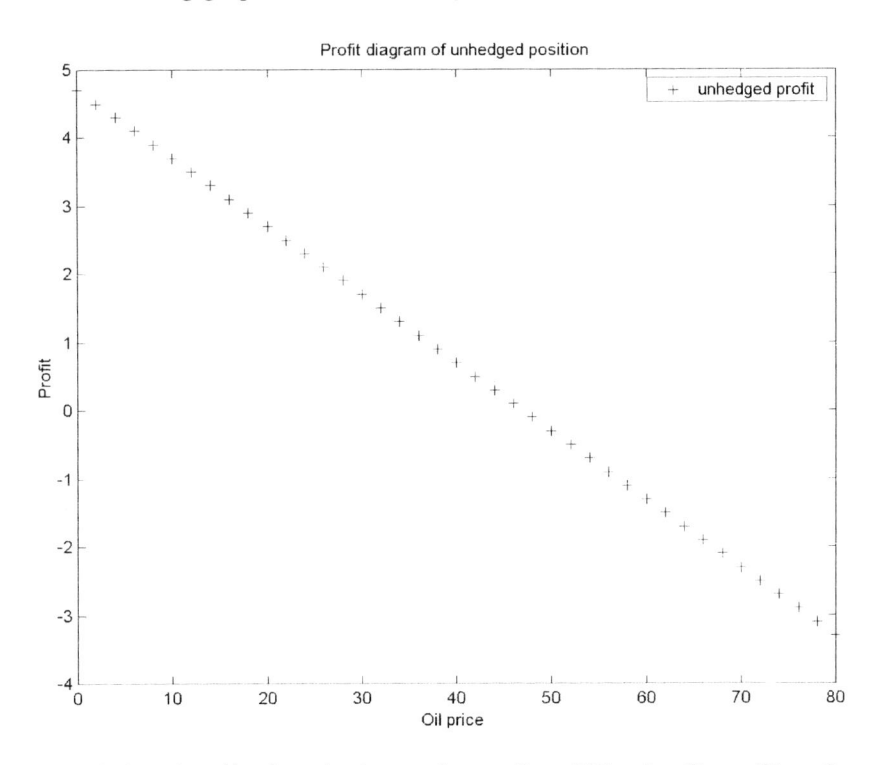

The higher the oil price, the lower the profits of Plastics Corp. Therefore, Plastics Corp. needs to buy futures to hedge their exposure.

4. We have seen in question 4.3 that the profit of Plastics Corp. can be described as:

$$P_{plastics} = \$4.70 - 0.1 \times p_{oil}$$

Therefore, we will need to buy 1/10 of a futures contract to completely remove the oil price risk from Plastics Corp.'s profits.

Oil Price in One Year	Unhedged Profit	Profit on 1/10 Long Forward	Hedged Profit
$25	$2.20	−$1.70	$0.50
$30	$1.70	−$1.20	$0.50
$35	$1.20	−$0.70	$0.50
$40	$0.70	−$0.20	$0.50
$45	$0.20	$0.30	$0.50
$50	−$0.30	$0.80	$0.50

We obtain the following profit diagrams:

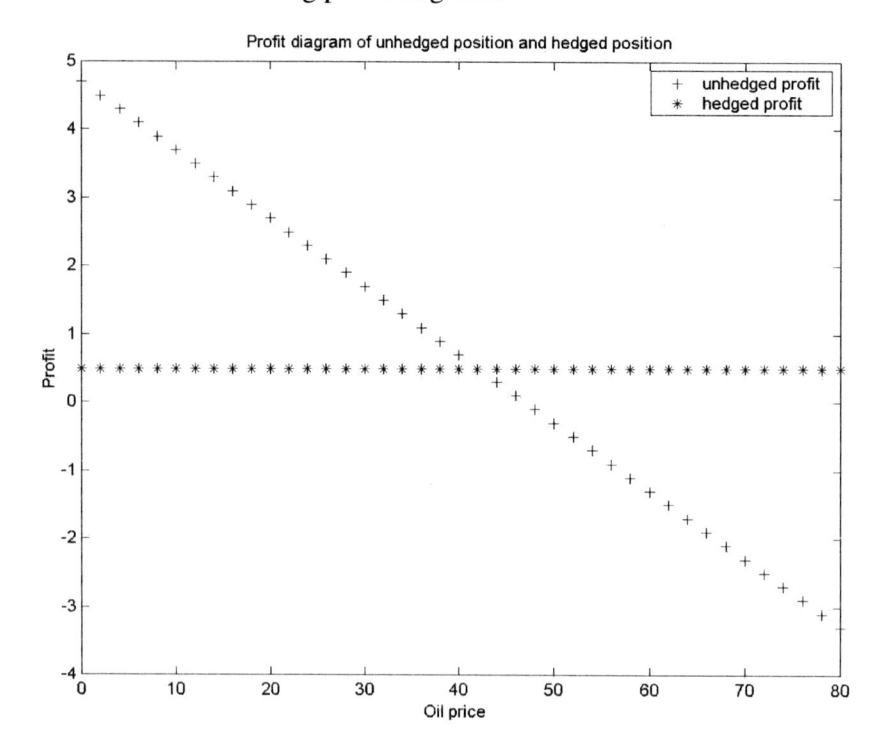

Profit diagram of unhedged position and hedged position

5. In this exercise, we need to first find the future value of the call premia. For the $35-strike call, it is: $8.085 × 1.0408 = $8.415. The following table shows the profit calculations of the $35.00-strike call and for one unit of resin. The calculations for the other call is similar.

Oil Price in One year	Unhedged Profit	Profit on 1/10 Long $35.00-Strike Call	Call Premium	Net Income on Hedged Profit
$25	$2.20	0	$0.8415	$1.3585
$30	$1.70	0	$0.8415	$0.8585
$35	$1.20	0	$0.8415	$0.3585
$40	$0.70	$0.50	$0.8415	$0.3585
$45	$0.20	$1.00	$0.8415	$0.3585
$50	−$0.30	$1.50	$0.8415	$0.3585

We obtain the following profit diagrams:

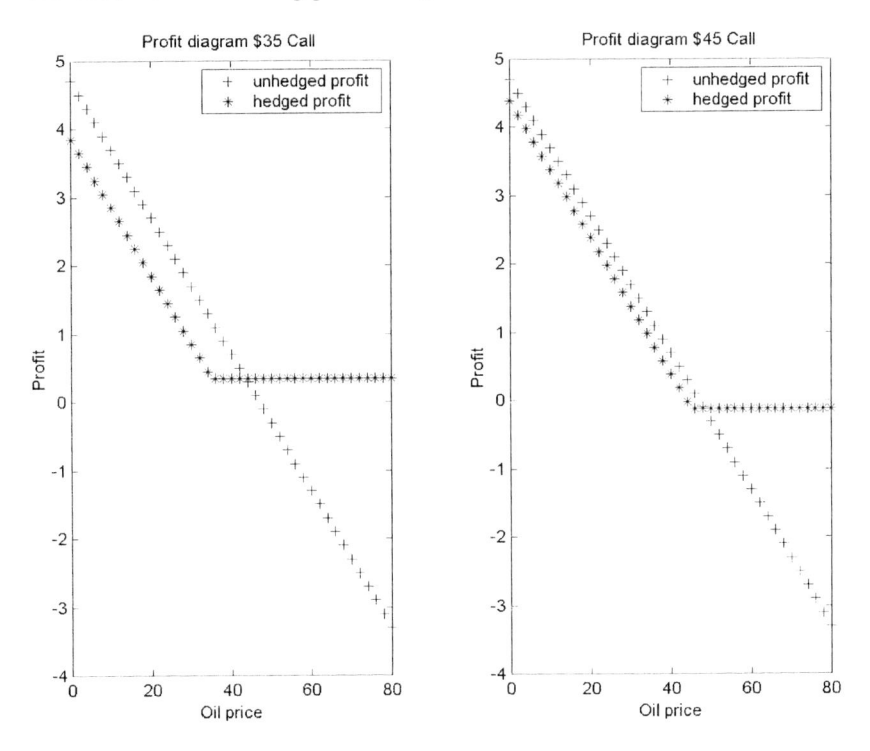

Profit diagram $35 Call

Profit diagram $45 Call

6. Plastics Corp. will sell a collar, which means that they buy the call leg and sell the put leg. We have to compute for each case the net option premium position, and find its future value. We have ($1.711 − $3.185) × 1.0408 = −$1.534. Note that the negative value means we have a cash inflow.

Oil Price in One Year	Unhedged Profit	Profit on 1/10 Short 40 Put	Profit on 1/10 Long 50 Call	Net Premium	Hedged Profit
$25	$2.20	−$1.50	0	−$0.153	$0.853
$30	$1.70	−$1.00	0	−$0.153	$0.853
$35	$1.20	−$0.50	0	−$0.153	$0.853
$40	$0.70	$0	0	−$0.153	$0.853
$45	$0.20	$0	0	−$0.153	$0.353
$50	−$0.30	$0	0	−$0.153	−$0.147

Profit diagram:

Profit diagram $40 put, $50 call collar

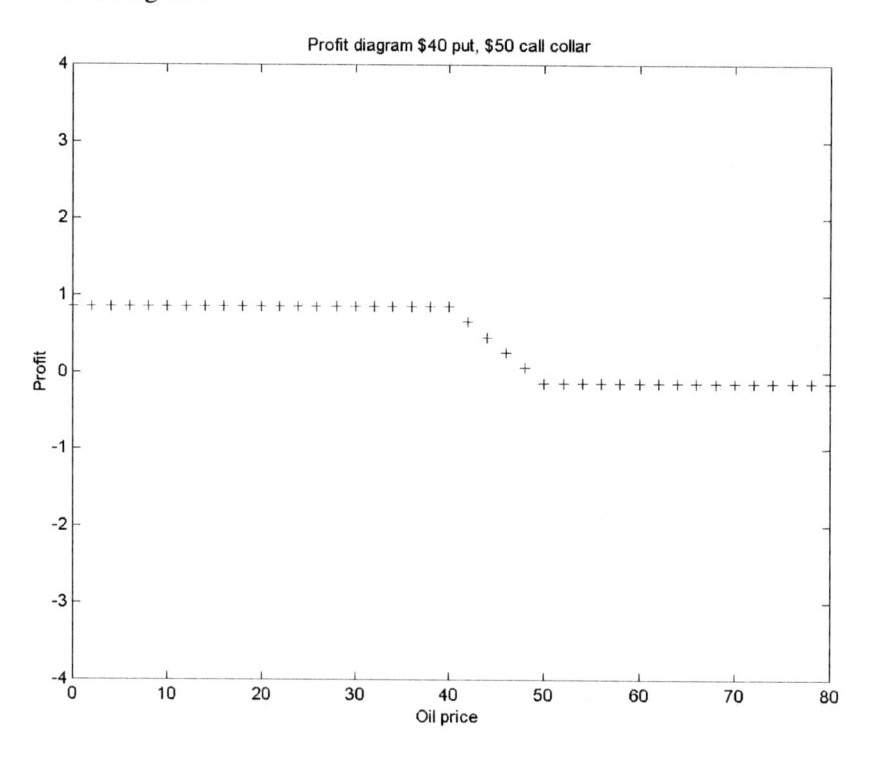

7. A good starting point is the table of call and put prices at the beginning of the questions to this chapter. We can see that the $45-strike call costs $3.032, and that the $40-strike put costs $3.185. Since the put prices are decreasing in the strike price, we know that we need to find a put that has a strike marginally lower than $40. Trial and error results in a strike price of $39.662. At that strike, the premium on the bought call and sold put cancel each other out.

8. (a) The hedged profit can be rewritten as:

    $$P = N_w P_w + (H - N_G) P_G - H \times F$$

    The last term is known and has no variance. Equation 4.4 is a direct application of the following rule for variance, with $b = (H - N_G)$

    $$Var(aX + bY) = a^2 Var(X) + b^2 Var(Y) + 2ab Cov(X, Y)$$

    (b) If we differentiate equation 4.4 with respect to H and set it equal to zero, we obtain:

    $$2(H - N_G)\sigma_G^2 + 2N_w \rho \sigma_w \sigma_G = 0$$
    $$\Leftrightarrow (H - N_G)\sigma_G^2 = -N_w \rho \sigma_w \sigma_G$$
    $$\Leftrightarrow H = N_G - \frac{N_w \rho \sigma_w \sigma_G}{\sigma_G^2} = N_G - \frac{N_w \rho \sigma_w}{\sigma_G}$$

    (c) We need to plug the optimal hedge ratio H* back into the equation of the hedged variance. Simplifying yields:

$$\sigma^2_{hedged} = N_w^2\sigma_w^2 + \left(N_G - \frac{N_w\rho\sigma_w}{\sigma_G} - N_G\right)^2\sigma_G^2 + 2\left(N_G - \frac{N_w\rho\sigma_w}{\sigma_G} - N_G\right)N_w\rho\sigma_w\sigma_G$$

$$\Leftrightarrow \quad = N_w^2\sigma_w^2 + (-1)^2 \times \left(\frac{N_w\rho\sigma_w}{\sigma_G}\right)^2\sigma_G^2 - 2\frac{N_w\rho\sigma_w}{\sigma_G}N_w\rho\sigma_w\sigma_G$$

$$\Leftrightarrow \quad = N_w^2\sigma_w^2 + (N_w\rho\sigma_w)^2 - 2(N_w\rho\sigma_w)^2$$

$$\Leftrightarrow \quad = N_w^2\sigma_w^2(1-\rho^2)$$

9. (a)

	Revenues (in Millions of Dollar)		
	Scenario A	Scenario B	Scenario C
35	3	−8.5	7.6
35	7.6	−1.6	5.3
45	19.6	16.3	16.3
45	13	26.2	14.32
50	18	25.6	16.1
50	25.6	40.8	13.44

Using Excel's formula stdevp, we get a standard deviation of S.O.'s revenues of $16.93.

(b) The correlation between oil price and the extraction schedule is negative—it is −0.8641. However, the correlation between oil price and the revenues is positive. It is: 0.8897.

This switch in signs is caused by the steep increase in oil prices: Although the extraction in scenario C decreases when oil prices increase, the price increase makes up for the smaller extraction, and total revenue actually increases with the oil price.

10. Using the equation of the book, we see that we need the standard deviation of the unhedged revenue, the standard deviation of the price of oil, and the correlation coefficient of oil and revenue. We calculated the correlation coefficient in part b2), it is 0.8897. The standard deviation of the oil price is 6.2361, and the standard deviation of the unhedged revenue is 4.2194. We obtain the following value for the variance minimizing hedge ratio:

$$H = -\frac{0.8897 \times 4.2194}{6.2361} = -0.602$$

If we sell short −0.602 futures, the revenue table for scenario C looks as follows:

	Revenues (in Millions of Dollar)		
	Scenario C Unhedged	Sell Forward 0.602 @$42	Scenario C Hedged
35	7.6	4.214	11.814
35	5.3	4.214	9.514
45	16.3	−1.806	14.494
45	14.32	−1.806	12.514
50	16.1	−4.816	11.284
50	13.44	−4.816	8.624

The standard deviation of the hedged revenue is $1.93. The standard deviation thus improved by $2.29.

Chapter 5 Financial Forwards and Futures

1. (a) Outright purchase—we enter a local pizzeria, choose a pizza that is already made and on display, and pay for it.

   (b) Fully leveraged purchase—we know the pizzeria owner very well, and eat there often. Therefore, we only pay for all pizzas eaten once at the end of the month. A pizza eaten on June 15th is thus not paid until June 30th.

   (c) Prepaid forward contract—we enter a local take-out pizzeria, choose a pizza from the menu, and pay. The pizzeria owner will prepare and bake the pizza, and we take delivery of the hot pizza 20 minutes later.

   (d) Forward contract—We call in to order the home-delivery of the pizza. We pay and receive the pizza 30 minutes after our order was placed.

2. (a) The owner of the stock is entitled to receive four dividends. As we will get the stock only one year from now, the value of the prepaid forward contract is today's stock price, less the present value of the four dividend payments:

   $$F_{0,T}^P = \$74 - \$0.75e^{-0.05 \times \frac{1}{12}} - \$0.75e^{-0.05 \times \frac{4}{12}} - \$0.75e^{-0.05 \times \frac{7}{12}} - \$0.75e^{-0.05 \times \frac{10}{12}}$$
   $$= \$74 - \$0.7469 - \$0.7376 - \$0.7284 - \$0.7194$$
   $$= \$74 - \$2.9323 = \$71.07$$

   (b) The forward price is equivalent to the future value of the prepaid forward. With an interest rate of 5 percent and an expiration of the forward in one year we thus have:

   $$F_{0,T} = F_{0,T}^P \times e^{0.05 \times 1} = \$71.068 \times e^{0.05 \times 1} = \$71.068 \times 1.0513 = \$74.71$$

3. (a) The owner of the stock is entitled to receive the dividends. We have to offset the effect of the continuous income stream in form of the dividend yield by tailing the position:

   $$F_{0,T}^P = \$74 e^{-0.05 \times 1} = \$74 \times 0.95123 = \$70.391$$

   (b) The forward price is equivalent to the future value of the prepaid forward. With an interest rate of 5 percent and an expiration of the forward in one year we thus have:

   $$F_{0,T} = F_{0,T}^P \times e^{0.05 \times 1} = \$70.391 \times e^{0.05 \times 1} = \$74$$

   The forward price is the same as the stock price. If we buy the forward, we have to forego dividend payments, because we do not own the stock. On the other hand, we can continue to earn interest on the amount the stock would cost today, because we have deferred payment. In this exercise, the cost and benefit of holding a forward contract cancel each other out.

4. (a) We plug the continuously compounded interest rate and the time to expiration in years into the valuation formula and notice that the time to expiration is 9 months, which equals 0.75 years. We have:

   $$F_{0,T} = S_0 \times e^{r \times T} = \$74 \times e^{0.05 \times 0.75} = \$74 \times 1.0382 = \$76.828$$

(b) The annualized forward premium is calculated as:

$$\text{annualized forward premium} = \frac{1}{T}\ln\left(\frac{F_{0,T}}{S_0}\right) = \frac{1}{0.75}\ln\left(\frac{\$77.00}{\$74}\right) = 0.0530$$

(c) For the case of discrete dividend payments, we have to solve:

$$F_{0,T} = S_0 e^{rT} - \sum_{i=1}^{n} D e^{r\times(T-t_i)}$$

$$= \$74 e^{0.05\times 0.75} - D\times e^{0.05\times(0.75-0.25_i)} - D\times e^{0.05\times(0.75-0.5_i)} - D\times e^{0.05\times(0.75-0.75_i)}$$

$$= \$76.828 - D\times(1.0253 + 1.0126 + 1)$$

$$\Leftrightarrow F_{0,T} - \$76.828 = -D\times(3.0379)$$

$$\Leftrightarrow \frac{(\$76.828 - \$75.309)}{3.0379} = D$$

$$\Rightarrow D = \$0.50$$

The constant quarterly dividend is $0.50.

5. First, we need to find the fair value of the forward price. We plug the continuously compounded interest rate, the dividends and the time to expiration in years into the valuation formula:

$$F_{0,T} = S_0 e^{rT} - \sum_{i=1}^{n} D e^{r\times(T-t_i)}$$

$$= \$66 e^{0.05\times 0.75} - 0.45\times e^{0.05\times(0.75-0.25_i)} - 0.45\times e^{0.05\times(0.75-0.5_i)} - 0.45\times e^{0.05\times(0.75-0.75_i)}$$

$$= \$68.522 - 0.45\times(1.0253 + 1.0126 + 1)$$

$$= \$68.522 - 0.45\times(3.0379)$$

$$= \$67.155$$

(a) If we observe a forward price of $67.50, we know that the forward is too expensive, relative to the fair value we have determined. Therefore, we will sell the forward at $67.50, and create a synthetic forward for $67.155, making a sure profit of $0.345. As we sell the real forward, we engage in cash and carry arbitrage:

Description	Today	in 3 Months	in 6 Months	in 9 Months
Short forward	0			$67.50 - S_T$
Buy stock	-$66.00			S_T
Borrow	$66.00	$66.00		-$68.522
Receive 1st dividend, invest dividend		$0.45 -$0.45		$0.4614
Receive 2nd dividend, invest dividend			$0.45 -$0.45	$0.4557
Receive 3rd dividend				$0.45
TOTAL	0	0	0	$0.345

This position requires no initial investment, has no MNO price risk, and has a strictly positive payoff. We have exploited the mispricing with a pure arbitrage strategy.

(b) If we observe a forward price of $66.75, we know that the forward is too cheap, relative to the fair value we have determined. Therefore, we will buy the forward at $66.75, and create a synthetic short forward for $67.155, thus making a sure profit of $0.405. As we buy the real forward, we engage in a reverse cash and carry arbitrage. Note that we have shorted MNO stock. Therefore, we are responsible for paying the dividends to the party we shorted from.

Description	Today	in 3 Months	in 6 Months	in 9 Months
Long forward	0			$S_T - \$66.75$
Short-sell stock	$66.00			$-S_T$
Lend	$66.00	–$66.00		$68.522
Borrow to pay 1st dividend to third party		$0.45 –$0.45		–$0.4614
Borrow to pay 2nd dividend to third party			$0.45 –$0.45	–$0.4557
Pay 3rd dividend				–$0.45
TOTAL	0	0	0	$0.405

This position requires no initial investment, has no MNO price risk, and has a strictly positive payoff. We have exploited the mispricing with a pure arbitrage strategy.

6. (a) We need to solve:

$$F_{0,T} = S_0 e^{rT} - \sum_{i=1}^{n} D e^{r \times (T-t_i)}$$

$$= \$44.25 e^{0.05 \times 0.50} - D \times e^{0.05 \times (0.50-0.25_i)} - D \times e^{0.05 \times (0.50-0.50_i)}$$

$$= \$45.37 - D \times (1.0126 + 1)$$

$$\Leftrightarrow F_{0,T} - \$45.37 = -D \times (2.0126)$$

$$\Leftrightarrow \frac{(\$45.370 - \$44.162)}{2.0126} = D$$

$$\Rightarrow D = \$0.60$$

(b) With a quarterly dividend payment of $1.00, the fair forward price would be:

$$F_{0,T} = S_0 e^{rT} - \sum_{i=1}^{n} D e^{r \times (T-t_i)}$$

$$= \$45.37 - \$1.00 \times (1.0126 + 1)$$

$$= \$43.357$$

Therefore, if we think that the dividend payment will be $1.00, we consider the observed forward price of 44.162 as too expensive. We will therefore sell the forward and create a synthetic long forward, capturing a certain amount of $0.805. We engage in a cash and carry arbitrage:

Description	Today	in 3 Months	in 6 Months
Short forward	0		$44.162 - S_T$
Buy stock	-$44.25		S_T
Borrow	$44.25	$44.25	-$45.37
Receive 1st dividend, invest dividend		$1.00 -$1.00	$1.0126
Receive 2nd dividend			$1.00
TOTAL	0	0	$0.805

(c) With a constant quarterly dividend of only $0.25, the fair forward price would be:

$$F_{0,T} = S_0 e^{rT} - \sum_{i=1}^{n} D e^{r \times (T-t_i)}$$

$$= \$45.37 - \$0.25 \times (1.0126 + 1)$$

$$= \$44.867$$

Therefore, if we think that the dividend payment will be $0.25, we consider the observed forward price of $44.162 as too cheap. We will therefore buy the forward and create a synthetic short forward, capturing a certain amount of $0.705. We engage in a reverse cash and carry arbitrage:

Description	Today	in 3 Months	in 6 Months
Long forward	0		$S_T - \$44.162$
Short-sell stock	$44.25		$-S_T$
Lend	$44.25	-$44.25	$45.37
Borrow to pay 1st dividend to third party		$0.25 -$0.25	-$0.2532
Pay 2nd dividend			-$0.25
TOTAL	0	0	$0.705

7. The S&P 500 E-mini index futures was introduced in September 1997. The contract size is $50 time the S&P 500 Index futures price. As such, it has a contract size that is 1/5th of the size of the regular S&P 500 index futures.

The minimum price fluctuation of the contract is 0.25 index points or $12.50 per contract. The futures contract is traded with expiration months of March, June, September, and December, and the last trading date is the third Friday of the contract months. The contract is cash-settled; brokers require an initial margin of 5 to 20%.

The contract is interesting for investors who do not have enough wealth to trade in the regular S&P 500 futures with an exposure of $250 times the index price. It also allows fine-tuning of index hedging strategies.

8. (a) The notional value of 3 contracts is $3 \times \$50 \times 900 = \$135,000$, because each index point is worth $50, and we buy three contracts.

(b) Since we have sold the futures contract, we would incur a loss if the index rose. The minimum tick size is 0.25 index points or $12.50 per contract. Therefore, the smallest possible loss we could endure is $37.50 at an index level of 900.25.

(c) The margin protects the counterparty against default. In our case, it is 15% of the notional value of our position, which means that we have to deposit an initial margin of:

$$\$135,000 \times 0.15 = \$20,250$$

(d) Let us calculate the details. We have the right to earn interest on our initial margin position. As the continuously compounded interest rate is currently 3%, after one week, our initial margin has grown to:

$$135,000 \times e^{0.03 \times \frac{1}{52}} = 135,077.91$$

We will get a margin call if the initial margin falls by 15%. We calculate 85% of the initial margin as:

$$\$135,000 \times 0.85 = \$114,750$$

3 short S&P 500 E-mini futures contracts obligate us to pay $150 times the forward price at expiration of the futures contract.

Therefore, we have to solve the following equation:

$$\$135,077.91 + (900 - F_{1W}) \times \$150 \geq \$114,750$$
$$\Leftrightarrow \quad (900 - F_{1W}) \times \$150 \geq -20,327.91$$
$$\Leftrightarrow \quad 900 - F_{1W} \geq -135.5194$$
$$\Leftrightarrow \quad F_{1W} \leq 1,035.5194$$
$$\Rightarrow \quad F_{1W} < 1,035.75$$

Therefore, the lowest S&P 500 index futures price at which we will receive a margin call is 1,035.75.

9. (a) The one-year futures price is determined as:

$$F_{0,1} = 900 \times e^{0.05} = 900 \times 1.0513 = 946.14$$

(b) One E-mini futures contract has the value of $\$50 \times 900 = \$45,000$. Therefore, the number of contracts needed to cover the exposure of $135,000 is: $\$135,00 \div \$45,000 = 3$. Furthermore, we need to adjust for the difference in beta. Since the beta of our portfolio is lower than one, our exposure is smaller than the exposure the index has. Therefore, we must decrease the number of contracts. The final hedge quantity is: $3 \times 0.75 = 2.25$. Therefore, it is advisable to short 2 (rather than 3) S&P 500 E-mini index future contracts.

10. (a) We need to use the formula for currency forwards:

$$F_{0,T} = x_0 \times e^{(r-r_f)T} = 0.84 \frac{\$}{E} e^{(0.03-0.045)0.5} = 0.8337 \frac{\$}{E}$$

(b) We can use the same formula, now treating the dollar interest rate as the foreign interest rate. However, we need to find the exchange rate for Euros/Dollar. It is 1/0.84 = 1.1905.

$$F_{0,T} = x_0 \times e^{(r-r_f)T} = 1.1905 \frac{E}{\$} e^{(0.045-0.03)0.5} = 1.1995 \frac{E}{\$}$$

Note that the footnote of the textbook is confirmed: The forward price exceeds the current exchange rate for the Frankfurt based forward, and it is less than the current exchange rate for the New York—based forward.

Chapter 6 Commodity Forwards and Futures

1. Contract specifications for mini-sized Silver Futures downloaded 10/20/2004

   Contract Size

   1,000 troy ounces.

   Deliverable Grades

   The contract grades for delivery shall be refined silver in a bar cast in a basic weight of either 1,000 troy ounces or eleven hundred troy ounces (the bar may vary no more than 10 percent more or less); assaying not less than 999 fineness; and made up of one of the brands and markings officially listed by the Exchange.

   Tick Size

   $.001/troy oz. (or $1.00 per contract).

   Price Quote

   Dollars and cents/troy ounce.

   Contract Months

   Jan, Feb, Mar, Apr, May, Jun, Jul, Aug, Sep, Oct, Nov, Dec.

   Last Trading Day

   On the business day immediately preceding the last two business days of the contract month. Trading in expiring contracts closes at 1:25 pm, Central Time, on the last trading day.

   (b) Even though silver is a commodity, it is produced in many different grades. The exchange would like to facilitate trading. Since the silver contract seller has an option to physically deliver the asset, the exchange must make sure that the buyer of the futures knows what he can expect to be delivered. Any uncertainty about the quality of the underlying asset could seriously hinder trading.

2. We can use the forward equation from the textbook to find the forward prices:

$$F_{0,T} = S_0 \times e^{(r-\delta_l) \times T}$$

Time to Expiration	Forward Price
1 month	7.309
3 months	7.327
5 months	7.346
7 months	7.364
13 months	7.420
25 months	7.532
37 months	7.646

The forward curve is upward sloping, thus the prices of Exercise 6.2. are an example of contango.

3. (a) You would want to know where to deliver, what kind of pork to deliver (inspected, weight), a particular kind of hog, temperature at delivery, etc.

   (b)

Trading Unit	40,000 pounds
Contract Months	Feb, Mar, May, Jul, Aug
Minimum Fluctuation	$.025 per cwt. $.0125 per cwt.
Price Limits	$2 or $3 per cwt., depending on price level; expandable by 150%
Termination of Trading	Business day prior to the last three business days of the contract month
Trading Hours	9:10 a.m. to 1 p.m. (12 p.m. on last trading day)
Position Limits:	*All months combined* *Any month* *Expiring contract*
	1000 contracts 800 contracts 15–25 contracts
Delivery specifications:	The CME futures contract calls for 40,000 pounds of 14–16 pound bellies, inspected by the USDA and stored in CME-approved warehouses. Delivery of lighter and heavier bellies may be made at specified discounts.

   (c) In the expiring month, it becomes more likely that the contract is actually physically settled. 25 contracts correspond to 1 million pounds of pork belly. For very high quantities, there might be a severe risk of some trader attempting to corner the market.

4. We can calculate the lease rates according to the formula:

$$\delta_l = r - \frac{1}{T} \ln\left(\frac{F_{0,T}}{S_0}\right)$$

Time to Expiration	Forward Price	Annualized Lease Rate
3 months	92.80	−0.019
4 months	92.80	−0.007
6 months	94.20	−0.022
8 months	97.20	−0.057

The lease rate is negative. Note that one reason for a negative lease rate might be the storage costs that you can save by not buying the frozen pork immediately. The forward curve is upward sloping, thus the prices are another example of contango.

5. Grandma, physically holding gold is valuable to some persons. You want the gold for investment, but you do not receive any benefit from holding the gold and looking at it each day. Furthermore, you will have to securely store your gold coins so that nobody can take them away from you. In order to do so, you need to rent a safe in your local bank. This is expensive—it will cost you approximately $60 per year. You can avoid all this by buying synthetic gold in the financial market.

6. (a) We can use the formula: $F_{0,T} \geq S_0 \times e^{(r)\times T} + \lambda(0, T)$. In particular, we know that 500 ounces can be stored for $250/ quarter, so one ounce can be stored for $0.50 per quarter. Since there is no possibility of loaning platinum, we can solve:

$$F_{0,T} \geq S_0 \times e^{(r)\times T} + \lambda(0, T)$$
$$\geq \$825 \times e^{0.04 \times 9/12} + \$0.50 \times e^{0.04 \times 6/12} + \$0.50 \times e^{0.04 \times 3/12} + \$0.50$$
$$\geq \$850.12 + \$0.50 \times (1.02 + 1.01 + 1)$$
$$\geq \$851.64$$

(b) It seems likely that there is a constant new supply of platinum, and that platinum is only stored in situations of extremely high uncertainty (i.e., political risk in one of the major producing countries). Therefore, the forward price is probably smaller than $851.64.

7. Our cash and carry arbitrage is:

Transaction	Time 0	Time T = 1
Short forward	0	$850.125 - S_T$
Buy platinum	−$825	S_T
borrow @ 0.05	$825	−$867.299
Total	0	−$17.174

The forward price bears an implicit lease rate. Therefore, if we try to engage in a cash and carry arbitrage, but if we do not have access to the platinum loan market, and thus to the additional revenue on our long platinum position, it is not possible for us to replicate the forward price. We incur a loss.

(b) We first need to find the implicit lease rate of the platinum contract.

$$\delta_l = r - \frac{1}{T}\ln\left(\frac{F_{0,T}}{S_0}\right) = 0.05 - \ln\left(\frac{850.125}{825}\right) = 0.02$$

If platinum can be loaned, we engage in the following cash and carry arbitrage, buying a tailed position in platinum and lending it out:

Transaction	Time 0	Time T = 1
Short forward	0	$850.125 - S_T$
Buy tailed platinum position, lend @0.02	−$808.664	S_T
borrow @ 0.05	$808.664	−$850.125
Total	0	0

Therefore, we now just break even.

8. We can calculate the convenience yield according to the formula:

$$F_{0,T} = S_0 \times e^{(r+\lambda-c)\times T}$$

$$\Leftrightarrow \quad \frac{F_{0,T}}{S_0} = e^{(r+\lambda-c)\times T}$$

$$\Leftrightarrow \quad \ln\left(\frac{F_{0,T}}{S_0}\right) = (r+\lambda-c)\times T$$

$$\Leftrightarrow \quad c = r+\lambda - \frac{1}{T}\ln\left(\frac{F_{0,T}}{S_0}\right)$$

$$\Rightarrow \quad c = 0.05 + 0.02 - \frac{1}{0.5}\ln\left(\frac{326.811}{320.34}\right)$$

$$c = 0.03$$

9. Note that the tailed position arises from us having to pay the convenience yield to the owner of the corn, and from receiving compensation for the storage cost (the owner of the corn is happy that he does not have to pay the storage costs, but we have to make him whole for the loss of his convenience yield).

Transaction	Today	in 6 Months
Long forward	0	$S_T - F_{0,T}$
Sell tailed position of spot (spot – convenience yield + storage cost)	+318.7423	$-S_T$
Lend net proceeds	–318.7423	326.8113
Total	0	$326.81 - F_{0,t}$

10. (a) You engage in a cash-and-carry arbitrage, but you will not be able to earn the convenience yield as an average investor. Furthermore, you will incur the storage cost of corn. Tabulated, this yields the following cash flows:

Transaction	Today	in 6 Months
Short forward	0	$F_{0,T} - S_T$
Buy tailed position of spot (spot + storage cost you need to pay	$-320.34 \times \exp(0.02 \times 0.5)$ = –323.559	S_T
Borrow money to buy tailed corn position	+323.559	–331.7504
Total	0	$F_{0,T} - 331.7504$

(b) The no-arbitrage region is: $326.811 \leq F_{0,T} \leq 331.750$. Only the price b2) allows arbitrage. You could profit at that price from a cash-and carry arbitrage which would yield a profit of $1.81. The two other prices are within the no-arbitrage region.

Chapter 7 Interest Rate Forwards and Futures

1. Using the bond valuation formulas (7.1), (7.3), (7.6) we obtain the following yields and prices:

Maturity	Zero-Coupon Bond Yield	Zero Coupon Bond Price	One-Year Implied Forward Rate	Par Coupon	Cont. Comp. Zero Yield
1	0.02000	0.98039	0.0200	0.0200	0.0198
2	0.02000	0.96117	0.0200	0.0200	0.0198
3	0.02500	0.92860	0.0351	0.0249	0.0247
4	0.02750	0.89717	0.0350	0.0273	0.0271
5	0.03000	0.86261	0.0401	0.0297	0.0296

2.

Maturity	Zero-Coupon Bond Yield	Zero Coupon Bond Price	One-Year Implied Forward Rate	Par Coupon	Cont. Comp. Zero Yield
1	0.0400	0.96153	0.0400	0.0400	0.03922
2	0.0450	0.91575	0.0500	0.0449	0.04400
3	0.0442	0.87841	0.0425	0.0441	0.04321
4	0.0406	0.85283	0.0300	0.0408	0.03979
5	0.0445	0.80455	0.0600	0.0443	0.04349

3. In order to be able to solve this problem, it is best to take equation (7.6) of the main text and solve progressively for all zero-coupon bond prices, starting with year one. This yields the series of zero-coupon bond prices from which we can proceed as usual to determine the yields.

Maturity	Zero-Coupon Bond Yield	Zero Coupon Bond Price	One-Year Implied Forward Rate	Par Coupon	Cont. Comp. Zero Yield
1	0.0500	0.9524	0.0500	0.0500	0.0488
2	0.0551	0.8982	0.0603	0.0550	0.0537
3	0.0551	0.8514	0.0550	0.0550	0.0536
4	0.0689	0.7659	0.1116	0.0675	0.0667
5	0.0964	0.6311	0.2136	0.0900	0.0921

4. (a) We have to take into account the interest we (or our counterparty) can earn on the FRA settlement if we settle the loan on initiation day, and not on the actual repayment day. Therefore, we tail the FRA settlement by the prevailing market interest rate of 4.5%. The dollar settlement is:

$$\frac{(r_{annually} - r_{FRA})}{1 + r_{annually}} \times \text{notional principal} = \frac{(0.045 - 0.0425)}{1 + 0.045} \times \$225,000.00 = \$538.2775$$

We receive money at the settlement, because the market interest rate we could lend at is 4.5%, but we have agreed via the FRA to a lending rate of only 4.25%. Interest rates moved in an unfavorable direction.

(b) If the FRA is settled on the date the loan is repaid (or settled in arrears), the settlement amount is determined by:

$$(r_{annually} - r_{FRA}) \times \text{notional principal} = (0.045 - 0.0425) \times \$225,000.00 = \$562.50$$

5. We can find the implied forward rates using the following formula:

$$[1 + r_0(t, t+s)] = \frac{P(0, t)}{P(0, t+s)}$$

This yields the following rates on the synthetic FRAs:

$$r_0(270, 360) = \frac{0.96579}{0.95012} - 1 = 0.01649$$

$$r_0(270, 720) = \frac{0.96579}{0.89421} - 1 = 0.08005$$

Note that these interest rates are not annualized.

6. We can find the implied forward rate using the following formula:

$$[1 + r_0(t, t+s)]^{(t+s)-t} = \frac{P(0, t)}{P(0, t+s)}$$

With the numbers of the exercise, this yields:

$$r_0(90, 360)^{0.75} = \frac{0.98965}{0.95012} - 1 = 0.04161$$

The following table recreates a long FRA position:

Transaction	t = 0	t = 90	t = 360
Portfolio A: enter long FRA		+50M	$-50M \times 1.04161$ $= -52.0805\,M$
Portfolio B:			
Buy 9.7943M Zero Coupons maturing at time t = 90	−49.4825M	+50M	
Sell (1 + 0.04161) * 50M * 0.95012 Zero coupons maturing at time t = 360	$+50M \times 1.04161$ $\times 0.95012 = 49.4825M$	0	$\frac{-49.4825}{0.95012}M$ $= -52.0805$
TOTAL	0	0	0

By entering in the above mentioned positions, we are perfectly recreating a synthetic FRA. We do not need our house bank in this case.

7.

$$\frac{\text{Change in bond price}}{\text{Unit change in yield}} = -\frac{1}{1+y/m}\left[\sum_{i=1}^{n}\frac{i}{m}\frac{C/m}{(1+y/m)^i} + \frac{n}{m}\frac{M}{(1+y/m)^n}\right]$$

$$\text{PVBP} = -\frac{1}{10,000} \times \frac{1}{1+y/m}\left[\sum_{i=1}^{n}\frac{i}{m}\frac{C/m}{(1+y/m)^i} + \frac{n}{m}\frac{M}{(1+y/m)^n}\right]$$

For a zero coupon, there are no intermediate coupon payments, so the sum is zero. We have annual payments, so m = 1. n = 1 * 3 = 3. The annualized yield to maturity of the zero-coupon bond is 5%. We therefore have:

$$\text{PVBP} = -\frac{1}{10,000} \times \frac{1}{1+0.05}\left[0 + \frac{3}{1}\frac{1}{(1+0.05)^3}\right] = -0.00025$$

Modified duration is the negative of the bond's change in bond price per unit change in yield multiplied by $1/B(y) = 2.85713$.

The Bond's Macaulay duration is modified duration times $1+y/m = 1.05$ in our example. We have: Macaulay Duration = 2.85713 times 1.05 = 3. This is the result in the text. A zero coupon bond's Macaulay duration is its time to maturity. The 1,080-day bond has three years to maturity.

8. (a) The Macaulay duration of a five year zero coupon bond is 5, its maturity.

(b) We can use the formula of the main text:

$$B(y+\varepsilon) = B(y) - [D_{\text{MAC}}/(1+y) \times B(y)\varepsilon]$$
$$= 792.92086 - 5/1.0475 \times 792.92086 \times 0.0040$$
$$B(0.0515) = 777.781560$$

(c)
$$B(0.0515) = \frac{1,000}{1.0515^5} = 777.953457$$

(d)
$$\text{Convexity} = \frac{1}{B(y)}\left[\sum_{i=1}^{n}\frac{i(i+1)}{m^2}\frac{C/m}{(1+y/m)^{i+2}} + \frac{n(n+1)}{m^2}\frac{M}{(1+y/m)^{n+2}}\right]$$
$$= \frac{1}{792.92086}\left[0 + \frac{5(5+1)}{1^2}\frac{1,000}{(1+0.0475/1)^{5+2}}\right]$$
$$= 27.34092$$

(e)
$$B(y+\varepsilon) = B(y) - [D_{\text{MAC}}/(1+y) \times B(y)\varepsilon] + 0.5 \times \text{Convexity} \times B(y) \times \varepsilon^2$$
$$= 792.92086 - 5/1.0475 \times 792.92086 \times 0.0040 + 0.5 \times 27.34092 \times 792.92086 \times 0.0040^2$$
$$B(0.0515) = 777.781560 + 0.173433$$
$$= 777.954994$$

The approximation is much better now compared to the result in part (b), and the true price in part (c).

9. (a) The implied forward rate is

$$(1+r_0(3,5))^{5-3} = \frac{B(0,3)}{B(0,5)}$$

$$\Leftrightarrow r_0(3,5) = \sqrt{\frac{0.86384}{0.79292086}} - 1 = 0.043763$$

(b) The market rate is larger than the implied rate. We want to lend at the cheaper market rate from year three to year five.

Let us sell the 5-year zero-coupon bond. We will create a synthetic borrowing opportunity at the zero-coupon implied forward rate of 4.3763 % and we will lend at 5%, thus creating an arbitrage opportunity. In particular, we will have:

Transaction Today	t = 0	t = 3	t = 5
Sell 1.08944 five-year zero-coupon bonds (1.043763 * 1,043763)	0.79292*1.08944 = 0.86384	0	−1.08944
Buy 1 three-year zero coupon bond	−0.86384	+1	
Lend 1 from year three to year five @ 1.05 * 1.05 − 1 = 10.25%		−1	+1.1025
TOTAL	0	0	0.01306

We see that we have created something out of nothing, without any risk involved. We have indeed found an arbitrage opportunity.

10.

$$B(y) = \sum_{i=1}^{n} \frac{C/m}{(1+y/m)^i} + \frac{M}{(1+y/m)^n}$$

$$= \sum F(y) \times G_i(y) + X(y) \times Z(y)$$

$$\frac{dB(y)}{dy} = \sum (F'(y) \times G_i(y) + G_i'(y) \times F(y)) + X'(y) \times Z(y) + X(y) \times Z'(y)$$

$$F(y) = C/m$$
$$G_i(y) = (1+y/m)^{-i}$$
$$X(y) = M$$
$$Z(y) = (1+y/m)^{-n}$$
$$F'(y) = 0$$
$$G_i'(y) = -\frac{i}{m}(1+y/m)^{-i-1}$$
$$X'(y) = 0$$
$$Z'(y) = -\frac{n}{m}(1+y/m)^{-n-1}$$

Plugging in all the terms above and rewriting yields the formula of the textbook.

Chapter 8 Swaps

1. We first solve for the present value of the cost per two barrels:

    $$\frac{\$50.85}{1.03} + \frac{\$45.94}{(1.035)^2} = 92.254$$

    We then obtain the swap price per barrel by solving:

    $$\frac{x}{1.03} + \frac{x}{(1.035)^2} = 92.254$$
    $$\Leftrightarrow \qquad x = 48.443$$

2. (a) We first solve for the present value of the cost per three barrels, based on the forward prices:

    $$\frac{\$50.85}{1.03} + \frac{\$45.94}{(1.035)^2} + \frac{\$42.97}{(1.0375)^3} = 130.731$$

    We then obtain the swap price per barrel by solving:

    $$x \times \left(\frac{1}{1.03} + \frac{1}{(1.035)^2} + \frac{1}{(1.0375)^3} \right) = 130.731$$
    $$\Leftrightarrow \qquad x = \frac{130.731}{2.7998} = 46.693$$

    (b) We first solve for the present value of the cost per two barrels (year 1 and year 3):

    $$\frac{\$50.85}{(1.03)} + \frac{\$42.97}{(1.0375)^3} = 87.846$$

    We then obtain the swap price per barrel by solving:

    $$\frac{x}{(1.03)} + \frac{x}{(1.0375)^3} = 87.846$$
    $$\Leftrightarrow \qquad x = 45.436$$

3. The fair swap rate was determined to be $46.693. Therefore, compared to the forward curve price of $50.85 in one year, we are underpaying $4.157. In year two, this underpayment has increased to:

    $$\$4.157 \times \frac{1.035^2}{1.03} = \$4.157 \times 1.04 = \$4.3234,$$

    where we used the appropriate forward rate to calculate the interest payment. In year two, we overpay by $46.693 − $45.94 = $0.753, so that our total accumulative underpayment is $4.3234–$0.753 = $3.5704. In year three, this underpayment has increased again to

    $$\$3.5704 \times \frac{1.0375^3}{1.035^2} = \$3.5704 \times 1.04252 = \$3.722.$$

    In year three, we receive a fixed payment of 46.693, which overpays relative to the forward curve price of $42.97 by $46.693 − 42.97 = 3.723. Therefore, our cumulative balance is indeed zero (except for the small rounding error).

    Note that whether we over- or underpay depends on the shape of the forward curve.

4. (a) We need to use the formula: $F_{0,T}^{euro} = 1/x_0 \times \exp(r_{euro} - r_\$)^T$

    From this, we have the following forward rates:

    $$F_{0,T} = 0.7874 \times \exp((0.04 - 0.0325) \times 1) = 0.7933$$
    $$F_{0,T} = 0.7874 \times \exp((0.04 - 0.0325) \times 2) = 0.7993$$
    $$F_{0,T} = 0.7874 \times \exp((0.04 - 0.0325) \times 3) = 0.8053$$

    (b) Since the firm will make debt payments in dollars, it should buy three euro forwards to eliminate currency exposure.

Year	Unhedged Dollar Cash Flow	Forward Exchange Rate	Hedged Euro Cash Flow
1	−8.125 million	0.7933	−6.4456
2	−8.125 million	0.7993	−6.4943
3	−258.125 million	0.8053	−207.8705

    (c)
    $$PV = \frac{-6.4456}{\exp(0.04)} - \frac{6.4943}{\exp(0.04 \times 2)} - \frac{207.8705}{\exp(0.04 \times 3)} = -196.8294 \text{ Euros}$$

    The value in dollars of this amount today is −$250 million, which is exactly the present value of the amount of debt Europia issued. This of course should not be surprising.

5.
Year	Dow Jones Total Return (which RF Asset Management Receives)	Fund's Bond Portfolio Return (which RF Pays to Counterparty)	Net Payment to RF Asset Management
1	+12	4.25	193.75 million
2	+8	4.25	93.75 million
3	0	4.25	−106.25 million
4	−12	4.25	−406.25 million

    Note that the last column multiplies the difference in return with the total exposure of the total return swap (half the $5 billion under management).

6. In order to answer this question, we use equation (8.13.) of the main text. We assumed that the interest rates and the corresponding zero-coupon bonds were:

Quarter	Interest Rate	Zero-Coupon Price
1	0.0070	0.9930
2	0.0140	0.9862
3	0.0210	0.9794
4	0.0280	0.9728
5	0.0350	0.9662
6	0.0420	0.9597
7	0.0490	0.9533
8	0.0560	0.9470

Then, the resulting swap prices are:

Quarter	Zero-Bond	Swap Price
1	0.9930	46.8800
2	0.9862	46.6608
3	0.9794	46.4222
4	0.9728	46.0629
5	0.9662	45.5079
6	0.9597	45.0643
7	0.9533	44.5514
8	0.9470	44.1020

7. The total costs of prepaid 4- and 8-quarter swaps are the present values of the payment obligations of the 4-quarter and 8-quarter oil swaps. They are:

$$\text{4-quarter prepaid swap price: } \$181.0932$$
$$\text{8-quarter prepaid swap price: } \$342.1243$$

8. Using the 8-quarter swap price of $44.102, we can calculate the net position by subtracting the swap price from the forward prices. The 1-quarter implied forward rate is calculated from the zero-coupon bond prices. The column implicit loan balance adds the net position of each quarter and the implicit loan balance plus interest of the previous quarter.

Quarter	Net Position	Implied Forward Rate	Implicit Loan Balance
1	2.7781	1.0070	2.7781
2	2.3381	1.0069	5.1353
3	1.8381	1.0069	7.0090
4	0.8681	1.0068	7.9246
5	−0.8519	1.0068	7.1268
6	−1.3019	1.0068	5.8731
7	−2.7019	1.0067	3.2106
8	−3.2319	1.0067	−0.0000

At the end of the eighth quarter, the implicit loan balance is of course zero.

9. We use equation (8.6) of the main text to answer this question:

$$X = \frac{\sum_{i=1}^{8} Q_{t_i} P_0(0,t_i) F_{0,t_i}}{\sum_{i=1}^{8} Q_{t_i} P_0(0,t_i)}, \quad \text{where} \quad Q = [1,1,1,1,2,2,2,2] \text{ or } [2,2,2,2,1,1,1,1]$$

After plugging in the relevant variables given in the exercise, we obtain a price for the first swap of $43.4364 and a price of $44.7615 for the second swap. The second swap price is higher because we require more delivery during the period where forward oil prices are higher.

10. From the given zero-coupon bond prices, from the zero coupon prices, we can calculate the one-quarter forward interest rates. They are:

Quarter	Forward Interest Rate
1	1.0110
2	1.0119
3	1.0126
4	1.0145
5	1.0009
6	1.0057
7	1.0066
8	1.0047

Now, we can calculate the deferred swap price according to the formula:

$$X = \frac{\sum_{i=3}^{6} P_0(0, t_i) r_0(t_{i-1}, t_i)}{\sum_{i=3}^{6} P_0(0, t_i)} = 0.85\%$$

Chapter 9   Parity and Other Option Relationships

1. This problem requires the application of put-call parity. We have:

$$C(12,15,9/12,4\%,2\%) = P(12,...) + e^{-\delta T} S_0 - e^{-rT} K$$
$$\Leftrightarrow C(12,15,0.75,4\%,2\%) = \$3.1422 + e^{-0.02 \times 0.75} \times 12 - e^{-0.04 \times 0.75} \times 15 = \$0.4069$$

2. This problem can be solved by applying the put-call parity. We have:

$$C(86,95,10/12) = P(86,...) + e^{-\delta T} S_0 - e^{-rT} K$$
$$\Leftrightarrow e^{-r \times 10/12} \times \$95 = \$14.6371 - \$5.7405 + e^{-0.04 \times 10/12} \times 86$$
$$e^{-r \times 10/12} = \$92.0772 / \$95$$
$$-r \times 10/12 = \ln(0.9692)$$
$$r = -0.03125 \times (-12/10)$$
$$= 0.0375$$

The continuously compounded interest rate is 3.75%.

3. We can make use of the put-call parity for currency options:

$$+C(K,T) = +e^{-r_f T} x_0 + P(K,T) - e^{-r_e T} K$$
$$\Leftrightarrow P(K,T) = e^{-0.02} 0.79 + 0.0587 - e^{-0.0375} \times 0.85 = 0.01434$$

A €0.85 strike European call option has a value of €0.01434.

Answer Section

4. (a) The current spot rate Euro/Can $ is $1/1.541 = 0.6489$.

   (b) We first find the price of a euro-denominated European call to buy one Canadian dollar with 6 months to expiration and a strike of €0.6667

   $$+C(K,T) = +e^{-r_f T}x_0 + P(K,T) - e^{-rT}K$$
   $$\Leftrightarrow C(K,T) = +e^{-0.02 \times 0.5} \times 0.6489 + 0.0352 - e^{-0.03 \times 0.5} \times 0.6667$$
   $$= 0.6424 + 0.0352 - 0.6567$$
   $$= 0.0209$$

   Then, we can apply Equation 9.7:

   $$C_{euro}(x_0, K, T) = x_0 K P_{Can\$}\left(\frac{1}{x_0}, \frac{1}{K}, T\right)$$

   $$\Leftrightarrow P_{Can\$}\left(\frac{1}{x_0}, \frac{1}{K}, T\right) = \frac{C_{Euro}(x_0, K, T)}{x_0 K}$$

   $$\Leftrightarrow P_{Can\$}(1.541, 1.5, 0.5) = \frac{0.0209}{0.6489 \times 0.6667} = 0.0483 \text{ Can\$/Euro}$$

5. We can use the boundary condition of equation 9.10 to write:

   $$55 \geq P\left(55, \frac{2}{12}\right) \geq \max[0, 55-54] \geq [0, 55 \times \exp(-0.13 \times 2/12) - 54]$$
   $$55 \geq P\left(55, \frac{2}{12}\right) \geq \max[0, 1] \geq [0, 53.82 - 54]$$
   $$55 \geq P\left(55, \frac{2}{12}\right) \geq 1$$

6. Because the options are American, we must ensure that a longer dated put option is worth more than a shorter dated put option. Thus, the P(55, 1-month) and P(55, 3-month) provide arbitrage bounds for P(55, 2-month).

   $$P(55, 1/12) \leq P(55, 2/12) \leq P(55, 3/12)$$
   $$4 \leq P(55, 2/12) \leq 8$$

7. From Equation 9.14, we have

   $P(60, 2/12) \geq P(55, 2/12)$ $P(55, 2/12) \geq P(50, 2/12)$
   $10 \geq P(55, 2/12)$ $P(55, 2/12) \geq 3$

   From Equation 9.16, we have

   $P(60, 2/12) - P(55, 2/12) \leq 60 - 55$ $P(55, 2/12) - P(50, 2/12) \leq 55 - 50$
   $10 - P(55, 2/12) \leq 5$ $P(55, 2/12) - 3 \leq 5$
   $P(55, 2/12) \geq 5$ $P(55, 2/12) \leq 8$

From Equation 9.18, we have

$$\frac{P(55, 2/12) - P(50, 2/12)}{55 - 50} \leq \frac{P(60, 2/12) - P(55, 2/12)}{60 - 55}$$

$$\frac{P(55, 2/12) - 3}{5} \leq \frac{10 - P(55, 2/12)}{5}$$

$$P(55, 2/12) - 3 \leq 10 - P(55, 2/12)$$

$$P(55, 2/12) \leq (10 + 3)/2$$

$$P(55, 2/12) \leq 6.5$$

8. The tightest boundaries for the 2-month 55-strike American put option are:

$$5.00 \leq P(55, 2/12) \leq 6.50$$

Therefore, (a) and (c) violate arbitrage bounds, but (b) does not.

We can exploit (a) by buying a bull spread: Buy one 2-month 55-strike option, and sell one 2-month, 60-strike option.

Transaction	t = 0	$S_T < 55$	$55 \leq S_T < 60$	$S_T \geq 60$
Buy 55 strike put	−4.25	$55 - S_T$	0	0
Sell 60 strike put	10	$S_T - 60$	$S_T - 60$	0
TOTAL	+5.75	−5	$S_T - 60 > -5$	0

Note that we are always protected against an early exercise against us from the 60-strike call. We initially receive $5.75, and our biggest possible exposure in the future is $5. We have found an arbitrage opportunity.

We can exploit (c) by buying a symmetric butterfly spread: Buy one 2-month 50-strike put option, sell two 2-month 55-strike put options, and buy one 2-month 60-strike option.

We can calculate lambda in order to know how many options to buy and sell when we construct the butterfly spread that exploits the mispriced 2-month 55-strike American put option at $8.25. Because the strike prices are symmetric around 55, lambda is equal to 0.5.

Therefore, we use a call and put butterfly spread to profit from these arbitrage opportunities.

Transaction	t = 0	$S_T < 50$	$50 \leq S_T \leq 55$	$55 \leq S_T \leq 60$	$S_T > 60$
Buy 1 50 strike put	−3	$50 - S_T$	0	0	0
Sell 2 55 strike puts	16.50	$2 \times S_T - 110$	$2 \times S_T - 110$	0	0
Buy 1 60 strike put	−10.00	$60 - S_T$	$60 - S_T$	$60 - S_T$	0
TOTAL	+3.50	0	$S_T - 50 \geq 0$	$60 - S_T \geq 0$	0

We initially receive $3.50 and have non-negative future payoffs. Therefore, we have found an arbitrage possibility, independent of the prevailing interest rate.

9. This contract pays Peter:

   max (0, $1 × (Peter's finance % – your marketing %))

   Therefore, you have to pay:

   – max (0, $1 × (Peter's finance % – your marketing %))

   Since we have a non-positive cash-outflow from the option Peter describes, we have sold the options no matter what the underlying is. If the underlying asset is your marketing percentage score, you have sold a put option with Peter's finance score as the strike price. If the underlying asset is Peter's finance percentage score, you have sold a call option with a strike of your marketing percentage score.

10. The financial expert has not fully understood equation 9.11 of the textbook. There is no benefit to early exercising the call option, even in a situation of substantially positive stock market returns. The stock does not pay a dividend, so we do not lose anything by waiting to take physical possession of the stock.

    First, note that the exercise does not mention the strike price – it might be set very high, even higher that the 52-week high.

    But even for a strike price that is small relative to the 52-week high price, there is no benefit to immediate exercise. We still lose the time value of money on the strike by paying immediately, and we lose the insurance against the stock crashing, and falling below the strike price.

    Finally, if you were of the same opinion as the expert, you should sell the option rather than early exercise it, because the all-time high of the underlying stock would be reflected in the option premium.

Chapter 10 Binomial Option Pricing: I

1. (a)/(b)

   Using the formulas given in the main text, we calculate the following values:

   for the European call option: for the European put option:

   $\Delta = 0.621$ $\Delta = -0.364$

   $B = -6.596$ $B = 7.744$

   price = 2.715   price = 2.278

2. (a) Using the formulas of the textbook, we obtain the following results:

   $\Delta = -0.544$

   $B = 11.568$

   price = 3.403

   (b) If we observe a price of $4, then the option price is too high relative to its theoretical value of $3.403. We sell the option for $4 and synthetically create a long put option for $3.403. We do so by selling 0.544 units of the share and by lending $11.568. We have created a risk-free profit of $0.597, and have hence demonstrated an arbitrage opportunity.

3. The stock prices evolve according to the following picture:

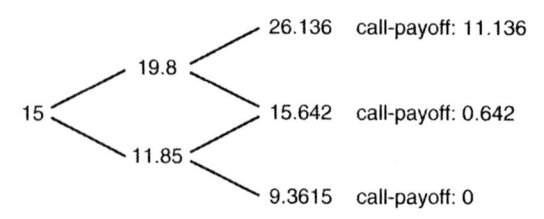

```
                 ┌─ 26.136   call-payoff: 11.136
          ┌ 19.8 ┤
          │      └─ 15.642   call-payoff: 0.642
    15 ───┤
          │      ┌─ 15.642
          └ 11.85┤
                 └─ 9.3615   call-payoff: 0
```

Since we have two binomial steps, and a time to expiration of 10 months, h is equal to 5/12. Therefore, we can calculate with the usual formulas for the respective nodes:

t = 0, S = 15	t = 1, S = 11.85	t = 1, S = 19.8
Δ = 0.591	Δ = 0.101	Δ = 0.9917
B = −6.627	B = −0.933	B = −14.63
price = 2.239	price = 0.268	price = 5.006

4. S(0) = 10:

	t = 0, S = 10	t = 1, S = 7.9	t = 1, S = 13.2
delta	0.189	0	0.344
B	−1.471	0	−3.524
premium	0.423	0	1.012

S(0) = 12:

	t = 0, S = 12	t = 1, S = 9.48	t = 1, S = 15.84
delta	0.385	0	0.698
B	−3.585	0	−8.59
premium	1.029	0	2.466

S(0) = 17:

	t = 0, S = 17	t = 1, S = 13.43	t = 1, S = 22.44
delta	0.714	0.380	0.9917
B	−8.318	−3.965	−14.630
premium	3.817	1.1388	7.624

S(0) = 25:

	t = 0, S = 25	t = 1, S = 19.75	t = 1, S = 33
delta	0.9834	0.9917	0.9917
B	−14.268	−14.63	−14.63
premium	10.318	4.956	18.096

The second part of the question asks why the delta of the option is not one. You might be tempted to think it should be one, because in all possible future states, we know that we exercise the option. Why don't we buy initially one unit of the share? We need to tail the stock position we buy by the dividend yield. The deltas you calculated are 1 share less the continuous dividend yield for the appropriate time period.

5. (a) u can be calculated to be 1.1735, d is 0.8694. This results in the following stock tree:

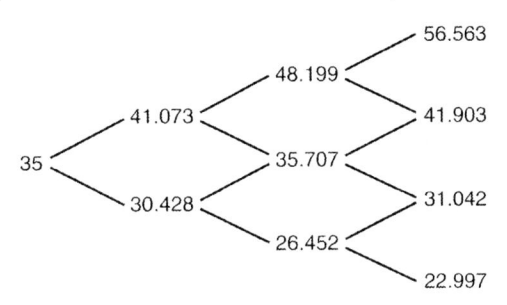

```
                              56.563
                    48.199 <
          41.073 <          41.903
  35 <            35.707 <
          30.428            31.042
                    26.452 <
                              22.997
```

(b) This is the printout from the software that comes with the book. The first two rows show the values for three up moves of the stock price. The first row shows the stock price, the second row shows the value of the option at that particular node. If the value of the option is printed in bold, it means that the option is early exercised. In the table below, we early exercise at the nodes dd (18.548), du(9.293), and d(14.572)—in all instances the value of immediate exercise is higher than the continuation value.

Time (yrs)	0.25	0.5	0.75
35.000	41.073	48.199	56.563
10.298	5.667	1.640	0.000
	30.428	35.707	41.903
	14.572	*9.293*	3.097
		26.452	31.042
		18.548	13.958
			22.997
			22.003

6. (a) We can calculate u and d as follows:

$$u = e^{(r-\delta)h + \sigma\sqrt{h}} = e^{(0.06-0.04)\times 4/12 + 0.3\times\sqrt{4/12}} = 1.1971$$

$$d = e^{(r-\delta)h - \sigma\sqrt{h}} = e^{(0.06-0.04)\times 4/12 - 0.3\times\sqrt{4/12}} = 0.8466$$

(b) We need to calculate the values at the relevant nodes in order to price the European call option:

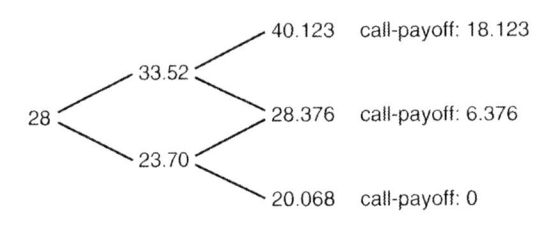

```
                      40.123   call-payoff: 18.123
           33.52  <
  28 <             28.376   call-payoff: 6.376
           23.70  <
                      20.068   call-payoff: 0
```

(c) In the following table, the first row of each two-row block shows the stock price, the value below shows the call premium at that particular node. For the European call, we have:

Time	4 Months	8 Months
28	33.51779	40.12293
6.673528	11.5095	18.1229
	23.70453	28.37583
	2.85485	6.37583
		20.06802
		0

For the American call, we have:

Time (yrs)	0.333333	0.666667
28	33.51779	40.12293
6.677249	**11.5178**	18.1229
	23.70453	28.37583
	2.85485	6.37583
		20.06802
		0

(d) There is a difference in premia for the two options, because it is optimal for us to exercise the American call option early after the first up node. This makes the American option slightly more valuable.

7. (a) We can calculate the price of the call currency option in a very similar way to our previous calculations. Please pay attention to the fact that we have a strike price and exchange rate in Euros, therefore the **foreign interest rate is the $ interest rate**!

For the European call option, we have:

Time (yrs)	0.416667	0.833333	1.25
0.79	0.936117	1.10926	1.314427
0.095828	0.17665	0.31197	0.51443
	0.677895	0.803277	0.95185
	0.03079	0.06837	0.15185
		0.581698	0.689288
		0	0
			0.499152
			0

The value of the option is 0.096€.

(b) for the European put option, we have:

Time (yrs)	0.416667	0.833333	1.25
0.79	0.936117	1.10926	1.314427
0.086435	0.031	0	0
	0.677895	0.803277	0.95185
	0.13698	0.05858	0
		0.581698	0.689288
		0.20903	0.11071
			0.499152
			0.30085

The value of the option is 0.086€.

8. (a) It is not optimal to exercise the American call early at any node. The value of early exercise is always smaller than the continuation value. Therefore, the price of the American call is identical to the price of the European call, or 0.096€.

(b) It is optimal to exercise the American put early at the node dd, at an exchange rate of 0.581698€/$. The value of immediate exercise is 0.2183€, while the continuation value is 0.20903€. This yields the following new tree:

Time (yrs)	0.416667	0.833333	1.25
0.79	0.936117	1.10926	1.314427
0.089029	0.031	0	0
	0.677895	0.803277	0.95185
	0.14188	0.05858	0
		0.581698	0.689288
		0.2183	0.11071
			0.499152
			0.30085

The value of the American put option is 0.089€.

9. We can use the information provided to calculate the price of two European call options with strike prices of 55 and 65. We have for the 55-strike option:

Time (yrs)	0.5	1
63	83.148	109.7395
15.42643	29.7735	54.7395
	50.68588	66.8957
	5.06143	11.8957
		40.7787
		0

The price for the 55-strike option is $15.426

We have for the 65-strike option:

Time (yrs)	0.5	1
63	83.148	109.7395
8.978617	20.069	44.7395
	50.68588	66.8957
	0.80659	1.8957
		40.7787
		0

The price for the 65-strike option is $8.979.

We construct a call bull spread by buying the low-strike option and selling the high-strike option. Therefore, it costs us $15.426 − $8.979 = $6.447 to enter into a long call bull spread.

10. The stock price tree looks as follows:

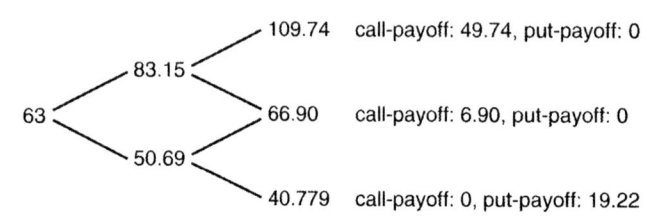

```
              109.74   call-payoff: 49.74, put-payoff: 0
       83.15
63            66.90    call-payoff: 6.90, put-payoff: 0
       50.69
              40.779   call-payoff: 0, put-payoff: 19.22
```

This yields the following continuation values at the first node, for both calls and puts:

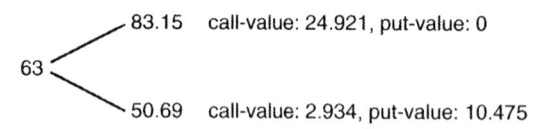

```
       83.15   call-value: 24.921, put-value: 0
63
       50.69   call-value: 2.934, put-value: 10.475
```

Since we are allowed to choose whether the option becomes a call or a put after the first node, we will choose a call option if the stock moved up, and we will choose a put option if the stock moved down in the first period. Now we can value the chooser option in our usual way by choosing Cu = 24.921 and Cd = 10.475. We calculate an option premium for the chooser option of $16.312, with a delta of 0.445 and B = −11.724.

Chapter 11 Binomial Option Pricing: II

1. (a) u = 1.4477; d = 0.7189, delta = 0.9608, B = 0, and the value of the European option is 96.079.
   (b) The value of immediate exercise is $100, which is larger than the continuation value of $96.079. We exercise immediately.
   (c) Recall the three economic considerations governing the decision to exercise early:
   The option holder:

- Receives the stock and therefore receives future dividends
- Pays the strike price prior to expiration (this has an interest cost)
- Loses the insurance implicit in the call. By holding the call instead of exercising, the option holder is protected against the possibility that the stock price will be less than the strike price at expiration.

The second and third bullet points do not have any value in this case. The strike is zero, so we do not pay anything and no interest is lost. We cannot lose insurance, because a stock has limited liability – it cannot fall below zero. There is only one benefit – receive the dividends, and no cost associated with early exercise. We exercise early. Note that the price for the European call option is equal to $C = S_0 \times \exp(-\delta \times h) = 100 \times \exp(-0.04)$.

2. (a) If r = 0%, the result in question 11.1 is not changed. We now forfeit the interest cost of giving up the strike price, but the strike price is already zero and no interest cost is borne.

   (b) If $\delta = 0\%$, there is no benefit from early exercising anymore. This yields the well known result that the European call and the American call have the same value—both are worth $100 now.

3. The main text tells us that if volatility is zero, the value of the insurance as one of the three economic considerations is zero—we know with certainty the stock price in the future, and the stock will not fall. We can apply the formula of the text:

$$\text{Exercise early if: } S > \frac{rK}{\delta}$$

$$\frac{rK}{\delta} = \frac{0.06 \times 90}{0.04} = 135$$

Therefore, we do not early exercise. The interest savings on the strike exceeds the dividends we lose by not early exercising.

4. (a) u = 1.3500, and d = 0.8187. We can derive a call premium of $16.653. The delta of the option position is 0.7528.

   (b) If we were to buy the amount of stock described by delta directly out of our wealth, we would have to pay 0.7528 * $100 = $75.28. Instead, we go to the bank and borrow $58.6319 so that we only have to contribute $16.653 out of our own wealth. This action is called leverage.

   (c) If the stock moves up, the return on the stock is $135.00/$100 – 1 = 35%. If the stock moves down, the return on the stock is $81.87/$100 – 1 = –18.13%.

   (d) If the stock moves up, the return on the option is $39.99/$16.65 – 1 = 240.1%. If the stock moves down, the return on the stock is $0/$16.65 – 1 = 0%.

   (e) The investment in the option is much riskier, because the variation in returns is much higher. The possible difference in returns for the stock is 53.13%, for option it is 240.1%.

5. We make use of the following inputs: S = $41, K = $40, sigma = 0.30, r = 0.08, T = 1.00 years, $\delta = 0$. Based on this values, u = 1.4623, and d = 0.8025.

   We can calculate therefore calculate the real probability as:

$$\alpha = 12\%: \quad p = \frac{\exp(\alpha h) - d}{u - d} = \frac{\exp(0.12) - 0.8025}{1.4623 - 0.8025} = 0.4926.$$

$$\alpha = 22\%: \quad p = \frac{\exp(\alpha h) - d}{u - d} = \frac{\exp(0.22) - 0.8025}{1.4623 - 0.8025} = 0.6723.$$

We calculate the expected payoff to the option in one period as:

$$\alpha = 12\%: \quad p \times C_u + (1-p) \times C_d = 0.4926 \times 19.954 + 0.5074 \times 0 = 9.8293.$$

$$\alpha = 22\%: \quad p \times C_u + (1-p) \times C_d = 0.6723 \times 19.954 + 0.3277 \times 0 = 13.4151.$$

We now use Equation 11.6 to calculate:

$$\alpha = 12\%: \quad \exp(\gamma) = \frac{0.738 \times \$41}{0.738 \times \$41 - \$22.405} \times \exp(0.12) + \frac{-\$22.405}{0.738 \times \$41 - \$22.405} \times \exp(0.08) = 1.254.$$

$$\alpha = 22\%: \quad \exp(\gamma) = \frac{0.738 \times \$41}{0.738 \times \$41 - \$22.405} \times \exp(0.22) + \frac{-\$22.405}{0.738 \times \$41 - \$22.405} \times \exp(0.08) = 1.711.$$

Taking natural logarithms, we have:

$$\alpha = 12\%: \quad \gamma = \ln(1.254) = 0.2260$$

$$\alpha = 22\%: \quad \gamma = \ln(1.711) = 0.5368$$

And finally, we can solve for the option price:

$$\alpha = 12\%: \quad C_{\alpha=12\%} = \exp(-0.2260) \times 9.8293 = 7.84$$

$$\alpha = 22\%: \quad C_{\alpha=22\%} = \exp(-0.5368) \times 13.4151 = 7.84$$

Indeed, it does not seem to matter which α we use, because we readjust the appropriate discount rate for the option.

6. In this case, the equation becomes:

$$\exp(\gamma) = \frac{S \times \Delta}{S \times \Delta + B} \times \exp(r) + \frac{B}{S \times \Delta + B} \times \exp(r)$$

$$= \left(\frac{S \times \Delta}{S \times \Delta + B} + \frac{B}{S \times \Delta + B} \right) \times \exp(r)$$

$$= \frac{S \times \Delta + B}{S \times \Delta + B} \times \exp(r)$$

$$= \exp(r)$$

$$\Rightarrow \gamma = r$$

We can see that if we use risk-neutral pricing, the discount rate of the stock is equal to the discount rate for the option is equal to the interest rate. This is what we mean when we say it is the simplest pricing procedure.

7–8. The following Table contains the answers to Questions 11.7 and 11.8.

Date	Price	Cont.comp. return
6-Jan-03	8784.89	
13-Jan-03	8586.74	–0.02281405
21-Jan-03	8131.01	–0.05453401
27-Jan-03	8053.81	–0.00953988
3-Feb-03	7864.23	–0.02382064
10-Feb-03	7908.8	0.005651434
18-Feb-03	8018.11	0.01372667
24-Feb-03	7891.08	–0.01596973
3-Mar-03	7740.03	–0.01932744
10-Mar-03	7859.71	0.015344147
17-Mar-03	8521.97	0.080897825
24-Mar-03	8145.77	–0.04514876
31-Mar-03	8277.15	0.015999932
7-Apr-03	8203.41	–0.00894878
Avg. monthly return		–0.00526794
Avg. annualized ret.		–0.27393311
Monthly standard deviation		0.033906043
Annualized standard deviation		0.244499954

9. We first calculate u and d for n = 50. If n = 50, h = 1/50 = 0.02. We have:

$$u = e^{(r-\delta)h+\sigma\sqrt{h}} = e^{(0.06-0.03)\times 0.02 + 0.4\times\sqrt{0.02}} = 1.0588$$

$$d = e^{(r-\delta)h-\sigma\sqrt{h}} = e^{(0.06-0.03)\times 0.02 - 0.4\times\sqrt{0.02}} = 0.9456$$

Now we can calculate $p^* = \dfrac{e^{(r-\delta)h} - d}{u - d} = 0.4859$

Here are the 10 first nodes from the tree:

n-i	Stock Price	Probability
0	871.704186	2.1166E-16
1	778.456447	1.1199E-14
2	695.183584	2.9034E-13
3	620.818566	4.9157E-12
4	554.408506	6.1121E-11
5	495.102447	5.9504E-10
6	442.140463	4.7226E-09
7	394.843915	3.1412E-08
8	352.606763	1.7867E-07
9	314.887794	8.8231E-07
10	281.203689	3.828E-06

The figure looks like:

Risk-neutral distribution of year-1 stock prices

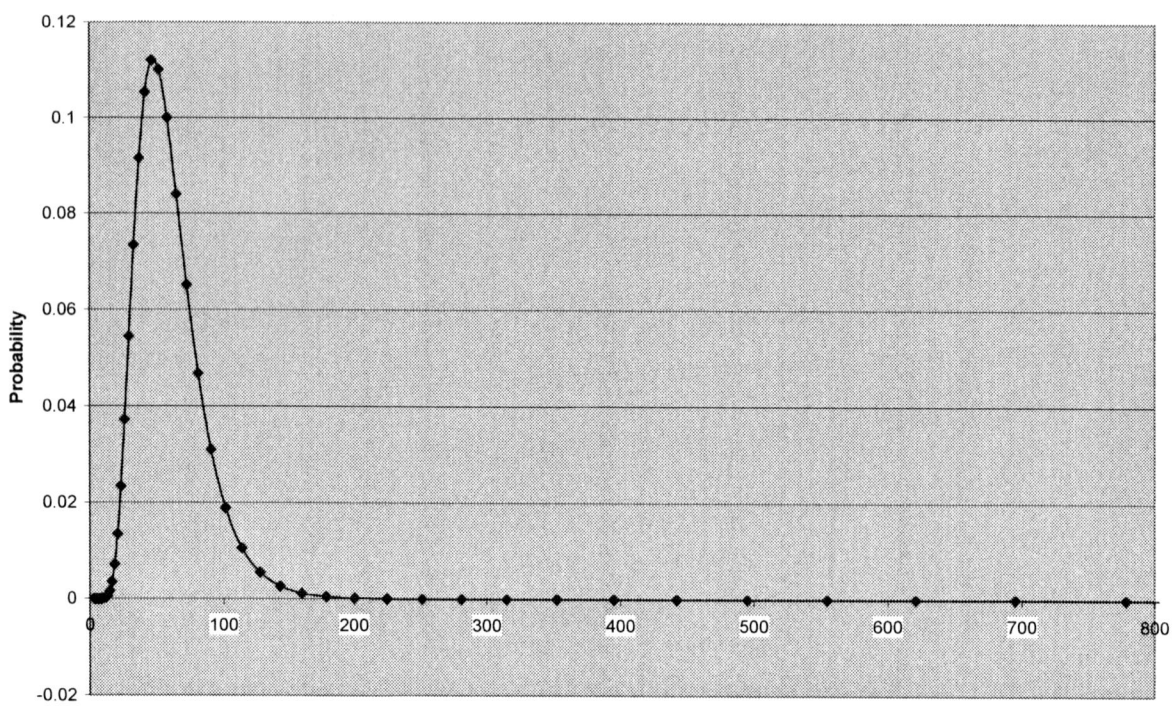

Now we calculate u and d for n = 100. If n = 100, h = 1/100 = 0.01. We have:

$$u = e^{(r-\delta)h+\sigma\sqrt{h}} = e^{(0.06-0.03)\times 0.01+0.4\times\sqrt{0.01}} = 1.0411$$

$$d = e^{(r-\delta)h-\sigma\sqrt{h}} = e^{(0.06-0.03)\times 0.01-0.4\times\sqrt{0.01}} = 0.9611$$

Now we can calculate $p^* = \dfrac{e^{(r-\delta)h} - d}{u - d} = 0.4900$

Here are the first ten nodes from the tree:

n-i	Stock Price	Probability
0	2813.04556	1.0465E-31
1	2596.76834	1.0892E-29
2	2397.1193	5.6114E-28
3	2212.82001	1.9079E-26
4	2042.69033	4.8154E-25
5	1885.64083	9.6229E-24
6	1740.66587	1.5858E-22
7	1606.83712	2.2164E-21
8	1483.29761	2.6818E-20
9	1369.25627	2.8532E-19
10	1263.98285	2.7024E-18

Here is the figure. The figure was truncated at 800 at the x-axis to make the figures better comparable.

Risk-neutral distribution of year-1 stock prices n = 100

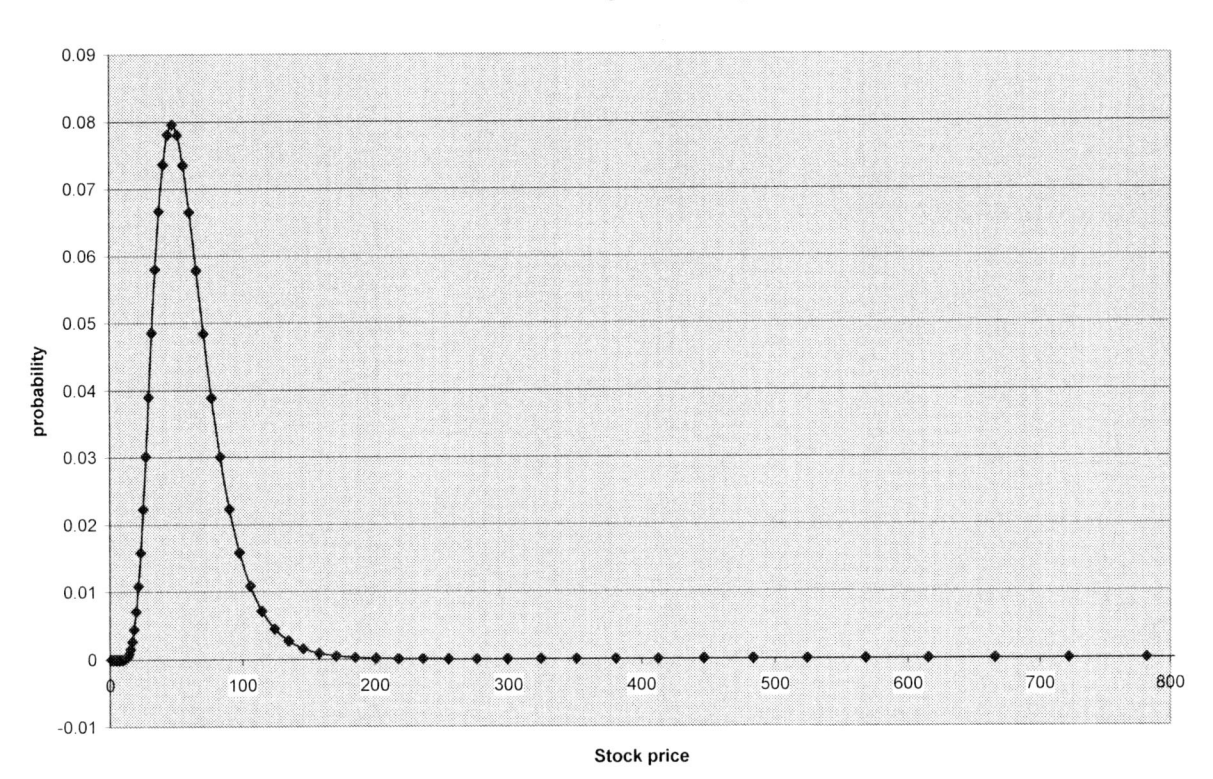

10. Based on the data given in the exercise, we can calculate:

    $h = 0.5/8 = 0.0625$, $u = 1.0645$, $d = 0.9394$, and $p^* = 0.5144$

    We have the following tree for the stock price:

Stock Tree								74.192
							69.697	
						65.475		65.475
					61.508		61.508	
				57.781		57.781		57.781
			54.280		54.280		54.280	
		50.992		50.992		50.992		50.992
	47.902		47.902		47.902		47.902	
45.000		45.000		45.000		45.000		45.000
	42.274		42.274		42.274		42.274	
		39.712		39.712		39.712		39.712
			37.306		37.306		37.306	
				35.046		35.046		35.046
					32.923		32.923	
						30.928		30.928
							29.054	
								27.294

European Call = American Call

								21.192
							16.896	
						12.871		12.475
					9.328		8.706	
				6.474		5.647		4.781
			4.337		3.502		2.450	
		2.822		2.106		1.256		0.000
	1.793		1.239		0.644		0.000	
1.117		0.717		0.330		0.000		0.000
	0.409		0.169		0.000		0.000	
		0.087		0.000		0.000		0.000
			0.000		0.000		0.000	
				0.000		0.000		0.000
					0.000		0.000	
						0.000		0.000
							0.000	
								0.000

European Put

								0.000
							0.000	
						0.000		0.000
					0.227		0.000	
				0.904		0.470		0.000
			2.072		1.628		0.972	
		3.651		3.325		2.868		2.008
	5.517		5.352		5.148		4.899	
7.550		7.537		7.541		7.604		8.000
	9.762		9.911		10.134		10.528	
		12.195		12.499		12.892		13.288
			14.709		15.101		15.495	
				17.165		17.558		17.954
					19.484		19.879	
						21.676		22.072
							23.747	
								25.706

American Put

									0.000
								0.000	
							0.000		0.000
						0.227		0.000	
					0.927		0.470		0.000
				2.151		1.675		0.972	
			3.834		3.465		2.964		2.008
		5.875		5.646		5.389		5.098	
8.200			8.083		8.000		8.000		8.000
		10.726		10.726		10.726		10.726	
			13.288		13.288		13.288		13.288
				15.694		15.694		15.694	
					17.954		17.954		17.954
						20.077		20.077	
							22.072		22.072
								23.946	
									25.706

The American put premium is higher than the European put premium, because the put is early exercised.

Chapter 12   The Black-Scholes Formula

1. You can use the NORMSDIST() function of Microsoft Excel to calculate the values for N(d1) and N(d2). NORMSDIST(z) returns the standard normal cumulative distribution evaluated at z. Here are the intermediate steps towards the solution:

D1	0.52583
D2	0.2997
N(d1)	0.7005
N(d2)	0.6178
N(–d1)	0.2995
N(–d2)	0.3822

2. (a)

T	Put Price
1	6.1841
10	23.5496
100	44.6801
200	44.9960
500	45.0000
1000	45.0000

The benefit to holding the put option is that we do not have to pay the underlying stock and that we continue to receive dividends on the underlying. On the other hand, the owner of the put option foregoes the interest payments he could receive if he "owned the strike" (i.e., received cash). As the interest rate is zero and the dividend yield is positive, the cost of holding the put is zero, and for the very long maturities, the put value approaches the value of the strike.

Looking at the BS-formula, we see that –d2 is positive and very large for a large T, and thus N(–d2) is close to one. The strike price does not get discounted, because r is zero.

$$P(\bullet) = \overline{K} \times \exp(-\overline{r}T) \times N\left(-\frac{\ln\left(\frac{\overline{S}}{K}\right) + (\overline{r} - \overline{\delta} - 0.5\sigma^2)T}{\sigma\sqrt{T}}\right) - \overline{S} \times \exp(-\overline{\delta}T) \times N\left(-\frac{\ln\left(\frac{\overline{S}}{K}\right) + (\overline{r} - \overline{\delta} + 0.5\sigma^2)T}{\sigma\sqrt{T}}\right)$$

(b)

T	Put Price
1	5.2258
10	12.2896
100	0.7567
200	0.0149
500	0.0000
1000	0.0000

Now, not receiving the strike has a cost in terms of lost interest, which is very high for long maturities. Therefore, the value of the put converges to zero. Looking at the BS-formula, we see that –d2 is positive and very large, and thus N(–d2) is still close to one. However, the strike price now gets discounted, because r is larger than zero. For very large T, exp(-rT) is very close to zero, and that's what explains the option price of zero.

$$P(\bullet) = \overline{K} \times \exp(-\overline{r}T) \times N\left(-\frac{\ln\left(\frac{\overline{S}}{K}\right) + (\overline{r} - \overline{\delta} - 0.5\sigma^2)T}{\sigma\sqrt{T}}\right) - \overline{S} \times \exp(-\overline{\delta}T) \times N\left(-\frac{\ln\left(\frac{\overline{S}}{K}\right) + (\overline{r} - \overline{\delta} + 0.5\sigma^2)T}{\sigma\sqrt{T}}\right)$$

3. (a) Using the Black-Scholes formula, we find a put-price of $0.6199.

   (b) We determine the one year forward price to be:

   $$F_{0,t} = S_0 \times \exp((r - \delta)T) = \$25 \times \exp((0.07 - 0) \times 0.5) = \$25.8905.$$

   (c) As the textbook suggests, we need to set the dividend yield equal to the risk-free rate when using the Black-Scholes formula. We can first calculate the call price, and then use put-call-parity for options on futures. Thus:

   $$C(25.8905, 22, 0.3, 0.07, 0.5, \mathbf{0.07}) = \$4.3766$$

   Now we use put-call parity to show:

   $$P(.) = C(.) + K * \exp(-rT) - F * \exp(-rT)$$
   $$= 4.3766 + 22 * \exp(-0.035) - 25$$
   $$= 0.6199$$

Answer Section 117

4.
$$C(\bullet) = S \times \exp(-\delta T) \times N(d_1) - K \times \exp(-rT) \times N(d_2)$$

$$= S \times \exp(-\delta T) \times N\left(\frac{\ln\left(\frac{S}{K}\right) + (r - \delta + 0.5\sigma^2)T}{\sigma\sqrt{T}}\right) - K \times \exp(-rT) \times N\left(\frac{\ln\left(\frac{S}{K}\right) + (r - \delta - 0.5\sigma^2)T}{\sigma\sqrt{T}}\right)$$

$$= 100 \times \exp(0) \times N\left(\frac{\ln\left(\frac{100}{100}\right) + (0.05)}{0\sqrt{1}}\right) - 100 \times \exp(-0.05) \times N\left(\frac{\ln\left(\frac{100}{100}\right) + (0.05 - 0 - 0) \times 1}{0\sqrt{1}}\right)$$

$$= 100 \times N\left(\frac{0 + 0.05}{0}\right) - 100 \times \exp(-0.05) \times N\left(\frac{0 + 0.051}{0\sqrt{1}}\right)$$

$$= 100 \times N(\infty) - 100 \times \exp(-0.05) \times N(\infty)$$

$$= 100 - 100 \times \exp(-0.05) = 4.8771$$

5. (a)

$$P(\bullet) = \overline{K} \times \exp(-\overline{r}T) \times N\left(-\frac{\ln\left(\frac{\overline{S}}{\overline{K}}\right) + (\overline{r} - \overline{\delta} - 0.5\sigma^2)T}{\sigma\sqrt{T}}\right) - \overline{S} \times \exp(-\overline{\delta}T) \times N\left(-\frac{\ln\left(\frac{\overline{S}}{\overline{K}}\right) + (\overline{r} - \overline{\delta} + 0.5\sigma^2)T}{\sigma\sqrt{T}}\right)$$

$$= 100 \times \exp(-0.05) \times N\left(-\frac{\ln\left(\frac{100}{100}\right) + (0.05 - 0 - 0)}{0 \times \sqrt{1}}\right) - 100 \times \exp(0) \times N\left(-\frac{\ln\left(\frac{100}{100}\right) + (0.05 - 0)}{0}\right)$$

$$= 100 \times \exp(-0.05) \times N(-\infty) - 100 \times \exp(0) \times N(-\infty)$$
$$= 0$$

(b) For a non-dividend paying stock, we have:

$$S_0 = C(\bullet) - P(\bullet) + \exp(-r \times T) \times K$$

$$\Leftrightarrow \quad C(\bullet) = S_0 - \exp(-r \times T) \times K + P(\bullet)$$

Since the call price of 12.4 is exactly equal to the first two terms, the put price must indeed be equal to zero.

118   McDonald • *Derivatives Markets, Second Edition*

6. (a)

$$C(\bullet) = S \times \exp(-\delta T) \times N(d_1) - K \times \exp(-rT) \times N(d_2)$$

$$= S \times \exp(-\delta T) \times N\left(\frac{\ln\left(\frac{S}{K}\right) + (r - \delta + 0.5\sigma^2)T}{\sigma\sqrt{T}}\right) - K \times \exp(-rT) \times N\left(\frac{\ln\left(\frac{S}{K}\right) + (r - \delta - 0.5\sigma^2)T}{\sigma\sqrt{T}}\right)$$

$$= 100 \times \exp(-0.07) \times N\left(\frac{\ln\left(\frac{100}{100}\right) - (0.02)}{0\sqrt{1}}\right) - 100 \times \exp(-0.05) \times N\left(\frac{\ln\left(\frac{100}{100}\right) + (0.05 - 0.07 - 0) \times 1}{0\sqrt{1}}\right)$$

$$= 100 \times \exp(-0.07) \times N\left(\frac{0 - 0.02}{0}\right) - 100 \times \exp(-0.05) \times N\left(\frac{-0.02}{0\sqrt{1}}\right)$$

$$= 100 \times N(-\infty) - 100 \times \exp(-0.05) \times N(-\infty)$$
$$= 0$$

(b)

$$P(\bullet) = \overline{K} \times \exp(-\bar{r}T) \times N\left(-\frac{\ln\left(\frac{\overline{S}}{\overline{K}}\right) + (\bar{r} - \bar{\delta} - 0.5\sigma^2)T}{\sigma\sqrt{T}}\right) - \overline{S} \times \exp(-\bar{\delta}T) \times N\left(-\frac{\ln\left(\frac{\overline{S}}{\overline{K}}\right) + (\bar{r} - \bar{\delta} + 0.5\sigma^2)T}{\sigma\sqrt{T}}\right)$$

$$= 100 \times \exp(-0.05) \times N\left(-\frac{\ln\left(\frac{100}{100}\right) + (0.05 - 0.07 - 0)}{0 \times \sqrt{1}}\right) - 100 \times \exp(-0.07) \times N\left(-\frac{\ln\left(\frac{100}{100}\right) + (0.05 - 0.07}{0}\right)$$

$$= 100 \times \exp(-0.05) \times N(\infty) - 100 \times \exp(-0.07) \times N(\infty)$$

$$= 95.123 - 93.239$$

$$= 1.884$$

(c) For a dividend-paying stock, we have:

$$S_0 \times \exp(-\delta \times T) = C(\bullet) - P(\bullet) + \exp(-r \times T) \times K$$

$$\Leftrightarrow \quad C(\bullet) = S_0 \times \exp(-\delta \times T) - \exp(-r \times T) \times K + P(\bullet)$$

$$= 93.239 - 95.123 + 1.884$$

$$= 0$$

(d) The difference is the following: The futures price for a stock is S*exp(r-d). In a world without risk, i.e., where the standard deviation is zero, we know for certain the future price of the stock. In exercise 12.4 and 12.5, where the dividend yield was zero, the future stock price exceeded the current stock price (S * exp(0.05) = 105.127). We knew for certain that we could exercise the call option, but not the put option. In this exercise, we know that the future stock price will be: S * exp(0.05 – 0.07) = 98.020, which is less than 100. Therefore, we would exercise the put option, but not the call option.

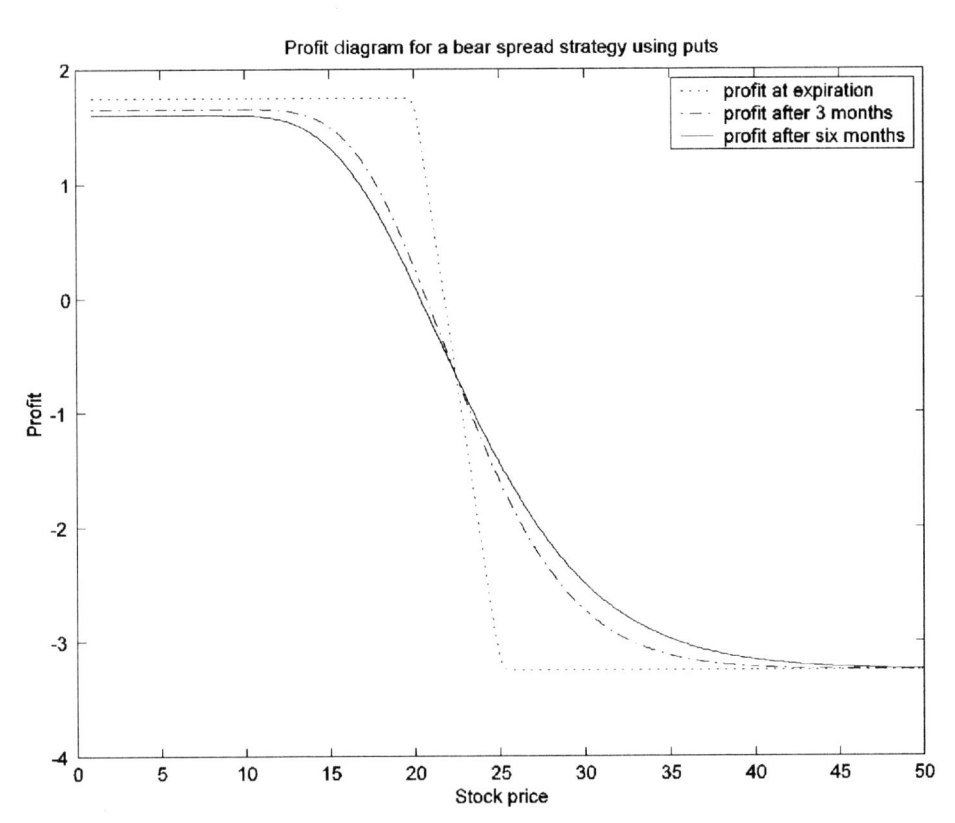

7.

Profit diagram for a bear spread strategy using puts

8. (a) For S = 5, we have the following. Note that the greeks of the bear spread are simply the sum of the greeks of the individual options. The greeks of the put with a strike of 20 enter with a negative sign because this option was sold.

	Sold 20-Put	Bought 25-Put	Bear Spread
Price	−14.3148	19.1187	4.8039
Delta	0.9802	−0.9802	−0.0000
Gamma	−0.0000	0.0000	−0.0000
Vega	−0.0000	0.0000	−0.0000
Theta	−0.0019	0.0024	0.0005
Rho	0.1922	−0.2402	−0.0480

We have very limited exposure to the greeks. The stock price is very low, and it is very likely that both options are exercised. A lot of greeks cancel each other out.

(b) For S = 50, we have:

	Sold 20-Put	Bought 25-Put	Bear Spread
Price	−0.0023	0.0297	0.0275
Delta	0.0005	−0.0056	−0.0051
Gamma	−0.0001	0.0011	0.0009
Vega	−0.0009	0.0080	0.0071
Theta	0.0000	−0.0003	−0.0003
Rho	0.0003	−0.0031	−0.0028

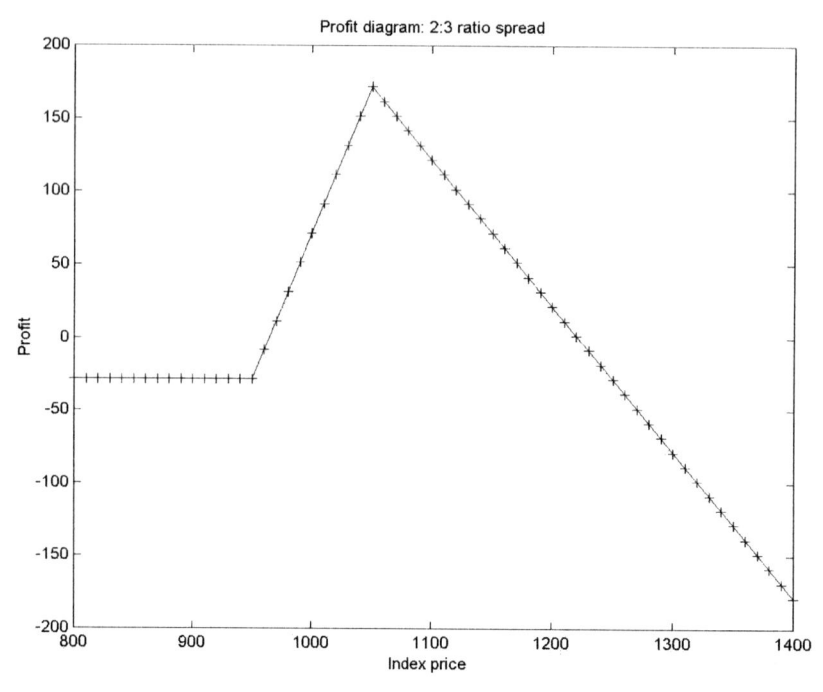

9. (a)

Profit diagram: 2:3 ratio spread

(b)

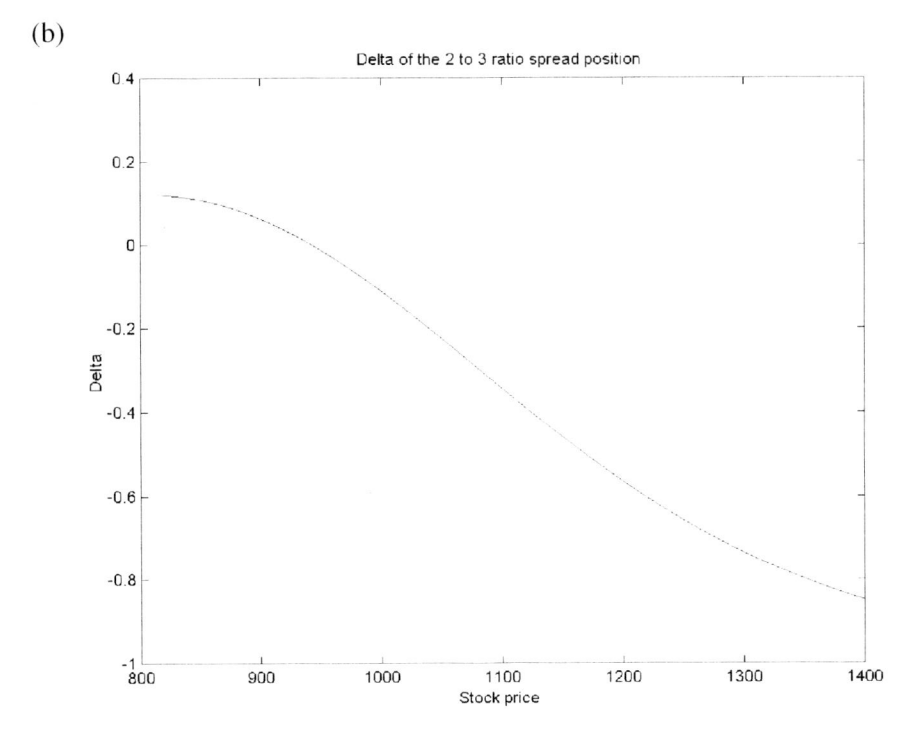

Delta of the 2 to 3 ratio spread position

(c)

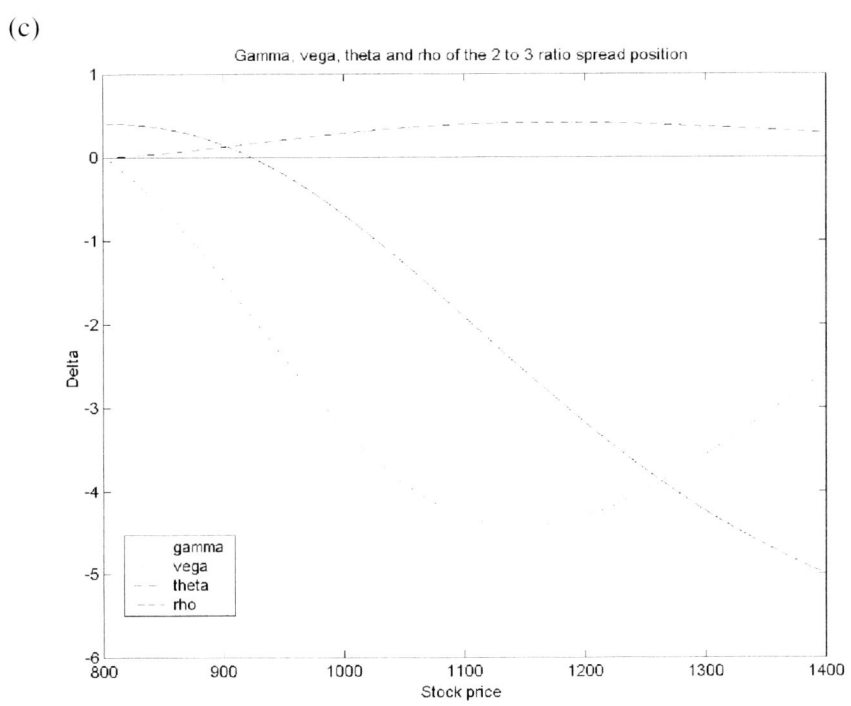

Gamma, vega, theta and rho of the 2 to 3 ratio spread position

10. The statement is not true. We have from put-call-parity on a dividend paying stock that:

$$S_0 \times \exp(-\delta \times T) = C(\bullet) - P(\bullet) + \exp(-r \times T) \times K$$
$$\Leftrightarrow \quad C(\bullet) = S_0 \times \exp(-\delta \times T) - \exp(-r \times T) \times K + P(\bullet)$$
$$\Rightarrow \quad C(\bullet) > P(\bullet) \text{ if } S_0 \times \exp(-\delta \times T) > \exp(-r \times T) \times K$$

Can we find a strike price/interest rate combination for which the above statement is not true? Suppose K = 98 and r = 0.02. Then we need to compare whether:

$$100 \times \exp(-0.05) > \exp(-0.02) \times 98$$

We find that in fact $100 \times \exp(-0.05) = 95.123 < 96.06 = 98 \times \exp(-0.02)$. There are many more combination of K and r for which the statement does not hold. The statement above neglects the costs and benefits that are associated with holding the respective put and call.

Chapter 13   Market-Making and Delta-Hedging

1. If we buy the call option, we have positive delta exposure. To hedge that exposure, we must sell shares and lend money initially.

   The delta of the option with the above characteristics is 0.7157, and its price (if the option is on 100 shares) is $358.42. We therefore sell 71.57 shares, and initially receive 1,789.37. We can lend these proceeds, less the option purchase price, and receive an overnight interest of $0.1568.

   If the stock price decreases to 24.55, we only need to repay $1,757.16 for the short stock position. Our option position is now worth $326.14, and we have interest income of $0.1568. Overall, our overnight profit is:

   $$1,789.37 - 1,757.16 - 358.42 + 326.14 + 0.1568 = +0.088$$

   If the stock price increases to 26.25, we have the following:

   $$1,789.37 - 1,878.84 - 358.42 + 451.64 + 0.1568 = \$3.915$$

2. If we buy the put option, we have negative delta exposure. To hedge that exposure, we must buy shares and borrow money initially.

   The delta of the option with the above characteristics is –0.2843, and its price (if the option is on 100 shares) is $113.00. We therefore buy 28.43 shares, and pay initially $710.63. We need to borrow that amount and the purchase price of the option and pay an overnight interest of (710.63 + 113.00) * exp(0.04 * 1/365) = $0.090.

   If the stock price decreases to 24.55, our share position is only worth $697.84. Our option position is now worth $125.97, and we have the interest expense of $0.09. Overall, our overnight profit is:

   $$-710.63 + 697.84 - 113.00 + 125.97 - 0.09 = +\$0.269$$

   If the stock price increases to 26.25, we have the following:

   $$-710.63 + 746.16 - 113.00 + 81.47 - 0.09 = +\$4.096$$

3. If we want to construct a put bear spread, we buy the put with the higher strike, and we sell the put with the lower strike.

We calculate the 25-strike put to cost 198.85 with a delta of – 0.42025. The 23-strike put costs 113.00 and has a delta of –0.2843. Since we buy the 25-strike put and sell the 23-strike put, we have an aggregate delta of –0.13600. Therefore, we need to buy shares initially and borrow an appropriate amount of money.

The initial investment is : –0.136 * 25 * 100 – 198.85 + 113.00 = –425.85. We pay $0.046 interest on that amount.

If the stock price decreases to $24.55, the put price becomes $218.01 for the 25-strike and $125.968 for the 23-strike.

Taking into account the change in our initial position (the 13.6 shares are worth now 333.88), we have an overnight profit of $0.1178.

If the stock price increases to $26.25, the 25-strike put is worth 151.05, and the 23-strike put is worth 81.47. The initial investment in shares is now worth 356.997, so our overnight profit is: $0.781.

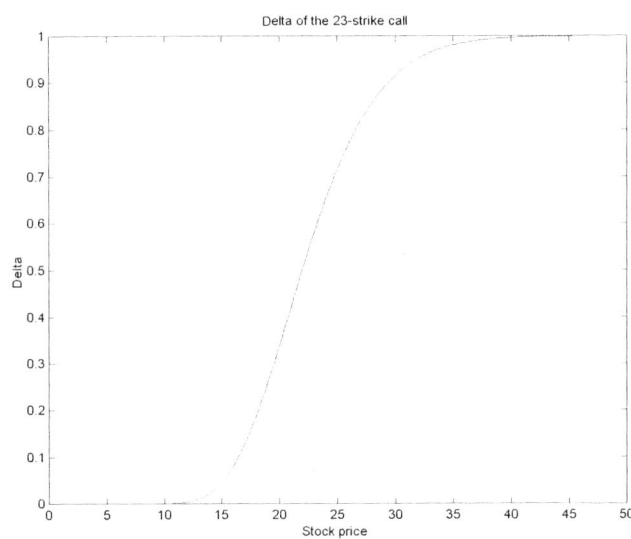

4. (a)

Delta of the 23-strike call

(b) You can see that the slope of delta is virtually zero until the stock price reaches $11. Then delta is increasing, and the slope is increasing at an ever higher rate until delta is about 0.5 and the stock price is about $23. Delta continues to increase, but at a decreasing rate. The above graph suggests that gamma is always larger than zero, but zero for small and very large stock price, and that it reaches a maximum around a stock price of $23.

(c)

Gamma of the 23-strike call

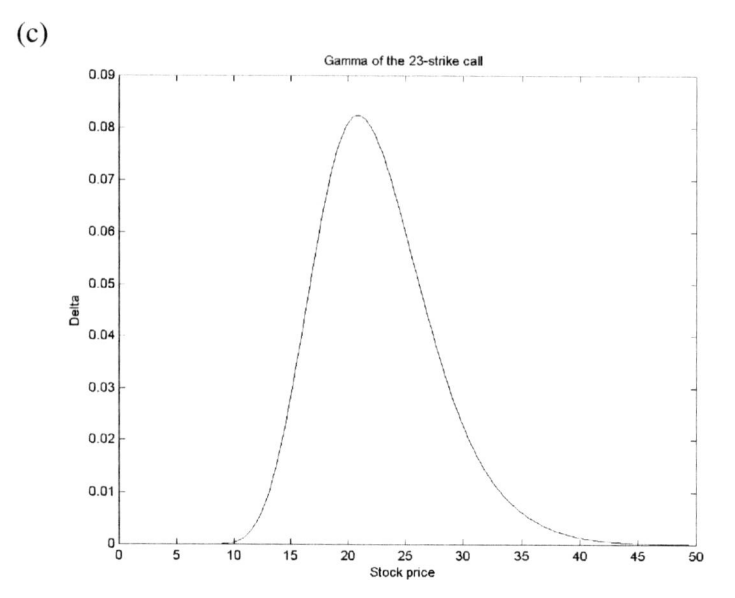

(d) We have for the two options:

	23-Strike Call	25-Strike Call
Price	3.5842	0.8451
Delta	0.7157	0.2724
Gamma	0.0600	0.0588
Price at 24.55	3.2614	0.7230
Price at 26.25	4.5164	1.2257

If we want to fully hedge the gamma risk, we must do so through the use of options. We have to sell 0.06/0.0588 = 1.0210 30-strike options to get rid off gamma risk. This means that we have to short 0.7157 − 1.021 * 0.2724 = 0.4376 shares. We receive $1,094.10 for the shorted stock. Overall, we can lend out $1,094.10 − 358.42 + 1.021 * 84.51 and receive interest of $0.09 on it.

If the stock price decreases to $24.55, our short stock position is worth $1,074.404. Together with the option prices of the table above, we have an overnight profit of −$0.0298.

If the stock price increases to $26.25, we have an overnight profit of: −$0.2498. Note the dramatic improvement compared to the only delta-hedged portfolio in exercise 13.1.

5. (a)

	S = 20	S = 25	S = 30	S = 35	S = 40
delta_c	0.0556	0.2724	0.5797	0.8115	0.9298
delta_p	−0.9444	−0.7276	−0.4203	−0.1885	−0.0702
gamma_c	0.0248	0.0588	0.0577	0.0341	0.0149
gamma_p	0.0248	0.0588	0.0577	0.0341	0.0149
vega_c	1.5838	5.8627	8.2818	6.6741	3.8004
vega_p	1.5838	5.8627	8.2818	6.6741	3.8004
put_theta	0.0017	−0.0026	−0.0057	−0.0051	−0.0030
call_theta	−0.0015	−0.0059	−0.0090	−0.0084	−0.0063
put_rho	−0.1416	−0.1169	−0.0748	−0.0375	−0.0155
call_rho	0.0051	0.0297	0.0719	0.1092	0.1311

We can clearly see that one bought put option and one short call option give a delta of −1, precisely the opposite delta we have from a long position in one share. Shares do not have gamma, or vega exposure, so these cancel each other out. The statement is indeed correct for the above share prices.

(b)

$$P = Ke^{-rT} - Se^{-\delta T} + C$$

$$\Leftrightarrow \quad P - C + S = Ke^{-rT}$$

$$\Rightarrow \quad \frac{\partial P}{\partial S} - \frac{\partial C}{\partial S} - \frac{\partial S}{\partial S} = \frac{\partial Ke^{-rT}}{\partial S}$$

$$\Delta_P - \Delta_C - 1 = 0$$

In the third line, we derive all terms with respect to S. We have shown that buying a put, selling a call (with the same strike and time to maturity) and buying a share has zero exposure to changes in the share price. Similarly, we can see that such a position is gamma neutral (by deriving the last line above again with respect to S) and vega neutral, but that it has exposure to theta and rho.

6. We can calculate:

$$\exp(rh + \sigma\sqrt{h}) = \exp(0.08 \times 1/365 + 0.30 \times \sqrt{1/365}) = 1.0160$$

$$\exp(rh - \sigma\sqrt{h}) = \exp(0.08 \times 1/365 - 0.30 \times \sqrt{1/365}) = 0.9846$$

We have the following Table:

	\multicolumn{6}{c}{Day}
	0	1	2	3	4	5
Stock price	40.000	39.385	38.780	39.403	40.035	40.678
Call price	278.040	241.788	208.636	239.291	273.081	310.101
Delta	0.582	0.541	0.499	0.541	0.583	0.625
Investment	2051.576	1888.98	1725.286	1891.612	2060.707	2230.662
new shares bought/sold		−4.140	−4.232	4.211	4.213	4.167
price for new shares		−163.056	−164.107	165.9431	168.6851	169.5189
Interest		−0.44971	−0.41407	−0.37819	−0.41465	−0.45171
Capital Gain		0.459336	0.414267	0.382894	0.409425	0.436237
Daily Profit		0.009626	0.000199	0.004707	−0.00522	−0.01547

The daily profit is again very close to zero.

7.

S	$\varepsilon \times \Delta$	$0.5 \times \varepsilon^2 \times \Gamma$	$\Theta \times h$	Predicted	Actual	Difference
23	−1.159	0.138	−0.111	1.350	1.367	−0.0168
23.1	−1.102	0.125	−0.111	1.395	1.410	−0.0150
23.2	−1.044	0.112	−0.111	1.440	1.453	−0.0134
23.3	−0.986	0.100	−0.111	1.486	1.498	−0.0119
23.4	−0.928	0.089	−0.111	1.532	1.543	−0.0105
23.5	−0.870	0.078	−0.111	1.580	1.589	−0.0091
23.6	−0.812	0.068	−0.111	1.628	1.635	−0.0079
23.7	−0.754	0.058	−0.111	1.676	1.683	−0.0067
23.8	−0.696	0.050	−0.111	1.726	1.731	−0.0056
23.9	−0.638	0.042	−0.111	1.776	1.780	−0.0046
24	−0.580	0.035	−0.111	1.826	1.830	−0.0037
24.1	−0.522	0.028	−0.111	1.878	1.880	−0.0028
24.2	−0.464	0.022	−0.111	1.930	1.932	−0.0020
24.3	−0.406	0.017	−0.111	1.983	1.984	−0.0013
24.4	−0.348	0.012	−0.111	2.036	2.037	−0.0007
24.5	−0.290	0.009	−0.111	2.090	2.090	−0.0001
24.6	−0.232	0.006	−0.111	2.145	2.145	0.0004
24.7	−0.174	0.003	−0.111	2.201	2.200	0.0009
24.8	−0.116	0.001	−0.111	2.257	2.256	0.0013
24.9	−0.058	0.000	−0.111	2.314	2.312	0.0017
25	0.000	0.000	−0.111	2.371	2.369	0.0021
25.1	0.058	0.000	−0.111	2.430	2.427	0.0024
25.2	0.116	0.001	−0.111	2.489	2.486	0.0027
25.3	0.174	0.003	−0.111	2.548	2.545	0.0029
25.4	0.232	0.006	−0.111	2.609	2.606	0.0032
25.5	0.290	0.009	−0.111	2.670	2.666	0.0034
25.6	0.348	0.012	−0.111	2.732	2.728	0.0037
25.7	0.406	0.017	−0.111	2.794	2.790	0.0039
25.8	0.464	0.022	−0.111	2.857	2.853	0.0042
25.9	0.522	0.028	−0.111	2.921	2.917	0.0045
26	0.580	0.035	−0.111	2.986	2.981	0.0048
26.1	0.638	0.042	−0.111	3.051	3.046	0.0051
26.2	0.696	0.050	−0.111	3.117	3.111	0.0055
26.3	0.754	0.058	−0.111	3.184	3.178	0.0059
26.4	0.812	0.068	−0.111	3.251	3.245	0.0064
26.5	0.870	0.078	−0.111	3.319	3.312	0.0069
26.6	0.928	0.089	−0.111	3.388	3.380	0.0075
26.7	0.986	0.100	−0.111	3.457	3.449	0.0082
26.8	1.044	0.112	−0.111	3.527	3.518	0.0089
26.9	1.102	0.125	−0.111	3.598	3.588	0.0097
27	1.159	0.138	−0.111	3.669	3.659	0.0107

8. (a)–(e).

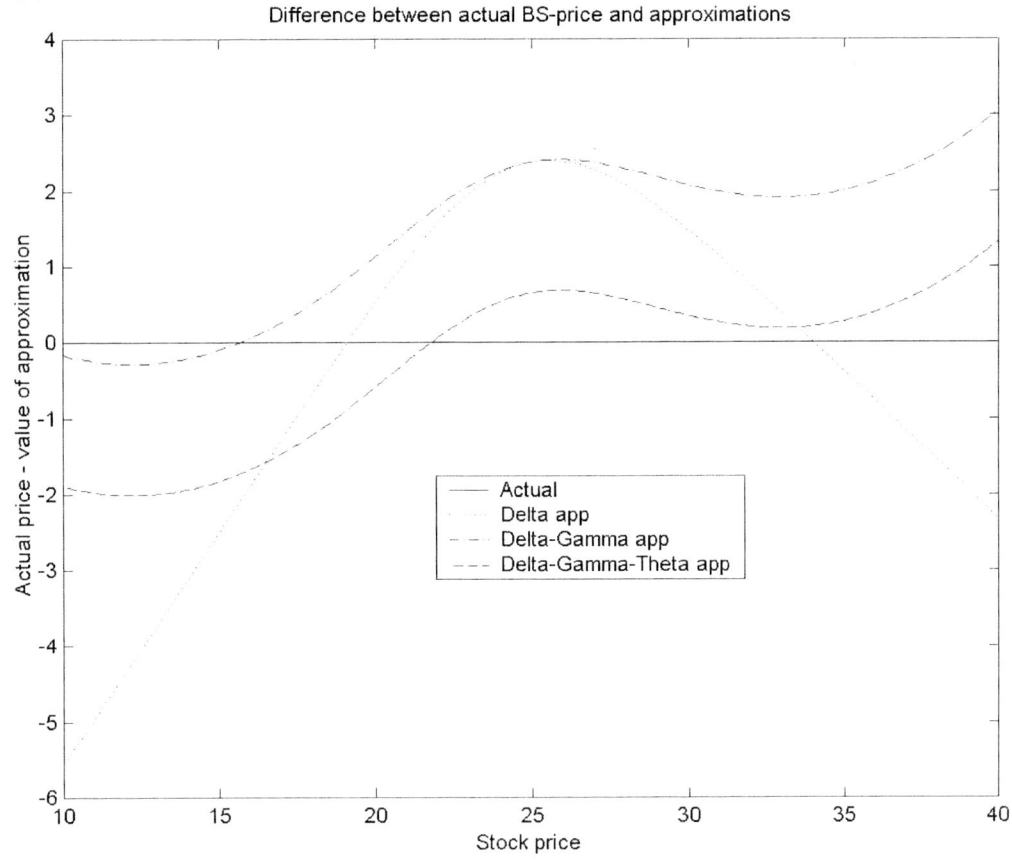

Difference between actual BS-price and approximations

(f) The time span between the original calculation and our approximation is very large at 315 days. Therefore, including theta in the approximation becomes very important. In general, it would not be a good idea to approximate the option price over such a long time span. You can see that even the theta approximation leads to considerable pricing errors.

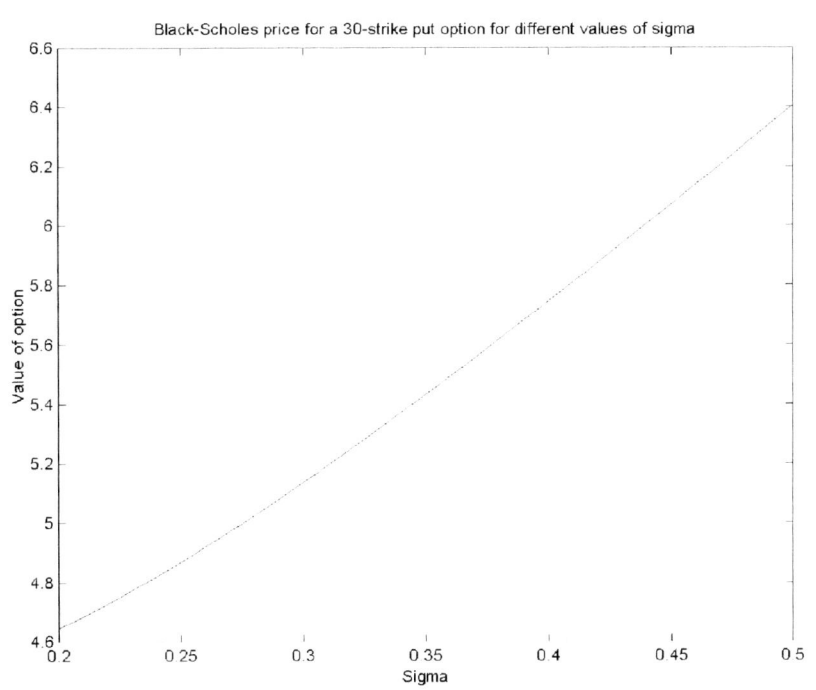

9. (a)

Black-Scholes price for a 30-strike put option for different values of sigma

Since we are long the option, and the option price increases as volatility increases, we make money as the volatility increases. Hence, we want to hedge against a fall in volatility.

We have for the two options:

	30-Strike Put	25-Strike Put
Price	5.2527	1.9885
Delta	–0.7276	–04203
Vega	0.0586	0.0690

Therefore, the necessary ratio to be vega-neutral is 0.0586/0.0690 = 0.8495. We need to short 0.8495 units of the 25-strike put.

(c) Buying one 30-strike put and selling 0.8495 25-strike puts yields a delta exposure of –0.7.276 + 0.8495 * 0.4203 = –0.3706.

We need to buy 0.3706 shares to make our portfolio delta-vega neutral.

(d) We now have:

	30-Strike Put	20-Strike Call	25-Strike Put
Price	5.2527	5.7535	1.9885
Delta	–0.7276	0.8827	–04203
gamma	0.0588	0.0348	0.0692
Vega	0.0586	0.0347	0.0690

However, we do not need the 20-strike call option. Since both put options are of the same maturity, the proportion of the 25-strike put we bought in part (c) also hedged gamma risk. The number of shares of stock and of the 25-strike put we need to buy/sell to create a delta-gamma-vega hedged position are identical to those in part (c).

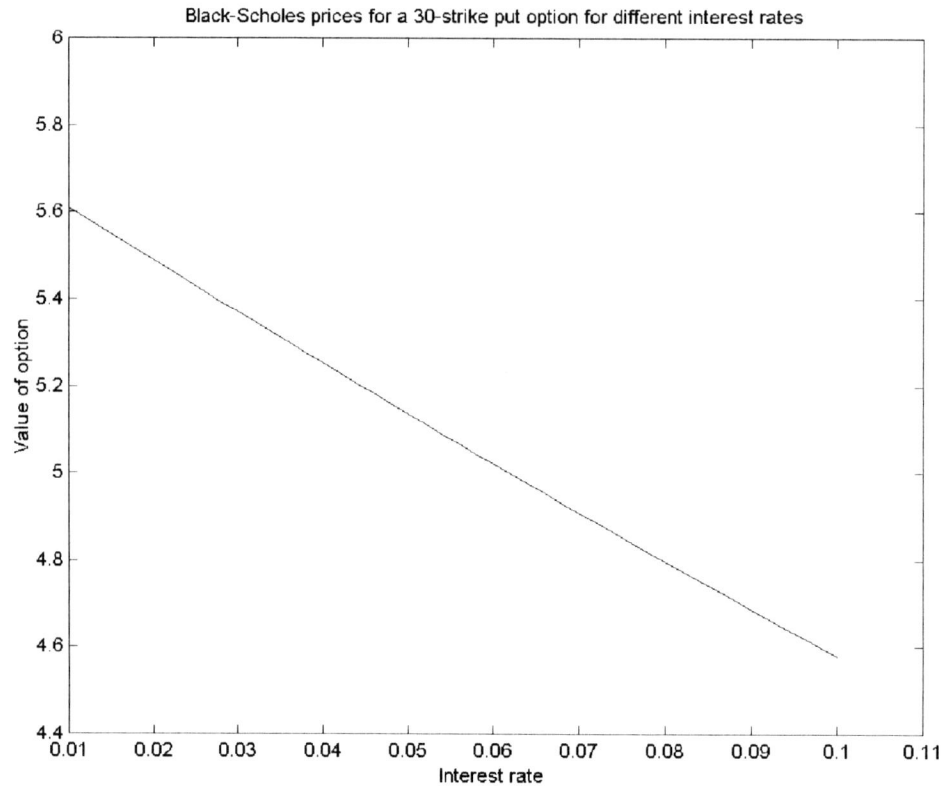

10. (a)

Black-Scholes prices for a 30-strike put option for different interest rates

If the interest rate increases, the put loses value. Since we are long the 30-strike put, we lose money.

(b) 30-strike put rho: –0.1169

25-strike put rho: –0.0623

Therefore, we need to short –0.1169/–0.0623 = 1.8764 units of the 25-strike put to create a rho-neutral position.

Chapter 14 Exotic Options: I

1. During your Google search, you should find the story of the Hunt brothers, two Texan billionaires who attempted to corner the silver market by buying vast quantities of silver. However, eventually the brothers lost more than 1 billion dollars. Cornering a market by manipulating prices is not easy, especially for a commodity like silver. Furthermore, it is illegal to do so. But frequently, people nevertheless try to manipulate prices. Using Asian options is helpful, because the market needs to be manipulated over a long period of time in order to make profits, and that is very expensive.

2. (a) u can be calculated to be 1.1735, d is 0.8694. This results in the following stock tree:

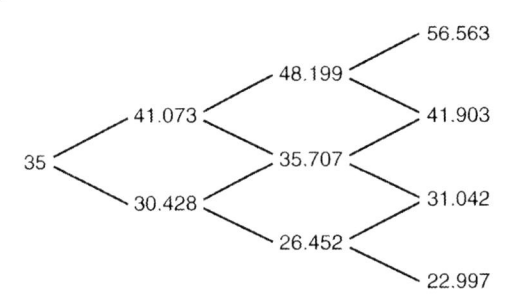

```
                          56.563
                 48.199
        41.073          41.903
35              35.707
        30.428          31.042
                 26.452
                          22.997
```

(b)–(c). The following are the possible geometric averages and the associated payoffs of the geometric average strike call option:

u	1.1735	p	0.4626
d	0.8694	1-p	0.5374

	Average Price	RNP	Stock Price	Payoff	Payoff *RNP	Discount Factor	Discounted
uuu	48.199	0.099	56.563	8.363	0.828	0.956	0.791
uud	43.613	0.115	41.903	0.000	0.000	0.956	0.000
udu	39.462	0.115	41.903	2.440	0.281	0.956	0.268
duu	35.707	0.115	41.903	6.196	0.712	0.956	0.681
udd	35.707	0.134	31.042	0.000	0.000	0.956	0.000
dud	32.309	0.134	31.042	0.000	0.000	0.956	0.000
ddu	29.234	0.134	31.042	1.808	0.242	0.956	0.231
ddd	26.452	0.155	22.997	0.000	0.000	0.956	0.000
					Option Price		1.972

Clearly, the average strikes are different for nodes that end in the same stock price; for example, the nodes uud and udu have average prices of 43.613 and 39.462, respectively. Note that averaging is done over the uncertain future stock prices after 3, 6, and 9 months.

130   McDonald • *Derivatives Markets*, Second Edition

3. (a)/(b).

   Now we have the following numbers:

	Average Price	RNP	Stock Price	Payoff	Payoff *RNP	Discount Factor	Discounted
uuu	48.612	0.099	56.563	7.951	0.787	0.956	0.752
uud	43.725	0.115	41.903	0.000	0.000	0.956	0.000
udu	39.561	0.115	41.903	2.342	0.269	0.956	0.257
duu	36.012	0.115	41.903	5.890	0.677	0.956	0.648
udd	35.941	0.134	31.042	0.000	0.000	0.956	0.000
dud	32.392	0.134	31.042	0.000	0.000	0.956	0.000
ddu	29.307	0.134	31.042	1.735	0.232	0.956	0.222
ddd	26.626	0.155	22.997	0.000	0.000	0.956	0.000
					Option Price		1.879

   (c) The price of the arithmetic call is slightly lower—arithmetic averaging leads to higher averages than geometric averaging. We are averaging the strike price, and this will lead to lower values for S − G(K). Therefore, the price of the geometric average strike call is higher than that of the arithmetic average strike call.

4. (a) Note that now the payoff is: Geometric average price−$37:

	Average Price	RNP	Stock Price	Payoff	Payoff *RNP	Discount Factor	Discounted
uuu	48.199	0.099	56.563	11.199	1.108	0.956	1.060
uud	43.613	0.115	41.903	6.613	0.760	0.956	0.727
udu	39.462	0.115	41.903	2.462	0.283	0.956	0.271
duu	35.707	0.115	41.903	0.000	0.000	0.956	0.000
udd	35.707	0.134	31.042	0.000	0.000	0.956	0.000
dud	32.309	0.134	31.042	0.000	0.000	0.956	0.000
ddu	29.234	0.134	31.042	0.000	0.000	0.956	0.000
ddd	26.452	0.155	22.997	0.000	0.000	0.956	0.000
					Option Price		2.057

   (b)

	Average Price	RNP	Stock price	Payoff	Payoff *RNP	Discount Factor	Discounted
uuu	48.612	0.099	56.563	11.612	1.149	0.956	1.099
uud	43.725	0.115	41.903	6.725	0.773	0.956	0.739
udu	39.561	0.115	41.903	2.561	0.294	0.956	0.282
duu	36.012	0.115	41.903	0.000	0.000	0.956	0.000
udd	35.941	0.134	31.042	0.000	0.000	0.956	0.000
dud	32.392	0.134	31.042	0.000	0.000	0.956	0.000
ddu	29.307	0.134	31.042	0.000	0.000	0.956	0.000
ddd	26.626	0.155	22.997	0.000	0.000	0.956	0.000
					Option Price		2.120

(c) The arithmetic call is more expensive. Arithmetic averages are larger than geometric averages, and we average the price in this exercise. The payoff in each state is G(S) – K, so a larger G(S) leads to larger payoffs.

5.

Today	Barrier hit S <= K	Barrier hit S > K	Barrier not hit S <= K	Barrier not hit S > K
Ordinary call option	0	S – K	0	S – K
Knock-in call option	0	S – K	—	—
Knock-out call option	—	—	0	S – K
Total	0	S – K	0	S – K

6. (a) The option is activated if the stock price rises above $30. We have to price an up-and-in call option. Based on the software package, the price is 2.191018.

   (b) The option is activated if the stock price rises above $30. We have to price an up-an-in put option. Based on the software package, the price is 0.588397

   (c) The price of an ordinary call option is 2.202767, the price of an ordinary put option is 2.375242. The call-option difference is 0.0117, the put-option difference is 1.7868. The put option difference is considerably larger. The knock-in put option is less valuable, because the stock price needs to increase above 30 to activate the option, but then needs to fall below $28 to ensure a positive payoff for the put option. For the call option, the movement to activate the barrier and the positive payoff region are aligned, and thus the difference in a regular and knock-in call is much smaller.

7. (a) The price of a standard European call is $3.507.

   (b) Based on the software package that comes with the book, the critical boundary for the stock price above which we will exercise is: $22.647.

   (c) The compound call is worth $2.563.

   (d) In the extreme case of an identical time to expiration, the critical boundary becomes K + strike price you pay to buy option = $28 + $1 = $29. You will only exercise the option on the option if you can recover the premium by immediately exercising of the underlying option.

8. (a) The price of a standard European put option is 2.876.

   (b) Using various values for the strike X in the software (or using Excel's goalseek function), we find a value of $3.28.

   (c) The price of this compound option is 0.538407.

9. (a) Implementing the formula of the textbook in Excel (you need to use the normdist() function), we get for the first gap option a value of 3.0244.

   (b) The gap call with a trigger of $15 has a value of 2.7654.

   (c) We are now obligated to pay out in some cases. For the second option, the option buyer has the "right" to receive S – K whenever S is bigger than $15. However, this is really an obligation for all values between 15 and 25, because S – K is negative. This makes the option of part (b) less valuable.

10. Using the spreadsheet software accompanying the book, and using a price level of 0.8 * 35 = 28 as input in the strike asset, we find a price of $4.35167 for this option.

    The second option has the same value. This is consistent with what is discussed in the book.

Chapter 15 Financial Engineering and Security Design

1. We need to find the prepaid forward contract price, which equals the price of the zero-coupon equity-linked bond:

$$F_{0,T}^P = S_0 - \sum_{i=1}^{t} P_{t_i} \times D_{t_i} = 46.22 - \sum_{i=1}^{20} P_{t_i} \times 0.53 = 46.22 - 0.53 \times 17.7641 = 36.805$$

2. We need to find the prepaid forward contract price, which equals the price of the zero-coupon equity-linked bond:

$$F_{0,T}^P = S_0 - \sum_{i=1}^{t} P_{t_i} \times D_{t_i} = 46.22 - \sum_{i=1}^{20} P_{t_i} \times D_{t_i}$$

The following Table shows the values of the quarterly zero coupons and of the growing dividend payments.

Exercise 15.2	
S(0)	46.22
annual cont comp irate	4.60%
quarterly cont comp irate	0.0115
constant dividend	0.53

Quarter	P(ti)	Dividend	P * Div
1	0.989	0.530	0.524
2	0.977	0.610	0.596
3	0.966	0.701	0.677
4	0.955	0.806	0.770
5	0.944	0.927	0.875
6	0.933	1.066	0.995
7	0.923	1.226	1.131
8	0.912	1.287	1.174
9	0.902	1.352	1.219
10	0.891	1.419	1.265
11	0.881	1.490	1.313
12	0.871	1.565	1.363
13	0.861	1.643	1.415
14	0.851	1.725	1.468
15	0.842	1.811	1.524
16	0.832	1.902	1.582
17	0.822	1.997	1.642
18	0.813	2.097	1.705
19	0.804	2.202	1.769
20	0.795	2.312	1.837
		Sum	24.844

Therefore, we can write the value of the zero-coupon equity-linked bond as:

$$F_{0,T}^P = S_0 - \sum_{i=1}^{t} P_{t_i} \times D_{t_i} = 46.22 - 24.84432 = 21.376$$

3. (a) The note should promise to pay a coupon equal to the quarterly dividend of $0.53. We can use equation 15.5 to show this formally:

$$c = \frac{S_0 - F_{0,T}^P}{\sum_{i=1}^{20} P_{t_i}} = \frac{46.22 - 36.805}{17.7641} = 0.53$$

(b) We can use the same formula to evaluate the appropriate coupon. Since we require a constant coupon when the dividend is growing at two different rates, it is more difficult to make a prediction about the coupon payment. We know that it must lie between 0.53 (the lowest dividend payment) and 2.312 (the highest dividend payment). The formula reveals that:

$$c = \frac{S_0 - F_{0,T}^P}{\sum_{i=1}^{20} P_{t_i}} = \frac{46.22 - 21.476}{17.7641} = 1.393$$

4. (a) We first need to find the prepaid forward price of the gold note. It is:

$$F_{0,T}^P = \$347.385 \times \exp(-0.0175 \times 3) = 329.618$$

Now we can use the formula of the textbook to calculate:

$$c = \frac{\$350 - \$329.618}{e^{-0.0125} + e^{-0.0125 \times 2} + e^{-0.0175 \times 3}} = \frac{20.382}{2.907} = 7.0114$$

(b) The annual coupon as a fraction of the spot price is 7.0114/350 = 2%.

(c) In this case, the yield on gold is higher than the yield on cash – the lease rate is 2%, the interest rate is 1.75%. The scenario of the exercise is similar to the one in Japan described in the textbook. The general level of interest rates is very low in the example.

5. We first need to calculate the one- and two-year forward prices for euros:

$$F_{0,t} = x_0 \times \exp(r(t) \times t) \times \exp(-r_f(t) \times t) = x_0 \frac{P_t^f}{P_t}$$

Using the relevant inputs from the text of the exercise, we obtain the 1-year forward rate as 0.862846 and the 2-year forward rate as 0.867171.

In the next step, we use formula 15.10 of the main text to calculate the foreign coupon (which is denoted in Euros). We also need the 1-year and 2-year dollar zero-coupon prices which are easily computed as P(1) = 0.946485 and P(2) = 0.88692.

$$c^f = M \times \frac{1 - P_T}{\sum_{i=1}^{2} F_{0,t_i} P_{t_i}}$$

Using the formula, we obtain a foreign coupon of Euro 71.30835. Note that the currency is indeed Euro, as the numerator is in dollar, and the denominator is in $/Euro. The dollar cancels out, the Euro prevails.

6. We need to use the inputs given in the section "pricing the CD". The S&P index today is 1,300, index volatility is 30%, the 5.5 year interest rate is 6%, the dividend yield is equal to 1.5%, and the strike price is equal to the index level.

We can plug these values into the Excel spreadsheet that comes with the main textbook, and use an averaging time of 5 during the life of the option in the appropriate field. We get as output:

Inputs	
Stock Price	1300
Exercise Price	1300
Volatility	30.000%
Risk-free interest rate	6.000%
Time to Expiration (years)	5.5
Dividend Yield	1.500%
# Prices in Average	5
Moneyness for Avg Strike	1
Number of simulations	6000

Geometric Average Price Asian Options

	Call	Put
Black-Scholes	441.441	178.98
Average Price, Continuous	200.252	119.87
Average Price, 5 Prices	**240.97**	133.44
Average Strike, Continuous	283.295	101.21
Average Strike, 5 Prices	242.731	87.803

Arithmetic Avg Asian (simple Monte Carlo)

Arithmetic Average Price	271.929	120.50
Arithmetic Average Strike	210.887	101.93
Iteration Number	6000	

Arithmetic Avg Asian (Control Variate)

Arithmetic Average Price	272.898	121.43
Arithmetic Average Strike	213.666	103.40
Iteration Number	6000	

Go to Sheet: Asian

The price of the geometric price Asian call option matches the price in the book exactly, because it is calculated analytically. The price of the arithmetic option diverges slightly. It is very close when we use the control variate approach. If you got a number that substantially deviates from the ones you see in this spreadsheet, try to increase the number of simulations. You should get much closer to the value of $273.12 mentioned in the textbook.

7. We can value this instrument today as

$$S_0 \times \exp(-0.04 \times 4) + 0.9 \times \text{AsianCall}\,(1300, 1300, 0.30, 0.04, 4, 0.015, 16\,\text{Averages})$$

The option we need to value is an arithmetic price Asian call option. We get from our software:

Inputs	
Stock Price	1300
Exercise Price	1300
Volatility	30.000%
Risk-free interest rate	4.000%
Time to Expiration (years)	4
Dividend Yield	1.500%
# Prices in Average	16
Moneyness for Avg Strike	1
Number of simulations	6000

Geometric Average Price Asian Options

	Call	Put
Black-Scholes	336.926	220.419
Average Price, Continuous	165.313	142.935
Average Price, 16 Prices	**174.604**	148.555
Average Strike, Continuous	213.197	119.069
Average Strike, 16 Prices	203.931	113.473

Now we just plug in the values of the formula above:
$$PV = 1300 \times \exp(-0.04 \times 4) + 0.9 \times 174.604$$
$$= 1282.39$$

The financial advisor earns a commission of 1.355%.

8. A holding company creates a wholly-owned 'shell' subsidiary, oftentimes a LLC or a Delaware Business Trust, capitalized with a minimal amount of cash in exchange for all of the common (voting) equity of the subsidiary (in the McKesson case, the 123,720 common shares), which is 3% of the value of the debentures.

The 123,720 shares of common stock issued by the trust to McKesson are convertible into McKesson common shares, and in that sense McKesson (potentially) holds shares in their own company, namely 166,000 (123,720 × 1.3418).

In related transactions, the subsidiary then issues trust preferred stock to investors for cash (in the McKesson case, 4 million preferred shares at $50 or $200 million. The holding company issues subordinated debentures in the same amount to the subsidiary in exchange for the $206,186,000 million proceeds of the trust preferred issue. The terms and yield of the debentures are identical to those of the trust preferred stock, so the debentures provide the cash to make the dividend payments to trust preferred holders. Note that the debentures pay 5% interest, and that the preferred stock is entitled to a 5% dividend.

The trust is a mere conduit between the holding company and the trust preferred investors, with interest payments from the holding company on the debentures equaling the dividends paid to the trust preferred investors. Note that the subsidiary trust has two classes of stock: trust preferred stock owned by outside investors, and common stock owned by the holding company.

Why do they exist-Tax treatment of TPS

As a limited liability corporation (LLC), the subsidiary trust is treated under U.S. tax law as a partnership, so it is not consolidated with McKesson for tax purposes (unlike for financial reporting purposes).

Since the subsidiary is a partnership and not a corporate subsidiary of the holding company for tax purposes, the holding company is able to deduct the interest payments it makes to the subsidiary.

Part of the information for this solution stems from the following article:

Engel, Ellen, Merle Erickson, and Edward Maydew, 2000, Debt-equity Hybrid Securities, Journal of Accounting Research, 37, 249-274.

9. **This is one of many possible answers, from www.riskinstitute.ch**

Liquid Yield Option Note (LYON)

A zero coupon convertible, callable (by the issuer), puttable (by the investor) bond issued by a corporation. The combination of LYON features usually assures that an investor will earn a positive return—at least until the expiration of the last opportunity to put the security back to the issuer—at a premium over the issue price. The total return, if the company prospers and the common stock performs well, will be less than the return earned by common shareholders. The payout pattern of a LYON is roughly similar to some types of equity-linked notes.

10. (a)
    Early February 2001: Lowe's issues LYON

    February 16th, 2004: First date investors are allowed to "put back" the security to the company, that is to require the company to buy the security back (the put feature).

    February 16th, 2004: First date the company can start buying back LYONs at their discretion (the call feature). Companies have the right to buy back the LYONs from that day on until maturity.

    February 16th, 2011: Second and last date the investors are allowed to require the company to buy the security back.

    February 16th, 2021: The LYONs mature, and investors receive back a principal of $1,000.

    Throughout the life of the LYON, that is, February 2001 to February 2021, investors can convert their LYON into 8.224 shares of Lowe's.

    An investor would like to convert his shares when the stock price times 8.224 exceeds the issue price plus accrued interest.

    Lowe's would like to buy the issue back if they can obtain cheaper financing.

(b) The yield to maturity is derived from

$$\$608.41 = \frac{\$1,000}{(1+y)^{20}} \Leftrightarrow (1+y) = \left(\frac{\$1,000}{\$608.41}\right)^{1/20} = 1.02516$$

so that the yield is indeed 2.5%.

(c) Lowe's is not allowed to buy back the LYONs prior to February 16th, 2004.

(d) Lowe's can buy the LYONs back at original issue price plus accrued interest, at a yield of 2.516%. Therefore, they would have to pay:

$$\$608.41 \times (1+0.02516)^4 = \$671.98$$

(e) Lowe's can buy the LYONs back at any time, they are not restricted to a February 16th date. In this case, they again have to pay the original issue price plus accrued interest:

$$\$608.41 \times (1+0.02516)^{4.5} = \$680.39$$

(f) The investor would again have achieved only the yield of 2.51%.

$$(1+y) = \left(\frac{\$780.01}{608.41}\right)^{1/10} = 1.02516$$

Chapter 16   Corporate Applications

1. (a) In general, there are two types of bonds: bearer bonds and registered bonds. With registered bonds, the company knows who the investors are, and they wire interest payments and redemption of principal to investors at the appropriate times. With bearer bonds, a company does not know who the investors are. The certificate contains a sheet with coupons that you cut out and present to any bank. Whoever presents the coupon gets paid. Hence, money is paid to the bearer of the certificate. Bearer bonds are very popular in Europe.

(b) While the interest rates change every period (that is the step-up feature), you know what the interest rates are. With floating rate notes, interest payments are tied to an unknown future reference interest rate such as LIBOR (London Interbank Offered Rate).

(c) The call feature is described in the bullet point "Bank's optional redemption." Investors have to be notified at least 10 business days before September 4th. The bank can call the bonds back once a year, on September 4th. If it decides to call the bonds back, it has to do so for the entire issue.

(d) The bank will call the bonds back if interest rates have decreased. At that point, the bonds are more valuable for investors. Therefore, the notes trade at a discount relative to a non-callable step-up issue.

(e) There is no conversion provision for investors.

2. (a) We can use Formula 16.4 to calculate the payoff at maturity:

$$B_T = \bar{B} - \max(0, \bar{B} - A_T) = \$150 - \text{Payoff Put}(150,150,...)$$

To find today's value, we need to price the put AND we need to discount the maturity value of the debt at the appropriate rate:

$$B_0 = 150 \times \exp(-0.06 \times 10) - BSPut(150,150,...)$$
$$= 82.3217 - 17.9223$$
$$= 64.3994$$

(b) The value of a 10-year zero coupon is equivalent to 82.3217, the first part of the formula we calculated in part (a). It is higher because a government bond does not carry default risk. The sold put option characterizes the default risk.

(c) The yield of the firm's debt is equal to

$$\rho = \frac{1}{T-t} \ln(\bar{B}/B_t) = \frac{1}{10} \ln(150/64.3994) = 0.08455$$

(d) da)
$$B_0 = 150 \times \exp(-0.06 \times 10) - BSPut(150,150, \sigma = 0.15,...)$$
$$= 82.3217 - 2.5352$$
$$= 79.7865$$

db) With the lower volatility, the risk of default is much smaller. Therefore, the value of the risky bond is much closer to the value of the government bond.

dc) The yield is now:

$$\rho = \frac{1}{T-t} \ln(\bar{B}/B_t) = \frac{1}{10} \ln(150/79.7865) = 0.06313$$

3. (a) The expected return on equity is: $r_E = r + (r_A - r) \times \Omega_E$

We can calculate the option's elasticity as: $\Omega_E = \dfrac{A_t \times \Delta_E}{E_t}$

(Alternatively, we can use the Excel software that comes with the book to read off the elasticity). Using the inputs above, we can calculate a value of 85.6006 for the firm's equity, and an option delta of 0.8641. The elasticity is thus equal to:

$$\Omega_E = \frac{A_t \times \Delta_E}{E_t} = \frac{150 \times 0.8641}{85.6006} = 1.51418$$

We can conclude that: $r_E = 0.06 + (0.12 - 0.06) \times 1.51418 = 0.1509$

138   McDonald • *Derivatives Markets*, Second Edition

(b) We can calculate the expected return on debt as: $r_B = r + (r_A - r) \times \Omega_B$
We can calculate the debt's elasticity as:

$$\Omega_B = \frac{A_t}{A_t - E_t} \times \Omega_A - \frac{E_t}{A_t - E_t} \times \Omega_E$$

$$= \frac{A_t}{A_t - E_t} - \frac{E_t}{A_t - E_t} \times \Omega_E$$

$$= \frac{150}{150 - 85.6006} - \frac{85.6006}{150 - 85.6006} \times 1.51418$$

$$= 0.3165$$

Therefore, the expected return on debt is equal to:

$$r_B = r + (r_A - r) \times \Omega_B = 0.06 + 0.06 \times 0.3165 = 0.07899$$

The expected return is smaller than the yield, because in some states of the world, bankruptcy occurs, and bonds do not pay the promised payoff.

(c) We can calculate: $r_E = r + (r_A - r) \dfrac{1}{\% \text{ Equity}} = 0.06 + (0.12 - 0.06) \times \dfrac{150}{85.6006} = 0.1651$

This number is higher than what we calculated it part (a) because it erroneously does not take into account the possibility of bankruptcy.

4. We can calculate the yields to maturity using our standard formula:

$$\rho = \frac{1}{T - t} \ln(\bar{B}/B_t)$$

For the senior bonds, we have: $\rho = \dfrac{1}{5} \ln(30/22.18) = 6.04\%$

For the intermediate bonds, we have: $\rho = \dfrac{1}{5} \ln(30/20.57) = 7.54\%$

It is more complicated to calculate the expected returns on the two tranches. We need the elasticity of each tranch. To find it, we look at a portfolio of the elements of the pricing and multiply the elasticity of each of the elements with the appropriate weight.

For the senior bond, we have: portfolio consists of assets and a sold 30-strike call. The overall portfolio value is: $A_t - C(30) = 90 - 67.82 = 22.18$. The appropriate weights are 90/22.18 and −67.82/22.18. The elasticity of the assets is one; the elasticity of the 30-strike call is: 1.3234.

$$\Omega_{\text{Senior}} = \frac{A_t}{A_t - C(30)} \times \Omega_A - \frac{C(30)}{A_t - C(30)} \times \Omega_{C(30)}$$

$$= \frac{90}{90 - 67.82} - \frac{67.82}{90 - 67.82} \times 1.3234$$

$$= 0.0111$$

The elasticity is extremely small; therefore, we already know that the expected return on the senior tranche is almost equal to the risk-free rate:

$$r_{Senior} = r + (r_A - r) \times \Omega_{Senior} = 0.06 + (0.10 - 0.06) \times 0.0111 = 0.06044$$

For the intermediate bond, we calculate: portfolio consists of a long position in the C(30) and a short position in the 60-strike call. The overall portfolio value is: 67.82 – 47.25 = 20.57. The appropriate weights are 67.82/20.57 and –47.25/20.57. The elasticity of the 30-strike call is 1.3234; the elasticity of the 60-strike call is: 1.7875.

$$\Omega_{Intermediate} = \frac{67.82}{20.57} \times 1.3234 - \frac{47.25}{20.57} \times 1.7875 = 0.2573$$

The expected return on the intermediate tranche is:

$$r_{Intermediate} = r + (r_A - r) \times \Omega_{Intermediate} = 0.06 + (0.10 - 0.06) \times 0.2573 = 0.0703$$

5. We can identify the respective values of the three tranches by writing out a table similar to Table 16.1:

Claim	Owns	Writes	Value	Yield	Expected Return
Senior Bonds	Assets	C(50)			
Intermediate Bonds	C(50)	C(100)			
Junior Bonds	C(100)	C(150)			
Equity	C(150)	—			

It is evident from the table above that the value of the equity and the expected return we calculated in Exercise 16.3 do not change—the equity is still equivalent to a 150-strike call option and has an expected return of 15.09%.

Using the Black-Scholes formula from the accompanying Excel spreadsheet, we can calculate the following prices and elasticities:

Instrument	Price	Elasticity
C(50)	123.6962	1.1951
C(100)	102.2618	1.3688
C(150)	85.6006	1.5142

Overall, we find:

Claim	Face Value	Value	Elasticity	Yield	Expected Return
Senior	50	26.3038	0.0825231	0.064231	0.064951
Intermediate	50	21.4344	0.3663913	0.084703	0.081983
Junior	50	16.6612	0.6217753	0.109894	0.097307
Equity		85.6006	1.5142		0.150852

6. (a) We can write:

Claim	Owns	Writes	Value	Yield	Expected Return
Senior Bonds	Assets	C(50)			
Intermediate Bonds	C(50)	C(100)			
Junior Bonds	C(100)	C(150)			
New Bonds	C(150)	C(170)			
Equity	C(170)	—			

We calculate the following:

	Face Value	Value	Elasticity	Yield	Expected Return
Senior	50	26.3038	0.0825	0.0642	0.0650
Intermediate	50	21.4344	0.3664	0.0847	0.0820
Junior	50	16.6612	0.6218	0.1099	0.0973
Subordinated	20	5.5924	0.7735	0.1274	0.1064
Equity		80.0082	1.5660		0.1540

(b) Now we have to write:

Claim	Owns	Writes	Value	Yield	Expected Return
New Tranche	Assets	C(20)			
Senior Debt	C(20)	C(70)			
Intermediate Bonds	C(70)	C(120)			
Junior Bonds	C(120)	C(170)			
Equity	C(170)	—			

	Face Value	Value	Elasticity	Yield	Expected Return
most senior	20	10.91943	0.013746	0.0605	0.0608
Senior	50	24.59927	0.189084	0.0709	0.0713
Intermediate	50	19.39043	0.475808	0.0947	0.0885
Junior	50	15.08267	0.708223	0.1198	0.1025
Equity		80.00819	1.565972		0.1540

(c) The equity owners do not care whether the new debt is junior or senior—they are the residual claimants, that is, they know that in case of bankruptcy, all debt holders have to be satisfied before they earn money.

(d) You can see that the seniority of the new tranche in part (b) has an effect on all following tranches. For example, the senior debt is reduced in value by 26.3038 – 24.59927. The covenant is valuable because it protects all existing bondholders.

7. (a) Without the conversion option, the entire issue is worth:

$$B_0 = 30,000 \times \$5,000 \times \exp(-0.05 \times 6) - \text{BSPut}(200M, 150M, 0.25, 0.05, 6, 0)$$
$$= 111.1227 - 7.9712$$
$$= 103.1515$$

This is equivalent to a per zero-coupon price of 103.1515M/30,000 = $3,438.3838.

To price the convertible bond, we first list:

n	= number of outstanding shares	= 4,000,000
q	= number of convertible shares	= 80
mq	= total number of shares if converted	= 80 * 30,000 = 2,400,000
n/(n + mq) = 4/6.4		= 0.625
M	= maturity payment	= 5,000
M/q * (n + mq)/n = 5,000/80 * 6.4/4		= 100
A(T)/n = 200M/4M		= 50

We can now use the formula given in the main textbook to write:

$$B_{Convertible} = mM \times \exp(-r \times T) - \text{BSPut}(A_t, mM, \ldots) + mq \times \frac{n}{n+mq} \times \text{BSCall}\left(\frac{A_T}{n}, \frac{M}{q}\frac{n+mq}{n}\right)$$

$$= 150M \times \exp(-0.05 \times 6) - \text{BSPut}(200M, 150M)$$
$$+ 2.4M \times 0.625 \times \text{BSCall}(50, 100, \ldots)$$
$$= 103.1515 + 1.5 \times 5.7190$$
$$= 111.7299$$

This corresponds to a price per bond of 111.7299/30,000 = 3724.3316.

(b) Each bond gives the shareholder the right to convert into 80 shares, so the strike price is $5,000/80 = 62.50. The value of one share today is (200M − 111.7299)/4 = 22.0675. The conversion premium is thus 62.50/22.0675 − 1 = 183%.

8. We need to first calculate the forward tree for the stock price. Based on the above numbers, we have:

$$u = \exp\left((r-\delta)h + \sigma\sqrt{h}\right) = \exp(0.05 + 0.32) = 1.4477$$

$$d = \exp\left((r-\delta)h - \sigma\sqrt{h}\right) = \exp(0.05 - 0.32) = 0.7634$$

$$p^* = \frac{\exp((r-\delta)h) - d}{u - d} = \frac{\exp(0.05) - 0.7634}{1.4477 - 0.7634} = 0.4034$$

We can then construct the following tables:

Stock Price Process

t = 0	t = 1	t = 2	t = 3
54.250	78.540	113.705	164.614
	41.413	59.956	86.800
		31.614	45.769
			24.134

Intrinsic Value

t = 0	t = 1	t = 2	t = 3
0.000	24.290	59.455	110.364
	0.000	5.706	32.550
		0.000	0.000
			0.000

One Period Option Value

t = 0	t = 1	t = 2	t = 3
9.720	26.935	62.100	0.000
	2.283	13.025	0.000
		0.000	0.000
			0.000

Reported Option Expense

t = 0	t = 1	t = 2	t = 3
9.720	2.646	2.646	0.000
	2.283	7.320	0.000
		0.000	0.000
			0.000

9. Suppose that the stock volatility is 25%, the continuously compounded interest rate is 5%, the dividend yield is zero, and the initial stock price is equal to $47.25.

We can value this exercise by relying on the formulas of the main text. First, we can find the value of an ordinary Black-Scholes option:

We have: BS(47.25, 47.25, 0.25, 0.05, 5, 0) = 13.6242

Then we can proceed and value the repriced option as:

$$\text{CallDownOut }(47.25, 47.25, 0.25, 0.05, 5, 0, 23.625)+$$
$$\text{CallDownIn }((47.25, 23.625, 0.25, 0.05, 5, 0, 23.625)=$$
$$13.5690 + 0.6707 = 14.2397$$

Therefore, the additional bonus cash payment necessary is $0.6155 per option.

10. (a)

WorldCom Price	Payoff
$S_T < 34$	$1.2206 * S_T$
$34 \leq S_T <= 40$	41.50
$S_T > 40$	$1.0375 * S_T$

(b)

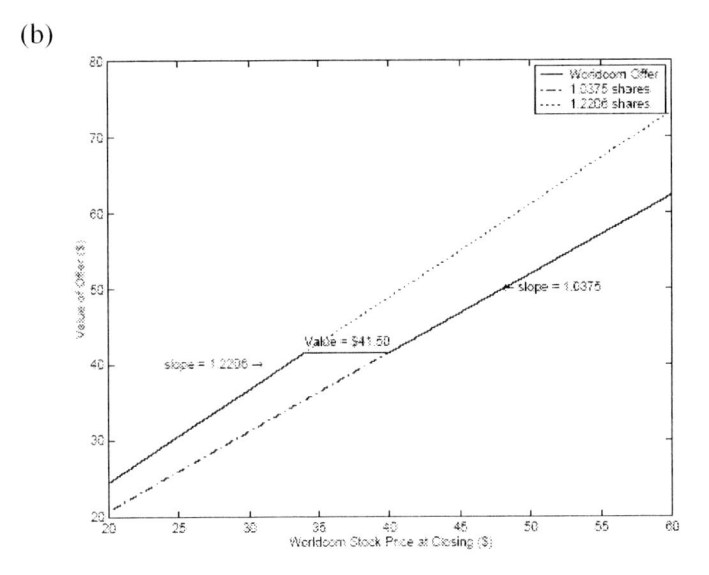

(c)

WorldCom Price	Bonds	Puts	Calls	Total
$S_T < 34$	41.50	$-1.2206(34 - S_T)$	0	$1.2206 * S_T$
$34 \leq S_T \leq 40$	41.50	0	0	41.50
$S_T > 40$	41.50	0	$1.0375(S_T - 40)$	$1.0375 * S_T$

Therefore, the offer of WorldCom is equivalent to 1.2206 short put options, 1.0375 long call options, and a long position in 41.50 riskless bonds.

(d) We can find the value of a 4-month European Call option on WorldCom by using the Black-Scholes formula with

$$C(35.4375, 40, 0.38, 0.055, 0.3333) = 1.6949$$

(e) In addition, we have to value a put option with strike of 34. We find:

$$P(35.4375, 34, 0.38, 0.055, 0.3333) = 2.0884$$

And we have to find the present value of the bonds:

$$41.50 * \exp(-0.055 * 0.3333) = 40.7462$$

Therefore, the WorldCom offer is valued at:

$$40.7462 - 1.2206 * 2.0884 + 1.0375 * 1.6949 = 39.9556$$

(f) The WorldCom offer is worth less than the GTE offer. Therefore, a rational shareholder should accept the GTE offer.

Chapter 17 Real Options

1.

$$NPV_{\text{Static}} = \$0.8 \times 3 \times \frac{1}{0.07 - 0.05} - 1.20 \times 3 \times \frac{1}{0.07} - 15$$

$$= 120 - 66.4286 = 53.5714$$

2. (a) We have to solve for the point where annual widget revenue is equal to marginal production cost plus opportunity cost of investing.

$$(1 + 0.05)^n \times 3 \times 0.80 = 3 \times 1.20 + 0.07 \times 15$$
$$(1.05)^n \times 2.40 = 4.65$$
$$\Rightarrow n = 13.556$$

We can calculate a modified NPV of:

$$\frac{1}{1.07^{13.556}} \times \left(\frac{1.05^{13.556} \times 3 \times 0.80}{0.07 - 0.05} - \frac{3 \times 1.20}{0.07} - 15 \right) = 66.36957$$

(b) Now we have to take into account the fact that the opportunity cost decreases each year due to advancements in technology. Since the opportunity cost decreases, we will attain the threshold of revenue equal to marginal cost sooner, that is, n should be smaller than in part (a).

$$(1 + 0.05)^n \times 3 \times 0.80 = 3 \times 1.20 + 0.07 \times 15 \times (1 - 0.03)^n$$
$$(1.05)^n \times 2.40 = 3.60 + 1.05 \times (0.97)^n$$
$$\Rightarrow n = 12.07935$$

The solution to the above equation was obtained using the function goalseek in Microsoft Excel. We can calculate the NPV as:

$$\frac{1}{1.07^{12.07935}} \times \left(\frac{1.05^{12.07935} \times 0.80 \times 3}{0.07 - 0.05} - \frac{1.20 \times 3}{0.07} - 15 \times (1 - 0.03)^{12.07935} \right) = 68.24474$$

3. We use as inputs $S = \frac{3 \times 0.80}{0.07 - 0.05} = 120 \quad K = \frac{1.20 \times 3}{0.07} + 15 = 66.4286$

$r = \ln(1.07) = 0.0677$, sigma = 0, and delta = $\ln(1.07) - \ln(1.05) = 0.01887$

We find an option value – NPV of 66.92472, which is higher than the value in Exercise 17.2 (a). The investment trigger is 243.5715, which corresponds to the value of the revenue stream after which it is optimal to exercise. We can use the following to back out the optimal time period:

$$\frac{3 \times 0.80 \times e^{0.04879 n}}{0.0676 - 0.04879} = 243.5715$$

$$e^{0.04879 n} = 101.488125 \times 0.01887$$

$$e^{0.04879 n} = 1.914927$$

$$n = 13.316$$

NOTE: This answer varies depending on how many leading zeros you choose as an input for sigma in the Excel spreadsheet.

4. (a) The statement is not correct. If we add uncertainty about project cash flows, the value of insurance (the implicit put option of the cost/benefit analysis of any option) influences the decision to delay the project because waiting to invest provides information about the value of the project.

   (b) For sigma = 10%, we have an option value of 68.6869 and a trigger of 261.7885. For sigma = 20%, we have an option value of 74.02798 and a trigger of 326.5908.

5. (a) We have to calculate the discount rate using the CAPM.

   We have:
   $$\alpha = 0.04 + 2.3 \times (0.10 - 0.04) = 0.178$$

   The expected cash flow is:
   $$E(X) = 0.4 \times 400 + 0.6 \times 120 = 232$$

   We can calculate V, which is the value of the project as
   $$V = \frac{E(X)}{(1+\alpha)^T} = \frac{232}{(1+0.178)} = 196.9440$$

   (b) In order to calculate the risk-neutral probability, we need
   $$F_{0,1} = 196.9440 \times 1.04 = 204.8218$$

   The risk-neutral probability is:
   $$p^* = \frac{F_{0,T} - X_d}{X_u - X_d} = \frac{204.8218 - 120}{400 - 120} = 0.30293$$

   Hence, we can use the formula to evaluate:
   $$V = \frac{0.30293 \times 400 + (1 - 0.30293) \times 120}{1.04} = 196.943$$

   The two methods yield equivalent results.

6. We can use the following ingredients in the calculation of the tree:

Inputs	
Stock Price	150
Exercise Price	100
Volatility	50.000%
Risk-free interest rate	6.766%
Time to Expiration (years)	2
Dividend Yield	11.333%
# Binomial steps	2
Type (0 = Eur, 1 = Amer)	1

This yields the following tree:

Times (yrs)

	1	2
150	236.2676	372.1493
55.65631	136.268	272.149
	86.91801	136.9061
	13.022	36.9061
		50.36494
		0

u = 1.5751; d = 0.5795
Risk-neutral prob of up = 0.3775
Forward tree

Hence, we would early exercise the investment option in the up node after one year. We would also exercise the option in the uu, ud nodes after one year and choose not to invest in the dd node. The small difference in option value compared to the Cox/Rubinstein tree is due to the fact that we are only using two binomial steps and rounding.

7. (a) We have to calculate the discount rate using the CAPM.

We have: $\alpha = 0.07 - 0.1 \times (0.06) = 0.064$

$$NPV_{Static} = \$12 \times \frac{1}{0.064 - 0.02} - 200$$

$$= 272.727 - 200 = 72.727$$

(b) Now we have to take into account the fact that the interest rates and dividend are given as effective annual rates and need to transform them first into continuously compounded rates.

We can calculate the dividend yield as $12/272.727 = 0.044$ or continuously compounded $\ln(1.044) = 4.306\%$. The continuously compounded interest rate is 6.766%. The initial project value or S is equal to 272.727 and the strike price is equal to $200. We have the following tree:

Time (yrs)	1	2
272.727	416.9934	637.5735
99.53332	216.993	437.574
	187.3672	286.4803
	32.4351	86.4803
		128.7239
		0

American Call
Strike = 200
Vol = 40.000%; r = 6.766%
Exp = 2 years; Div = 4.306%
u = 1.5290; d = 0.6870
Risk-neutral prob of up = 0.4013
Forward tree

We early exercise the project in nodes u, uu, and ud. The value of the investment option increased to $99.533.

Answer Section   147

8. (a) We have:

Time (yrs)	1	2	3	4	5
272.727	416.9934	637.5735	974.8355	1490.502	2278.94316
113.0723	226.406	437.574	774.836	1290.5	2078.94316
	187.3672	286.4803	438.0218	669.7255	1023.99517
	50.3234	111.328	238.022	469.726	823.995171
		128.7239	196.8159	300.9271	460.11069
		15.3149	39.4187	101.328	260.11069
			88.43508	135.2152	206.741059
			0.94826	2.52829	6.7410595

American Call   60.75613   92.8947461
Strike = 200   0   0
Vol = 40.000%; r = 6.766%   41.7403
Exp = 5 years; Div = 4.306%   0
u = 1.5290; d = 0.6870
Risk-neutral prob of up = 0.4013
Forward tree

The option is more valuable. The possibility to postpone investment until a later time keeps the insurance put option alive longer, and this is reflected in a higher investment option price.

(b) We can use the formula for perpetual call options to find that the option has a value of $143.5738, and we exercise the option if the project cash flow is above 808.0545. It is interesting to compare the prices of the cash flow at which you exercise in part (a) with the trigger price of 808.0545. You can see from the five-period tree above that you already exercise the option early if the cash flow is 438.0218 in period t = 2. The option to wait for a very long time increases the boundary dramatically.

9. (a) Using the perpetual option price method, we can find that the value of the option is $220. As the trigger price is below the current spot price (3 * 325 = 975), we exercise immediately for a value of 975 − 755 = 220.

(b)

Inputs		Perpetual Options		
			Call	Put
Stock Price	975			
Exercise Price	755	Option Price	339.1912	110.0523
Volatility	20.000%	Exercise at:	1649.259	429.9538
Risk-free interest rate	4.879%			
Dividend Yield	3.922%			

We exercise if the price of 3 ounces of gold has grown to 1,649.259, which is after approximately 19.87 years.

10. (a) We can calculate the present value of 5 ounces of gold per year forever—it is, according to Formula 17.7 of the main text, $325*5/0.04 = $40,625. The present value of the investment and extraction costs is $250*5/0.05 + 12,000 = $37,000.

We can use the perpetual call formula to value the option as being worth 4,776.442 and a barrier of 46,027.62. We start extraction if the per ounce gold price hits 0.04 * 46,027.62/5 = 368.22.

148   McDonald • *Derivatives Markets*, Second Edition

(b) We can then use the same perpetual call formula with a volatility of 25% to value the option. The option is worth 14,356.17 and the barrier is 94,483.71. This corresponds to a gold price per ounce of 0.04 * 94,483.71/5 = 755.86.

Chapter 18   The Lognormal Distribution

1.

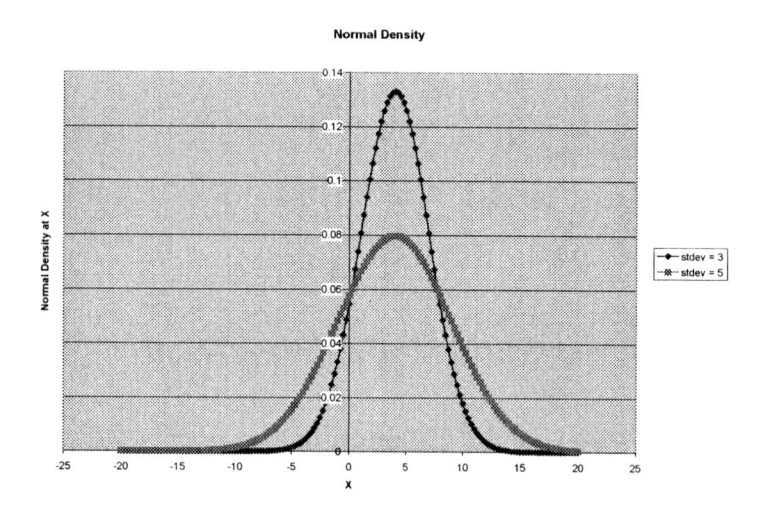

Normal Density

2.

Cumulative Normal Distribution Function

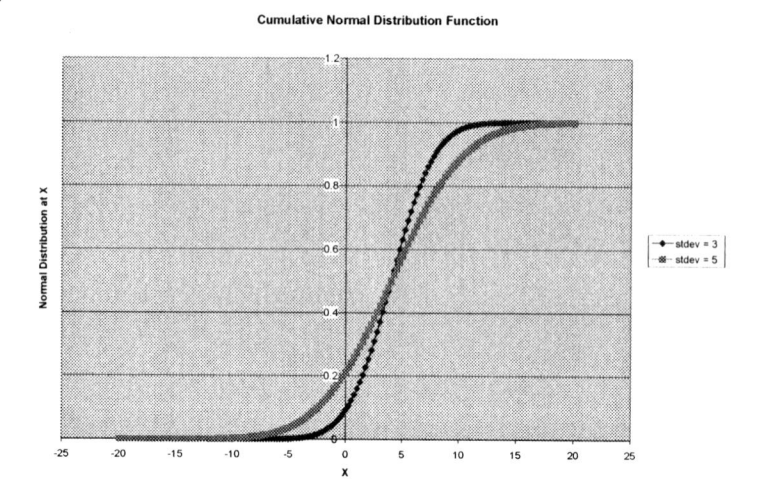

3. We can calculate the values using the formula $x = \mu + \sigma \times z$ to get:

z	$x = \mu + \sigma^*z$
0.32	−3.18981
0.01	−4.94343
−1.2	−11.7882
−0.33	−6.86676
0.42	−2.62412

4. We can use the formula of the text to show that

$$ax_1 + bx_2 \sim N(a\mu_1 + b\mu_2,\ a^2\sigma_1^2 + b^2\sigma_2^2 + 2ab\rho\sigma_1\sigma_2)$$

$$x_1 - 2x_2 \sim N(3 - 2\times 2,\ 1 + 4\times 0.64 - 4\times 0.2\times 1\times 0.8)$$

$$\sim N(-1,\ 2.92)$$

5. (a) We can use Formula 18.13 to find:

$$E(e^x) = e^{m + 0.5\times v^2} = e^{0 + 0.5*1} = e^{0.5} = 1.648721$$

(b) We can use Formula 18.14 to find

$$Var(e^x) = e^{2m+v^2}(e^{v^2} - 1) = e^{0+1}(e^1 - 1) = 4.670774$$

6. (a) We can use Formula 18.20 to write:

$$S_t = S_0 \times e^{(a - \delta - 0.5\sigma^2)t + \sigma\sqrt{t}z}$$
$$S_3 = \$35 \times e^{(0.06 - 0.02 - 0.5\times 0.04)3 + 0.2\times\sqrt{3}z}$$
$$= \$35 \times e^{0.06 + 0.34641z}$$

(b) For the expectation, we have

$$E(S_3) = S_0 e^{(a-\delta)3} = \$35 \times e^{(0.06 - 0.02)\times 3} = \$35 \times e^{(0.12)} = \$39.46239$$

(c) For the median, we have:

$$Median(S_3) = S_0 e^{(a - \delta - 0.5\sigma^2)3} = \$35 \times e^{(0.06 - 0.02 - 0.02)\times 3} = \$35 \times e^{(0.06)} = \$37.16428$$

7. We can use the formula of the book to calculate:

$$prob(S_t < K) = N\left(\frac{\ln(K) - \ln(S_0) - (a - \delta - 0.5\sigma^2)t}{\sigma\sqrt{t}}\right)$$

$$= N\left(\frac{\ln(28) - \ln(35) - (0.06 - 0.02 - 0.5\times 0.04)\times 2}{0.2\times\sqrt{2}}\right)$$

$$= N(-1.86071) = 0.031393$$

8. We can use the formula in the book to calculate:

$$\text{prob}(S_t > K) = N\left(\frac{\ln(S_0) - \ln(K) + (a - \delta - 0.5\sigma^2)t}{\sigma\sqrt{t}}\right)$$

$$= N\left(\frac{\ln(35) - \ln(45) + (0.06 - 0.02 - 0.5 \times 0.04) \times 4}{0.2 \times \sqrt{4}}\right)$$

$$= N(-1.71314) = 0.043343$$

9. We can use Formula 18.30 in the main text to write:

$$E(S(t)|S(t) > K) = Se^{(a-\delta)t} \frac{N(\hat{d}_1)}{N(\hat{d}_2)}, \quad \text{where} \quad \hat{d}_1 = \frac{\ln(S_0) - \ln(K) + (a - \delta + 0.5\sigma^2)t}{\sigma\sqrt{t}}$$

$$\text{and} \quad \hat{d}_2 = \frac{\ln(S_0) - \ln(K) + (a - \delta - 0.5\sigma^2)t}{\sigma\sqrt{t}}$$

Therefore,

$$E(S(t)|S(t) > 35) = 35e^{(0.06-0.02)4} \frac{N(\hat{d}_1)}{N(\hat{d}_2)}, \quad \text{where} \quad \hat{d}_1 = \frac{\ln(35) - \ln(35) + (0.06 - 0.02 + 0.02)4}{0.2\sqrt{4}}$$

$$\text{and} \quad \hat{d}_2 = \frac{\ln(35) - \ln(35) + (0.06 - 0.02 - 0.02)4}{0.2\sqrt{4}}$$

We can calculate:

d1 = 0.8, N(0.8) = 0.7881 and d2 = 2.4 and N(2.4) = 0.991802). This yields an expectation of 51.68618.

10. (a) Here are the first five returns. It is important to use split- and dividend-adjusted prices:

Date	Price	Return
4-Jan-99	28.78	
5-Jan-99	29.39	0.020974
6-Jan-99	29.97	0.019542
7-Jan-99	29.46	–0.01716
8-Jan-99	29.3	–0.00545

(b) The mean is 0.000153, the standard deviation is 0.020939.

(c) Please use the help function of Excel if you are stuck here.

(d)

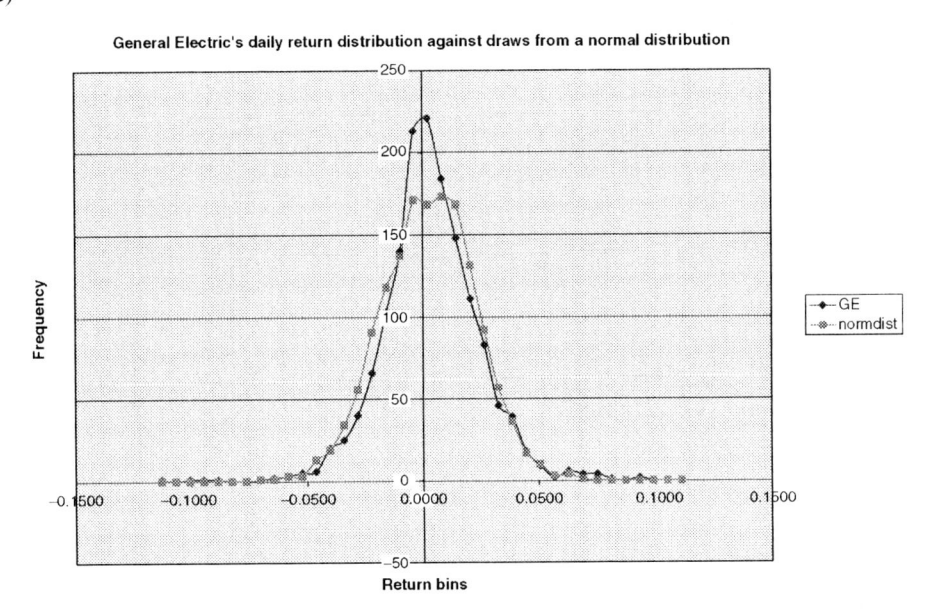

General Electric's daily return distribution against draws from a normal distribution

(e) We observe the same results for GE that the textbook describes for the S&P and IBM. The daily returns display leptokurtosis; if you look at the bins of the histogram, you also see fat tails (none of the extreme bins has observations from the random numbers, but several observations from GE).

Chapter 19 Monte Carlo Valuation

1.

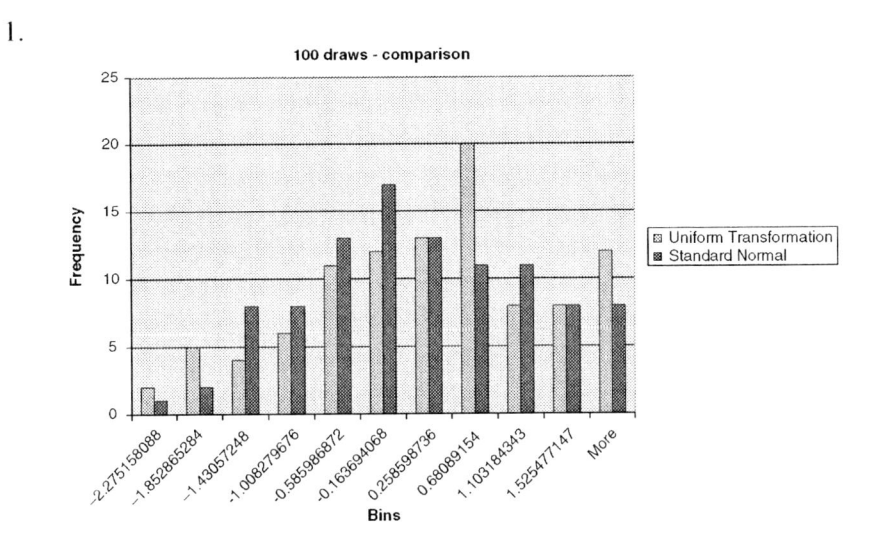

100 draws - comparison

And for 500 draws, we have:

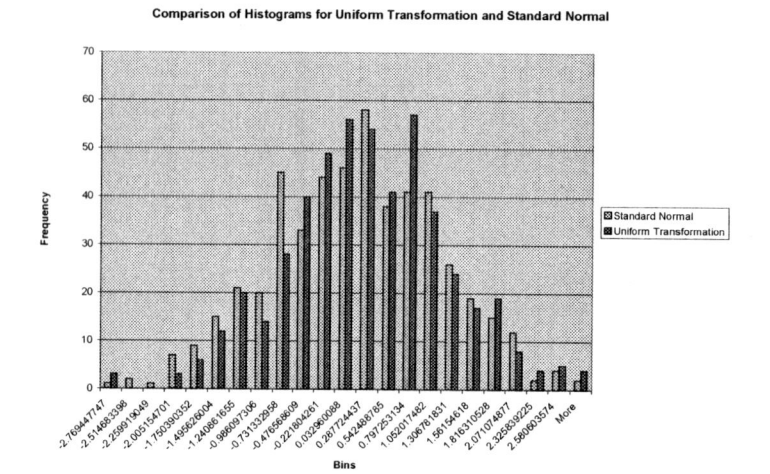

To conclude, even for 100 draws, the two distributions are relatively close. However, in order to approximate the bell shape, we need to sample many more observations.

2. (a)
$$E(e^x) = e^{m+0.5 \times v^2} = e^{-0.2+0.5*4} = 1.868246$$

$$\text{Var}(e^x) = e^{2m+v^2}(e^{v^2}-1) = e^{-1+2.25}(e^{2.25}-1) = 29.62511$$

(b) The mean of a random sample of 5,000 draws was 1.8502, the variance was 23.3525. The bottom line is that estimates of the variance can be quite far off even if we sampled 5,000 times.

(c) It looks like a lognormal distribution should look.

3.

S(0)	45
alpha	0.08
sigma	0.3
T	3
E(R(0, 2))	0.24
STD(R(0, 2))	0.519615

A random sample yielded the return of 0.245253, and a standard deviation of 0.527979.

4. In this case, h = 0.0833(1/12). The other inputs stay the same.

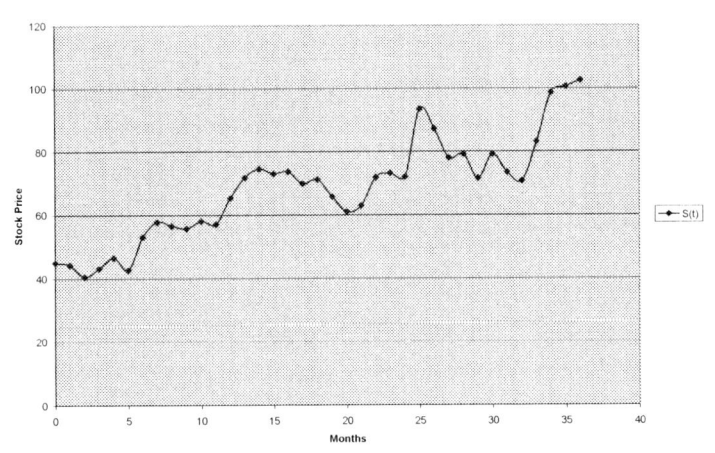

One path of the stock price over 36 months

5. A typical result of the simulation is an option price of 1.2034, a dollar standard deviation of this price of $3.489, and a standard deviation of 0.064.

    By increasing t, we increase the option value. An increase in option value leads to an increase in the dollar standard deviation. Since we leave the number of draws constant, the standard deviation increases.

6. In three trials of 3,000 simulations, the following results were obtained:

	Trial 1	Trial 2	Trial 3
Option Price	7.439706	7.203332	7.366159
$ Stdev	6.075981	5.949075	5.985313
Sample Stdev	0.110932	0.108615	0.109276

    If we assume a $ standard deviation of 6 as representative, we would need 360,000 simulations to achieve a standard deviation of 0.01.

7. (a) Here are the first five draws for your reference:

Draw	S(0)	Epsilon	S(t = 0.5)	S^(1/4)
1	28	1.22009	38.95076	2.49821
2	28	0.983646	36.43106	2.456789
3	28	−1.91649	16.04085	2.001275
4	28	−0.23321	25.82238	2.254234
5	28	−1.34888	18.83436	2.083232

    Don't forget to discount the average of S^(1/4) by exp(−0.05 * 0.5) when you determine the option's price.

We have for three representative runs of 3,000 simulations:

	Trial 1	Trial 2	Trial 3
Option Price	2.246446	2.241237	2.23729
$ Stdev	0.164826	0.1626	0.165539
Sample Stdev	0.003009	0.002969	0.003022

(b) Here are the first five simulations:

Draw	S(0)	Epsilon	S(t = 0.5)	S^4
1	28	−0.30204	25.32454	411307.5
2	28	1.46112	41.69877	3023380
3	28	0.246547	29.57527	765093.7
4	28	−0.8139	21.91123	230497.9
5	28	0.716203	33.77691	1301606

We have for three representative trials of 3,000 simulations:

	Trial 1	Trial 2	Trial 3
Option Price	1077089	1050936	1048998
$ Stdev	1889356	1580492	1654824
Sample Stdev	34494.76	28855.7	30212.82

8. (a) This is 1 minus the probability of no crashes in a given year. We can calculate

$$1 - P(0, 0.04 * 1) = 1 - 0.960789 = 0.039211$$

(b) This is 1 minus the probability of no crash or one crash over a period of 20 years.
We have Prob(X >= 2; 0.04 * 20) = 1 − Prob(X < 2; 0.04 * 20) = 1 − 0.449329 − 0.359463 = 0.191208.

(c) You would classify the draws from the uniform distribution into the following bins:

m	Probability	Cumulative Probability
0	0.301194	0.301194212
1	0.361433	0.662627266
2	0.21686	0.879487099
3	0.086744	0.966231032
4	0.026023	0.992254212
5	0.006246	0.998499775
6	0.001249	0.999748887537412
7	0.000214	0.999963021132094
8	3.21E-05	0.999995141171296
9	4.28E-06	0.999999423843190
10	5.14E-07	0.999999937763817

Note how small the probabilities for even six crashes in 30 years are.

9. (a)

Path	t = 0	t = 1	t = 2	t = 3
1	1	**1.09**	**1.08**	1.34
2	1	1.16	1.26	1.54
3	1	1.22	**1.07**	**1.03**
4	1	**0.93**	**0.97**	**0.92**
5	1	**1.11**	1.56	1.52
6	1	**0.76**	**0.77**	**0.9**
7	1	**0.92**	**0.84**	**1.01**
8	1	**0.88**	1.22	1.34

(b) The relevant paths for early exercise are 1, 3, 4, 6, and 7. We have to calculate the discounted continuation values for these two paths, and estimate a regression.

Regression

Path	t = 2	S^2	Payoff t = 2	PV(Continuation)	Payoff t = 3	Fitted Continuation Value
1	1.08	1.1664	0.07	0	0	0.0580
3	1.07	1.1449	0.08	0.113011744	0.12	0.0703
4	0.97	0.9409	0.18	0.216605843	0.23	0.1639
6	0.77	0.5929	0.38	0.235441133	0.25	0.1962
7	0.84	0.7056	0.31	0.131847035	0.14	0.2084

S^2	S	Intercept
−2.59	4.34	−1.61
4.301	8.013	3.672
0.56528	0.087682	#N/A

The regression is equal to

fitted continuation value at time 2 = −1.61 + 4.34 * S −2.59 * S^2

The fitted continuation values are smaller then the value of immediate payoff at t = 2. We exercise in all paths: 1, 3, 4, 6, and 7.

(c) The American put option is in the money at nodes 1, 4, 5, 6, 7, and 8. Therefore, we can calculate the relevant values as follows:

Relevant nodes for regression at t = 1

Path	t = 0	t = 1	Payoff t = 1	PV(Continuation Value)	Fitted Continuation Value
1	1	1.09	0.06	0.0000	0.0103
4	1	0.93	0.22	0.1224	0.1089
5	1	1.11	0.04	0.0000	0.0027
6	1	0.76	0.39	0.3108	0.2858
7	1	0.92	0.23	0.2449	0.1172
8	1	0.88	0.27	0.0000	0.1532

S^2	S	Intercept
1.288	**−3.218**	**1.988**
3.526	6.700	3.143
0.571351	0.116446	#N/A

The fitted values are based on a regression analysis that yields the following results:
Continuation value at (t = 1) = 1.988 + 1.288 * S − 3.218 * S^2
All the fitted continuation values are smaller than the payoffs for immediate exercise. We early exercise for all paths: 1, 4, 5, 6, 7, and 8.

10. (a) We have to verify whether early exercise is optimal at t = 0. We can write:

Path	S(0)	S(2)	Payoff	pv (continuation)	t = 1	t = 2	t = 3
1	1	1	0.15	0.056505872	0.06	0	0
2	1	1	0.15	0	0	0	0
3	1	1	0.15	0.070953635	0	0.08	0
4	1	1	0.15	0.207188197	0.22	0	0
5	1	1	0.15	0.037670581	0.04	0	0
6	1	1	0.15	0.367288168	0.39	0	0
7	1	1	0.15	0.216605843	0.23	0	0
8	1	1	0.15	0.254276424	0.27	0	0

0	0	0.151311
0	0	0.045491
1.19752E-16	0.128668	#N/A

The fitted continuation value is a constant—it is 0.1513. This is bigger than the value of immediate exercise (0.15), so it is never optimal to exercise in period t = 0. We can write down the final cash-flow and average them to obtain the value of the American put option:
1/8 * [0.056505872 + 0 + 0.070953635 + 0.207188197 + 0.037670581 + 0.367288168 + 0.216605843 + 0.254276424] = 0.1513.

(b)

Payoff t = 3	PV (payoff t = 3)
0	0
0	0
0.12	0.100232
0.23	0.192112
0	0
0.25	0.208818
0.14	0.116938
0	0
European Put:	0.077262

Chapter 20 Brownian Motion and Ito's Lemma

1. The one-hour expected return is equal to $0.08/(365 \times 24) = 0.000009132$.

   The one-day variance is equal to $0.3^2/(365 \times 24) = 0.000010274$.

   Thus, $r_{1hour} \sim N(0.000009132, 0.000010274)$

   In order to have a one-day return of less than -100%, we would need to draw from a standard normal distribution a value less than

   $$\frac{-1 - 0.000009132}{\sqrt{0.000010274}} = -311.9857547$$

   The probability $N(-311.986)$ is essentially zero.

2. (a) We start out with:

   $$Z(t+h) - Z(t) = Y(t+h)\sqrt{h}$$

   Since $h = 1/12$, $t_0 = 0$, $T = 0.25$, $n = 3$. We have three terms over which we need to sum:

   $$Z(1/12) - Z(0) = Y(1/12)\sqrt{1/12}$$
   $$\Leftrightarrow \quad Z(1/12) = Z(0) + Y(1/12)\sqrt{1/12}$$

   $$Z(2/12) - Z(1/12) = Y(2/12)\sqrt{1/12}$$
   $$\Leftrightarrow \quad Z(2/12) = Z(1/12) + Y(2/12)\sqrt{1/12}$$

   $$Z(3/12) - Z(2/12) = Y(3/12)\sqrt{1/12}$$
   $$\Leftrightarrow \quad Z(0.25) = Z(2/12) + Y(3/12)\sqrt{1/12}$$

   Now, we can replace some terms in the equation twice to write:

   $$Z(0.25) = Z(0) + Y(1/12)\sqrt{1/12} + Y(2/12)\sqrt{1/12} + Y(3/12)\sqrt{1/12}$$
   $$\Leftrightarrow \quad Z(0.25) - Z(0) = Y(1/12)\sqrt{1/12} + Y(2/12)\sqrt{1/12} + Y(3/12)\sqrt{1/12}$$
   $$= \sqrt{1/12} \times \sum_{i=1}^{3} Y(i \times 1/12)$$

   Since $h = T/n$ or $1/12 = 0.25/3$, we can slightly rewrite:

   $$Z(0.25) - Z(0) = \frac{\sqrt{0.25}}{\sqrt{3}} \times \sum_{i=1}^{3} Y(i \times 1/12)$$

   $$\sqrt{0.25}\left[\frac{1}{\sqrt{3}} \times \sum_{i=1}^{3} Y(i \times 1/12)\right]$$

(b) We again have h = 1/12, so n = 3, and we need three terms. We have:

$$X(1/12) = X(0) + 0.1 \times 1/12 + 0.3Y(1/12)\sqrt{1/12}$$

$$X(2/12) = X(1/12) + 0.1 \times 1/12 + 0.3Y(2/12)\sqrt{1/12}$$

$$X(3/12) = X(2/12) + 0.1 \times 1/12 + 0.3Y(3/12)\sqrt{1/12}$$

We can replace in the above equation twice to get:

$$X(3/12) = X(0) + 0.1 \times 1/12 + 0.3Y(1/12)\sqrt{1/12} + 0.1 \times 1/12 + 0.3Y(2/12)\sqrt{1/12}$$

$$+ 0.1 \times 1/12 + 0.3Y(3/12)\sqrt{1/12}$$

$$\Leftrightarrow X(3/12) - X(0) = 0.1 \times (1/12 + 1/12 + 1/12) + 0.3 \times \sqrt{1/12} \times [Y(1/12) + Y(2/12) + Y(3/12)]$$

Knowing that h = T / n, we can simplify the above equation to:

$$X(T) - X(0) = 0.1 \times 0.25 + 0.3 \left(\sqrt{0.25/3} \sum_{i=1}^{3} Y(i \times 1/12) \right)$$

$$= 0.1 \times 0.25 + 0.3 \times \sqrt{0.25} \left(\sum_{i=1}^{n} \frac{Y(i \times 1/12)}{\sqrt{3}} \right)$$

3. (a) False. Only a pure Brownian motion does not have a drift.
   (b) True.
   (c) False. Lambda measures the speed of mean reversion.
   (d) False. Brownian motion has the infinite crossing property. You cannot draw a Brownian motion.
   (e) False. The main drawback of arithmetic Brownian motion is that the process can become negative. The small time interval is irrelevant.
   (f) True, as discussed in the book.
   (g) False.

4. We can write:

Period Length	h	Alpha * h	Sigma * sqrt(h)	Ratio
14 years, 22 days, and 20 hours	14.06256	1.12500	1.12500	1.00000
10 years	10.00000	0.80000	0.94868	1.18585
5 years	5.00000	0.40000	0.67082	1.67705
1 year	1.00000	0.08000	0.30000	3.75000
1 month	0.08333	0.00667	0.08660	12.99038
1 day	0.00274	0.00022	0.01570	71.64365
1 hour	0.00011	0.00001	0.00321	350.98077

Equality is achieved if h is above 14 years. We can clearly see that this is too long of an interval to model stock prices. Therefore, the conclusion of the main text is validated. It is the standard deviation that is important and determines the movement of the Brownian motion.

5. We can address this question by using Equation 20.31. We have:

$$\frac{dS^a}{S^a} = \left[a(\alpha-\delta) + \frac{1}{2}a(a-1)\sigma^2\right]dt + a\sigma\,dZ$$

with $a = 4$:

$$= \left[4(0.08-0.04) + \frac{1}{2}4\times(4-1)0.09\right]dt + 4\times 0.3\,dZ$$

$$= 0.7\,dt + 1.2\,dZ$$

6.
$$\frac{dS^a}{S^a} = \left[a(\alpha-\delta) + \frac{1}{2}a(a-1)\sigma^2\right]dt + a\sigma\,dZ$$

with $a = 1/4$:

$$= \left[0.25(0.08-0.04) + \frac{1}{2}0.25\times(0.25-1)0.09\right]dt + 0.25\times 0.3\,dZ$$

$$= -0.02375\,dt + 0.075\,dZ$$

The drift term is negative, suggesting that the process is trending downwards over time.

7. (a) We can show in very general terms the process followed by $\frac{dS^a}{S^a}$ for an arithmetic BM:

$$dS = \alpha\,dt + \sigma\,dZ$$

$$V = S^a \Rightarrow \frac{\partial V}{\partial S} = aS^{a-1} \Rightarrow \frac{\partial^2 V}{(\partial S)^2} = a\times(a-1)S^{a-2} \Rightarrow \frac{\partial V}{\partial t} = 0$$

$$dV(S,t) = V_S\,dS + \frac{1}{2}V_{SS}(dS)^2 + V_t\,dt$$

Then we have:

$$dS^a = aS^{a-1}(\alpha\,dt + \sigma\,dZ) + \frac{1}{2}a\times(a-1)S^{a-2}\sigma^2\,dt = 0$$

$$dS^a = \left[aS^{a-1}\alpha + \frac{1}{2}a(a-1)S^{a-2}\sigma^2\right]dt + aS^{a-1}\sigma\,dZ$$

(b)
$$dS^a = \left[aS^{a-1}\alpha + \frac{1}{2}a(a-1)S^{a-2}\sigma^2\right]dt + aS^{a-1}\sigma dZ$$

with $a = 4$:

$$dS^4 = \left[4 \times S^3 \times 0.08 + \frac{1}{2}4(4-1)S^2 \times 0.09\right]dt + 4 \times S^3 \times 0.3 dZ$$
$$= [0.32 \times S^3 + 0.54 \times S^2]dt + 1.2 \times S^3 dZ$$

(c)
$$dS^a = \left[aS^{a-1}\alpha + \frac{1}{2}a(a-1)S^{a-2}\sigma^2\right]dt + aS^{a-1}\sigma dZ$$

with $a = 1/4$:

$$dS^4 = \left[1/4 \times S^{1/4-1} \times 0.08 + \frac{1}{2} \times \frac{1}{4}\left(\frac{1}{4}-1\right)S^{1/4-2} \times 0.09\right]dt + \frac{1}{4} \times S^{1/4-1} \times 0.3 dZ$$
$$= [0.02 \times S^{-3/4} - 0.0084 \times S^{-7/4}]dt + 0.075 \times S^{-3/4} dZ$$

8.
$$\frac{dS}{S} = [(\alpha_S - \delta_S)]dt + \sigma_S dZ_S$$

$$\frac{dQ}{Q} = [(\alpha_Q - \delta_Q)]dt + \sigma_Q dZ_Q$$

$$\frac{d(S^a Q^b)}{S^a Q^b} = \left[a(\alpha_S - \delta_S) + b(\alpha_Q - \delta_Q) + \frac{1}{2}a(a-1)\sigma_S^2 + \frac{1}{2}b(b-1)\sigma_Q^2 + ab\rho\sigma_S\sigma_Q\right]dt +$$
$$a\sigma_S dZ_S + b\sigma_Q dZ_Q$$

with $a = 1$ and $b = -2$:

$$\frac{d(S^1 Q^{-2})}{S^1 Q^{-2}} = [(\alpha_S - \delta_S) - 2(\alpha_Q - \delta_Q) + 3\sigma_Q^2 - 2\rho\sigma_S\sigma_Q]dt + \sigma_S dZ_S - 2\sigma_Q dZ_Q$$

9. (a) With $V(X, Y) = XY$,

$$\frac{\partial V}{\partial X} = Y \quad \frac{\partial V}{\partial Y} = X \quad \frac{\partial^2 V}{(\partial X)^2} = \frac{\partial^2 V}{(\partial Y)^2} = 0 \quad \frac{\partial^2 V}{(\partial Y)(\partial X)} = 1 \quad \frac{\partial V}{\partial t} = 0$$

Then,

$$dXY = V_X dX + V_Y dY + \frac{1}{2} \times 2 \times 1 \times dXdY + 0 + 0 + 0$$
$$= Y \times (\alpha dt + \beta dZ_X) + X \times (\lambda dt + v dZ_Y) + (\alpha dt + \beta dZ_X) \times (\lambda dt + v dZ_Y)$$
$$(\alpha Y + \lambda X + \beta v \rho)dt + Y\beta dZ_X + Xv dZ_Y$$

(b) With $V(X,Y) = X/Y$,

$$\frac{\partial V}{\partial X} = 1/Y \quad \frac{\partial V}{\partial Y} = \frac{-X}{Y^2} \quad \frac{\partial^2 V}{(\partial X)^2} = 0 \quad \frac{\partial^2 V}{(\partial Y)^2} = \frac{2X}{Y^3} \quad \frac{\partial^2 V}{(\partial Y)(\partial X)} = \frac{-1}{Y^2} \quad \frac{\partial V}{\partial t} = 0$$

Then

$$dXY = \frac{1}{Y}dX + \frac{-X}{Y^2} \times dY + \frac{1}{2} \times 0 \times dXdX + \frac{1}{2} \times \frac{2X}{Y^3} \times dYdY + 1 \times \frac{-1}{Y^2} \times dXdY + 0$$

$$= \frac{1}{Y}(\alpha dt + \beta dZ_X) - \frac{X}{Y^2} \times (\lambda dt + v dZ_Y) + \frac{X}{Y^3} \times v^2 dt - \frac{1}{Y^2} \times \rho \beta v dt$$

$$= \left(\frac{\alpha}{Y} - \lambda \frac{X}{Y^2} - \frac{1}{Y^2}\beta v \rho + \frac{X}{Y^3} \times v^2\right)dt + \frac{1}{Y}\beta dZ_X - \frac{X}{Y^2}v dZ_Y$$

10. Using Ito's Lemma and implementing the values we know from the two equations above, we can write:

$$dV(S, r, t) = \left(V_t + \mu S V_S + \lambda(\alpha - r) + \frac{1}{2}\sigma_r^2 r V_{rr} + \frac{1}{2}\sigma_S^2 S^2 V_{SS} + \rho \sigma_S \sigma_r S\sqrt{r} V_{rS}\right)dt$$
$$+ \sigma_r \sqrt{r} V_r dZ_r + \sigma_S S V_S dZ_S$$

Chapter 21 The Black-Scholes Equation

1. We can do this using Ito's Lemma:

   With $V(S) = \ln S$,

   $$\frac{\partial V}{\partial S} = 1/S \quad \frac{\partial^2 V}{(\partial S)^2} = -\frac{1}{S^2} \quad \frac{\partial V}{\partial t} = 0$$

   Then

   $$d\ln S = \frac{1}{S}dS - \frac{1}{2} \times \frac{1}{S^2} \times dSdS + 0$$

   $$= \frac{1}{S}((r-\delta)Sdt + \sigma S dZ^*) - 0.5\frac{1}{S^2} \times (\sigma^2 S^2 dt) + 0$$

   $$= ((r-\delta) - 0.5 \times \sigma^2)dt + \sigma dZ^*$$

2. (a) $\ln(S(t)/S(0))$ is normally distributed with mean $(r - \delta - 0.5\sigma^2)t$ and variance $\sigma^2 t$

   (b)
   $$S(T) = S(t)e^{(r-\delta-0.5\sigma^2)\times(T-t)+\sigma\sqrt{T-t}y}$$

   Where $y \sim N(0, 1)$

3. (a) We integrate over the interval K to infinity, because the call option expires valueless if K > S(T).
   (b) We have:

$$C[S(t), K, \sigma, r, T-t, \delta] = e^{-r(T-t)} \int_K^\infty S(T) f^*[S(T), \sigma, r, \delta; S(t)] dS(T)$$
$$- e^{-r(T-t)} \int_K^\infty K f^*[S(T), \sigma, r, \delta; S(t)] dS(T)$$

4. (a) The second integral becomes:

$$-Ke^{-r(T-t)} \int_K^\infty f^*[S(T), \sigma, r, \delta; S(t)] dS(T)$$
$$\Leftrightarrow -Ke^{-r(T-t)} \times \text{prob}[S(T) > K]$$

(b) with

$$S(V) = S(t) e^{(r-\delta-0.5\sigma^2) \times (T-t) + \sigma\sqrt{T-t}y}$$

$$-Ke^{-r(T-t)} \times \text{prob}\left[S(t) e^{(r-\delta-0.5\sigma^2) \times (T-t) + \sigma\sqrt{T-t}y} > K\right]$$

Solving: $S(t) e^{(r-\delta-0.5\sigma^2) \times (T-t) + \sigma\sqrt{T-t}y} > K$

$$\Leftrightarrow e^{(r-\delta-0.5\sigma^2) \times (T-t) + \sigma\sqrt{T-t}y} > K/S(t)$$

$$\Leftrightarrow (r-\delta-0.5\sigma^2) \times (T-t) + \sigma\sqrt{T-t}y > \ln[K/S(t)]$$

$$\Leftrightarrow y > \frac{\ln[K/S(t)] - (r-\delta-0.5\sigma^2) \times (T-t)}{\sigma\sqrt{T-t}}$$

$$\Leftrightarrow y > \frac{\ln K - \ln S(t) - (r-\delta-0.5\sigma^2) \times (T-t)}{\sigma\sqrt{T-t}}$$

$$\Leftrightarrow y > -\frac{\ln S(t) - \ln K + (r-\delta-0.5\sigma^2) \times (T-t)}{\sigma\sqrt{T-t}}$$

(c) First, we can conclude that $-\dfrac{\ln S(t) - \ln K + (r-\delta-0.5\sigma^2) \times (T-t)}{\sigma\sqrt{T-t}} = -d_2$, that is, we have found the negative of Equation 12.2(b).

Now, we can show:
$$\text{prob}(y > -d_2) = 1 - \text{prob}(y < -d_2)$$
$$\text{Since } y \sim N(0, 1)$$
$$\Leftrightarrow \qquad = 1 - N(-d_2)$$

By property of the standard normal distribution
$$\Leftrightarrow \qquad = N(d_2)$$

(d) We should conclude that we have just derived half of the Black-Scholes formula.
$$-Ke^{-r(T-t)} \times N(d_2)$$

5. (a)
$$e^{-r(T-t)} \int_K^\infty S(T) f^*[S(T), \sigma, r, \delta; S(t)] dS(T)$$

with
$$S(T) = S(t) e^{(r-\delta-0.5\sigma^2) \times (T-t) + \sigma \sqrt{T-t} y}$$

We have:
$$e^{-r(T-t)} \int_K^\infty S(t) e^{(r-\delta-0.5\sigma^2) \times (T-t) + \sigma \sqrt{T-t} y} f^*[S(T), \sigma, r, \delta; S(t)] dS(T)$$

(b) We can write:
$$e^{-r(T-t)} \int_K^\infty S(t) e^{(r-\delta-0.5\sigma^2) \times (T-t) + \sigma \sqrt{T-t} y} f^*[S(T), \sigma, r, \delta; S(t)] dS(T)$$

$$e^{-r(T-t)} S(t) e^{(r-\delta-0.5\sigma^2) \times (T-t)} \times \int_{-d_2}^\infty e^{\sigma \sqrt{T-t} y} f^*[y] dy$$

Since y is standard normally distributed, we can replace the abstract function f* with the density for the standard normal distribution:
$$e^{-r(T-t)} \int_K^\infty S(t) e^{(r-\delta-0.5\sigma^2) \times (T-t) + \sigma \sqrt{T-t} y} f^*[S(T), \sigma, r, \delta; S(t)] dS(T)$$

$$e^{-r(T-t)} S(t) e^{(r-\delta-0.5\sigma^2) \times (T-t)} \times \int_{-d_2}^\infty e^{\sigma \sqrt{T-t} y} \times \frac{1}{\sqrt{2\pi}} e^{-\frac{1}{2} y^2} dy$$

$$S(t) e^{(-\delta-0.5\sigma^2) \times (T-t)} \times \frac{1}{\sqrt{2\pi}} \int_{-d_2}^\infty e^{\sigma \sqrt{T-t} y - \frac{1}{2} y^2} dy$$

(c) Multiply out the second equation to see that it is equivalent to the first.

(e) By defining $b = y - \sigma \sqrt{T-t}$, we change the lower limit of integration. We previously were interested in $y \geq -d_2$. Now, let's replace y by $b + \sigma \sqrt{T-t}$.

This means for the lower limit of integration:

$$b + \sigma\sqrt{T-t} \geq -d_2$$

$$\Leftrightarrow \quad b \geq -d_2 - \sigma\sqrt{T-t}$$

$$\Leftrightarrow \quad b \geq -(d_2 + \sigma\sqrt{T-t})$$

and using one of the hints, we can write:

$$\Leftrightarrow \quad b \geq -(d_1)$$

Using the second hint, we write:

$$\Leftrightarrow \quad b < (d_1)$$

Therefore, we can indeed conclude that

$$S(t)e^{(-\delta)\times(T-t)} \times \frac{1}{\sqrt{2\pi}} \int_{-\infty}^{d_1} e^{-\frac{1}{2}(b)^2} db$$

(f) You should conclude that you have just derived the first part of the Black-Scholes formula. Taken together with the results of Exercise 21.4, you have derived the Black-Scholes formula. Congratulations!

6. The Black-Scholes formula for a European put option is:

$$P(S, K, \sigma, r, T, \delta) = Ke^{-r\times(T-t)}N(-d_2) - Se^{-\delta T}N(-d_2)$$

with

$$-d_1 = \frac{-\ln(S/K) - \left(r - \delta + \frac{1}{2}\sigma^2\right)(T-t)}{\sigma\sqrt{T-t}}$$

$$-d_1 = \frac{\ln(K/S)}{\sigma\sqrt{T-t}} - \frac{\left(r - \delta + \frac{1}{2}\sigma^2\right)\sqrt{T-t}}{\sigma}$$

$$-d_2 = -d_1 + \sigma\sqrt{T-t}$$

At expiration, the second term in the second equation of $-d_1$ is equal to zero. We need to consider two possibilities for the first term:

K > S: The first term of $-d_1$ goes to positive infinity because $\ln(K/S) > 0$, and $N(\infty) = 1$.

K < S: The first term of $-d_1$ goes to negative infinity because $\ln(K/S) < 0$, and $N(-\infty) = 0$.

At expiration, there is no difference in the behavior of $-d_1$ and $-d_2$. Therefore, if K > S, we can conclude that the Black-Scholes formula yields K − S, and when K < S, we see that it yields zero. We have the desired result.

7. We have $b = 0.5$, and $\eta = 0.01$, $\delta^* = 0.07625$, and the price of the claim as 888.8545.

    Proposition 20.4 states that the claim has a value of:

    $$V = \exp(-rT) \times [S_0 e^{(r-\delta)T} (Q_0^b e^{[b(r-\delta_Q)+0.5b(b-1)\sigma_Q^2]T} \times e^{b\rho\sigma_S\sigma_Q T})],$$ which yields the same result.

8. We have $b = -2$. Therefore, $\eta = 0.16$, $\delta^* = -0.53$, and the price of the claim is 0.024504.

9. We have to evaluate the Black-Scholes formula for a European call option at the modified dividend yield, and calculate the equation of Proposition 21.1 using $b = 1$.

    We have $\eta = 0.04 - 1 * 0.4 * 0.3 * 0.5 = -0.02$, and $\delta^* = 0.01$

    Furthermore, $C(100, 105, 0.3, 1, 0.08, -0.02) = 14.57829$

    Therefore, the claim is worth 1,250.827.

10. We have:

    $$P(S, K, \sigma, r, T, \delta) = Ke^{-r \times (T-t)} N(-d_2) - Se^{-\delta T} N(-d_1)$$

    We need to calculate the following derivatives:

    $$\frac{\partial P}{\partial S} = \Delta_P = e^{-\delta T} \times [1 - N(d_1)]$$

    $$\frac{\partial^2 P}{(\partial S)^2} = \Gamma_P = \frac{e^{-\delta T} N'(d_1)}{S\sigma\sqrt{T}}$$

    $$\frac{\partial P}{\partial t} = \theta_P = rKe^{-rT} \times [1 - N(d_2)] + \delta e^{-\delta T} S \times N(d_1) - \delta Se^{-\delta T} - \frac{Ke^{-rT} N'(d_2)\sigma}{2\sqrt{T}}$$

    Equation 21.10 states that:

    $$V_t + \frac{1}{2}\sigma^2 S^2 V_{SS} + (r-\delta) S V_S - rV = 0$$

    Plugging in the greeks,

    $$rKe^{-rT} \times [1 - N(d_2)] + \delta e^{-\delta T} S \times N(d_1) - \delta Se^{-\delta T} - \frac{Ke^{-rT} N'(d_2)\sigma}{2\sqrt{T}} + \frac{1}{2}\sigma^2 S^2 \times \frac{e^{-\delta T} N'(d_1)}{S\sigma\sqrt{T}}$$

    $$+ (r-\delta) S \times e^{-\delta T} \times [N(d_1) - 1] - r[Ke^{-r \times (T-t)} N(-d_2) - Se^{-\delta T} N(-d_1)] = 0$$

$$rKe^{-rT} \times [1-N(d_2)] + \delta e^{-\delta T} S \times N(d_1) - \delta S e^{-\delta T} - \frac{Ke^{-rT}N'(d_2)\sigma}{2\sqrt{T}} + \frac{1}{2}\sigma^2 S^2 \times \frac{e^{-\delta T}N'(d_1)}{S\sigma\sqrt{T}}$$

$$+(r-\delta)S \times e^{-\delta T} \times [N(d_1)-1] - r[Ke^{-r \times (T)}N(-d_2) - Se^{-\delta T}N(-d_1)] = 0$$

$$\Leftrightarrow rKe^{-rT}N(-d_2) - rKe^{-r \times (T)}N(-d_2) + \delta e^{-\delta T} S \times N(d_1) - \delta S \times e^{-\delta T} \times N(d_1) - \delta Se^{-\delta T} + \delta S \times e^{-\delta T}$$

$$-rS \times e^{-\delta T} \times N(-d_1) + rSe^{-\delta T} N(-d_1) - \frac{Ke^{-rT}N'(d_2)\sigma}{2\sqrt{T}} + \frac{1}{2}\sigma^2 S^2 \times \frac{e^{-\delta T}N'(d_1)}{S\sigma\sqrt{T}} = 0$$

$$\Leftrightarrow -\frac{Ke^{-rT}N'(d_2)\sigma}{2\sqrt{T}} + \frac{1}{2}\sigma^2 S^2 \times \frac{e^{-\delta T}N'(d_1)}{S\sigma\sqrt{T}} = 0$$

$$\Leftrightarrow \frac{\sigma}{2\sqrt{T}}\left[Se^{-\delta T}N'(d_1) - Ke^{-rT}N'(d_2)\right] = 0$$

$$\Leftrightarrow +\frac{\sigma}{2\sqrt{T}}\left[Se^{-\delta T}N'(d_1) - Ke^{-rT}N'(d_1 - \sigma\sqrt{T})\right] = 0$$

$$\Leftrightarrow \frac{\sigma}{2\sqrt{T}}\left(Se^{-\delta T}\frac{1}{\sqrt{2\pi}}e^{-0.5d_1^2} - Ke^{-rT}\frac{1}{\sqrt{2\pi}}e^{-0.5(d_1-\sigma\sqrt{T})^2}\right) = 0$$

Let's use $d_1 = \frac{\ln(S/K) + (r-\delta+0.5\sigma^2)T}{\sigma\sqrt{T}}$. Solve for S:

$$S = Ke^{d_1\sigma\sqrt{T}-(r-\delta+0.5\sigma^2)T}$$

Therefore,

$$\Leftrightarrow \frac{\sigma}{2\sqrt{T}}\left(Ke^{d_1\sigma\sqrt{T}-(r-\delta+0.5\sigma^2)T}e^{-\delta T}\frac{1}{\sqrt{2\pi}}e^{-0.5d_1^2} - Ke^{-rT}\frac{1}{\sqrt{2\pi}}e^{-0.5(d_1-\sigma\sqrt{T})^2}\right) = 0$$

$$\Leftrightarrow \frac{\sigma}{2\sqrt{T}}\left(\frac{K}{\sqrt{2\pi}}\left[e^{d_1\sigma\sqrt{T}-(r+0.5\sigma^2)T-0.5d_1^2} - e^{-rT-0.5(d_1-\sigma\sqrt{T})^2}\right]\right) = 0$$

$$\Leftrightarrow \frac{\sigma}{2\sqrt{T}}\left(\frac{K}{\sqrt{2\pi}}\left[e^{d_1\sigma\sqrt{T}-(r+0.5\sigma^2)T-0.5d_1^2} - e^{-rT-0.5d_1^2-0.5\sigma^2 T+d_1\sigma\sqrt{T}}\right]\right) = 0$$

We have verified that the Black-Scholes equation satisfies the pde.

Chapter 22 Exotic Options: II

1. (a) Using the *CashCall* function of the software that comes with the book, we can easily see that the value of a claim that pays $1 if S > K in four months is equal to 0.5113. The value of a claim that pays $5 is five times that amount, or $2.5564.

    (b) Using the *CashPut* function of the software that comes with the book, we can easily see that the value of a claim that pays $1 if S < K in four months is equal to 0.4722. The value of a claim that pays $5 is five times that amount, or $2.2361.

    (c) The value of the portfolio is the sum of its individual components, which equals $4.9174. You are paid $5 independently of the stock price because you are paid both if the stock goes up and if the stock goes down. The value of that portfolio should equal the present value of $5 four months from now, which it indeed does:

    $$PV(\$5) = \$5 \times \exp\left(-0.05 \times \frac{4}{12}\right) = 4.9174.$$

2. (a) Using the *AssetCall* function of the software that comes with the book, we can easily see that the value of a claim that pays one share if S > K in four months is equal to $43.66757. The value of a claim that pays five shares is five times that amount, or $218.3378.

    (b) Using the *AssetPut* function of the software that comes with the book, we can easily see that the value of a claim that pays one share if S < K in four months is equal to $27.85403. The value of a claim that pays five shares is five times that amount, or $139.2702.

    (c) The value of your portfolio is the sum of the individual components, which equals $357.608.

    (d) You know that you will receive for sure one share in four months. However, you do not receive the benefits associated with the share before you actually own it, which means that you do not receive the dividends. The value of your portfolio is five times the current stock price, less the present value of the dividends that will accrue to the stock during the next four months. Mathematically,

    $$PV(\text{Portfolio}) = 5 \times \$72 \times \exp\left(-0.02 \times \frac{4}{12}\right) = 357.608$$

3. (a) Using the formula, we can calculate the following price:

    CashDICall(72, 70, 0.4, 4/12, 0.02, 65) = 2.143817

    (b) This statement is not correct. The value of a down and in option with a strike of K = H is lower than the value of a regular Black-Scholes option with a strike price of K = H. Imagine the following situation: The stock price is 72 [as above in part (a)], and the strike and barrier are equal to 70. Suppose that during the next four months, the stock price continues to go up, without ever going down to $69.99 or lower. The Black-Scholes option expires in the money and is worth S(T) − K. The CashDICall is worthless because the barrier that activates the call was never hit. Therefore, the CashDICall must be worth less than a regular Black-Scholes option.

4. The statement is false. While the exact time over which we have to discount the price is unknown, we know that it is at most T − t, or the remaining life of the option. The deferred rebate option's value is always discounted over T − t years. The longer the time period over which we discount, the smaller the present value.

168 McDonald • *Derivatives Markets*, Second Edition

5. (a) We have BSCALL(72, 70, 0.4, 1, 0.02) = 12.97861

   (b) We can proceed as in Example 22.6 of the main text and price the above option package as an up and out call plus 35 up rebate options with a barrier of $105.

   The up and out call is worth $2.094, and the 35 up rebate options are worth $10.440. The total price of the package is $12.534. The investment bank is offering us a package for $10.884 that has a fair price of $12.534. We should accept the deal!

6. (a) We can use the spreadsheet to value the option part of the compensation package. Note that the cash strike is 1,500,000/75,000 = $20. We will have to add the base salary of $1,000,000 to the package.

Inputs			Rainbow Option		
Asset 1				Call	Put
	Price	29	Price	32.66007	18.33841
	Volatility	35.000%			
	Dividend Yield	0.000%			
Asset 2					
	Price	28		2449505	
	Volatility	30.000%			
	Dividend Yield	0.000%			
Other					
	Cash Strike	20			
	Correlation	0.4			
	Risk-free rate	0.05			
	Time to Expiration (years)	1			

   Therefore, we have an overall value of $3,449,505 for the compensation package.

   (b) Now, the option part is worth $2,597,404 and the overall package is worth $3,597,404. The value of the package increased because choosing the maximum of two negatively correlated assets is more advantageous: Whenever one asset is low, the other one tends to be high. This makes the option to choose especially valuable.

7. We know that the price of a Black-Scholes European Call is equal to:

   $$\text{BSCall}(S, K, \sigma, r, T, \delta) = S \times e^{-\delta(T)} \times N(d_1) - K \times e^{-r(T)} \times N(d_2)$$

   With

   $$d_1 = \frac{\ln S(0) - \ln K + (r - \delta + 0.5\sigma^2) \times (T)}{\sigma\sqrt{T}}$$

   $$d_2 = \frac{\ln S(0) - \ln K + (r - \delta - 0.5\sigma^2) \times (T)}{\sigma\sqrt{T}}$$

   Our strategy is to replace all values of the right hand side and to show that this is identical to what is written above.

   We have:

   $$\text{BSCall}(Se^{-\delta T}, Ke^{-rT}, \sigma, 0, T, 0) = S \times e^{-\delta(T)} \times N(\hat{d}_1) - K \times e^{-r(T)} \times N(\hat{d}_2)$$

With

$$\hat{d}_1 = \frac{\ln[S(0)e^{-\delta T}] - \ln(Ke^{-rT}) + (0.5\sigma^2) \times (T)}{\sigma\sqrt{T}}$$

$$= \frac{\ln[S(0)] - \delta T - \ln(K) - (-rT) + (0.5\sigma^2) \times (T)}{\sigma\sqrt{T}} = d_1$$

$$\hat{d}_2 = \frac{\ln[S(0)e^{-\delta T}] - \ln(Ke^{-rT}) - (0.5\sigma^2) \times (T)}{\sigma\sqrt{T}} = d_2$$

Where we have used that $\ln(SK) = \ln(S) + \ln(K)$ and $\ln[\exp(-rT)] = -rT$.

8. This answer uses the same input variables as the McDonald textbook. You should set up your spreadsheet dynamically so that you can compare your answers with those presented here.

First, we can calculate the intermediary steps suggested in Section 22.4:

Inputs		Variables as in McDonald				
Nikkei	20000	x_A	0.01095	u	1.0949522
Currency	0.01	x_B	0.009506	d	0.9505536
T	1				
Sigma_Nikkei	0.15	Q_A	22893.85	A	1.1446927
Sigma_Currency	0.1	Q_B	18597.41	B	0.9298706
dt	0.5	Q_C	21942.87	C	1.0971433
n	2	Q_D	17824.89	D	0.8912447
div_Nikkei	0.02				
r_dom	0.08	p	0.48233		
r_for	0.04	p*	0.469366		
corr(Nik, Curr)	0.2				
PV	0.960789				

In the next step, we set up the tree:

x1	Q1	x2	Q2	rnp	Weighted Q2
			26206.43	0.051252	1343.1321
		0.011989202			
			21288.32	0.0579422	1233.4914
	22893.85				
			25117.84	0.0550073	1381.664
		0.010408108			
			20404.03	0.0621876	1268.8779
0.01095					
			21288.32	0.0579422	1233.4914
		0.011989202			
			17293.19	0.0655056	1132.8006
	18597.41				
			20404.03	0.0621876	1268.8779
		0.010408108			
20000			16574.84	0.0703052	1165.2985
0.01			25117.84	0.0550073	1381.664
		0.010408108			
			20404.03	0.0621876	1268.8779
	21942.87				
			24074.47	0.0590377	1421.3013
		0.009035522			
			19556.46	0.0667441	1305.2795
0.009506					
			20404.03	0.0621876	1268.8779
		0.010408108			
			16574.84	0.0703052	1165.2985
	17824.89				
			19556.46	0.0667441	1305.2795
		0.009035522			
			15886.34	0.08	1198.7287
			Quanto forward:		**20342.941**

The last price is the sum of the probability-weighted individual nodes. It is indeed equal to the price we calculated using the formula.

9. (a) To answer the question, use the following input variables:

Input Variables			
Nikkei	8500	r_dom	0.014
K_foreign	7650	r_for	0.005
Currency (USD/JPY)	0.008	corr(Nik, Curr)	0.1
T	0.192308	Position Size	1
Sigma_Nikkei	0.22	pseudodiv	0.02065
Sigma_Currency	0.075	div_Nikkei	0.01

We can then use the Black Scholes formula with the following inputs:

S   = Q_0 (Nikkei)
K   = K_foreign
R   = r_domestic
div = div+corr*sig_cur*sig_Nik+r_dom-r_for
vol = sig_Nik
T   = T

	In Yen	Translated at a fixed exchange rate (assume the spot rate)
Black-Scholes Call Price	892.3097627	7.138478102
Black-Scholes Put Price	55.42918319	0.443433465

We obtain the final amount by multiplying the above amount by 10,000: $4,434.33.

(b) The hedging portfolio is complicated. First, we have to hedge the Nikkei risk by buying a delta-weighted position in Nikkei futures. This position in Nikkei futures generates a dividend in Nikkei. At the same time, we have to hedge our currency risk, by buying or selling an appropriate amount of dollar. We earn interest on that portfolio. The key insight is that we have to remain hedged in two dimensions in each hedging interval: We have to adjust the Nikkei position, and we have to adjust the currency position.

10. We used a correlation of 0.1 in Question 22.9. Therefore, here are the answers for rho = 0.3 and rho –0.1:

Rho = 0.3

	In Yen	Translated at a fixed exchange rate (assume the spot rate)
Black-Scholes Call Price	887.6398379	7.101118703
Black-Scholes Put Price	56.13040574	0.449043246

Rho = –0.1

	In Yen	Translated at a fixed exchange rate (assume the spot rate)
Black-Scholes Call Price	896.9901253	7.175921003
Black-Scholes Put Price	54.73498863	0.437879909

The put option becomes more valuable whenever the correlation goes up, and becomes less valuable when the correlation goes down. This is because whenever the correlation goes up, the pseudo-dividend goes up, and the higher the dividend, the higher the put option value. For more info, see the discussion above Example 22.8 of the book.

Chapter 23 Volatility

1. (a) Let's add a bond price column to the above table:

Period	Yield to Maturity	Bond Price	1-Year Forward Price Volatility
1	0.05	0.9524	—
2	0.055	0.8985	0.12
3	0.06	0.8396	0.12
4	0.07	0.7629	0.128

   Therefore, the two-year forward price is F = P(0, 3)/P(0, 2) = 0.8396/0.8985 = 0.9344

   (b) Using Black's Formula, we can write:

   BSCall($0.8396, 0.92 * 0.8985, 0.12, 0, 2, 0) = 0.06306

   (c) Using Black's Formula for put options, we can write:

   BSPut($0.8396, 0.92 * 0.8985, 0.12, 0, 2, 0) = 0.05008

2. We can price this as a series of three bond put options with a strike of: 1/(1 + 0.072) = 0.9328
   Using Formula 23.7 of the main text, we can write down the three individual options as:

   Caplet(year 1, 7.2%) = (1.072) * BSPut(0.8985, 0.9328 * 0.9524, 0.12, 0,1,0) = 0.037885

   Caplet(year 2, 7.2%) = (1.072) * BSPut(0.8396, 0.9328 * 0.8985, 0.12, 0,2,0) = 0.055989

   Caplet(year 3, 7.2%) = (1.072) * BSPut(0.7629, 0.9328 * 0.8396, 0.128, 0,3,0) = 0.078847

   Therefore, the three-year cap is worth $0.1727.

3. (a) Let's add the bond price column to the above table:

Period	Yield to Maturity	Bond Price	1-Year Forward Price Volatility
1	0.06	0.9434	—
2	0.065	0.9070	0.14
3	0.072	0.8117	0.13
4	0.075	0.7488	0.12
5	0.08	0.6806	0.11

   Therefore, the four-year forward price for a one-year bond is

   F = P(0, 5)/P(0, 4) = 0.6806 / 0.7488 = 0.9089

(b) Using Black's Formula, we can write:

$$\text{BSCall}(\$0.6806, 0.85 * 0.7488, 0.11, 0, 4, 0) = 0.082386$$

(c) Using Black's Formula for put options, we can write:

$$\text{BSPut}(\$0.6806, 0.85 * 0.7488, 0.11, 0, 4, 0) = 0.038266$$

4. The volatility for the CIR model is: $\sigma_{CIR} = 12\%/\sqrt{0.06} = 48.99\%$

Using the software that comes with the book, we can calculate for the five-year zero-coupon bond:

Zero Coupon Bonds ($1 Maturity)

	Vasicek	CIR
Bond Price	0.69544	0.68674
Long-Term Yield	3.480%	7.602%
Interest Rate Delta	–0.01985	–0.01341
Interest Rate Gamma	0.05664	0.73655
Yield to Maturity	7.264%	7.516%

To find the values of the $1,000 zero-coupon, we have to multiply the bond price, interest rate delta, and interest rate gamma by $1,000:

Zero Coupon Bonds ($1,000 Maturity)

	Vasicek	CIR
Bond Price	$695.44	$686.74
Interest Rate Delta	–19.85	–13.41
Interest Rate Gamma	56.64	736.55

Using the software that comes with the book, we can calculate for the 15-year zero-coupon bond:

Zero Coupon Bonds ($1 Maturity)

	Vasicek	CIR
Bond Price	0.43166	0.32088
Long-Term Yield	3.480%	7.602%
Interest Rate Delta	–0.01686	–0.00650
Interest Rate Gamma	0.06586	0.73655
Yield to Maturity	5.601%	7.578%

To find the values of the $1,000 zero-coupon, we have to multiply the bond price, interest rate delta, and interest rate gamma by $1,000:

Zero Coupon Bonds ($1,000 Maturity)

	Vasicek	CIR
Bond Price	$431.66	$320.88
Interest Rate Delta	–16.86	–6.50
Interest Rate Gamma	65.86	$736.55

5. We will value the coupon bond as a series of zero-coupon bonds with the following face value–maturity combinations:

($70, 1 year)

	Vasicek	**CIR**
Bond Price	65.90335	65.90063

($70, 2 years)

	Vasicek	**CIR**
Bond Price	62.38919	62.31107

($70, 3 years)

	Vasicek	**CIR**
Bond Price	59.68196	59.27360

($70, 4 years)

	Vasicek	**CIR**
Bond Price	57.77299	56.62966

($1070, 5 years)

	Vasicek	**CIR**
Bond Price	864.73576	829.08764

Therefore, by adding up the five values for the CIR and the Vasicek processes, we obtain the following bond prices:

(a) The Vasicek bond is worth $1,110.483
(b) The CIR bond is worth $1,073.203

6.

Period	Yield to Maturity	Volatility in One Year	Bond Prices
1	0.1	—	0.90909
2	0.11	0.19	0.81162
3	0.12	0.18	0.71178
4	0.125	0.17	0.62430
5	0.13	0.16	0.54276

Node 1   r(0) =   0.909091

			Two Criteria According 23.51 and 23.52			Target Values
			The cells in bold are changed in solver			
Node 2		rd (= Rh)	**0.09792 (G18)**	bond yield	0.8116 (J18)	0.811622 (K18)
		sigma	**0.19000 (G19)**	volatility	0.1900 (J19)	0.19(K19)
	=>	ru (= Rh * exp(2*sigma*sqrt(h)))	0.14318			

CRITERION FUNCTION

0.00000 = (J18-K18)^2+(J19-K19)^2

Excel's Solver minimizes the criterion function by changing the values for rd and sigma in G18 and G19. ru is then just calculated.

Node 3

		Two Criteria According to 23.52 and 23.53		
				Target
r(dd) (=R(2h))	0.09760			
sigma2	0.17199	bond	0.71178	0.71178
r(ud) (=r(dd)*exp(2*sigma2*sqrt(h)))	0.13767	yield volatility	0.18000	0.18
r(uu) (=r(dd) * exp(4*sigma2*sqrt(h)))	0.19419			

Criterion Function   8.60812E-16

The following screen shot demonstrates how to use the solver tool:

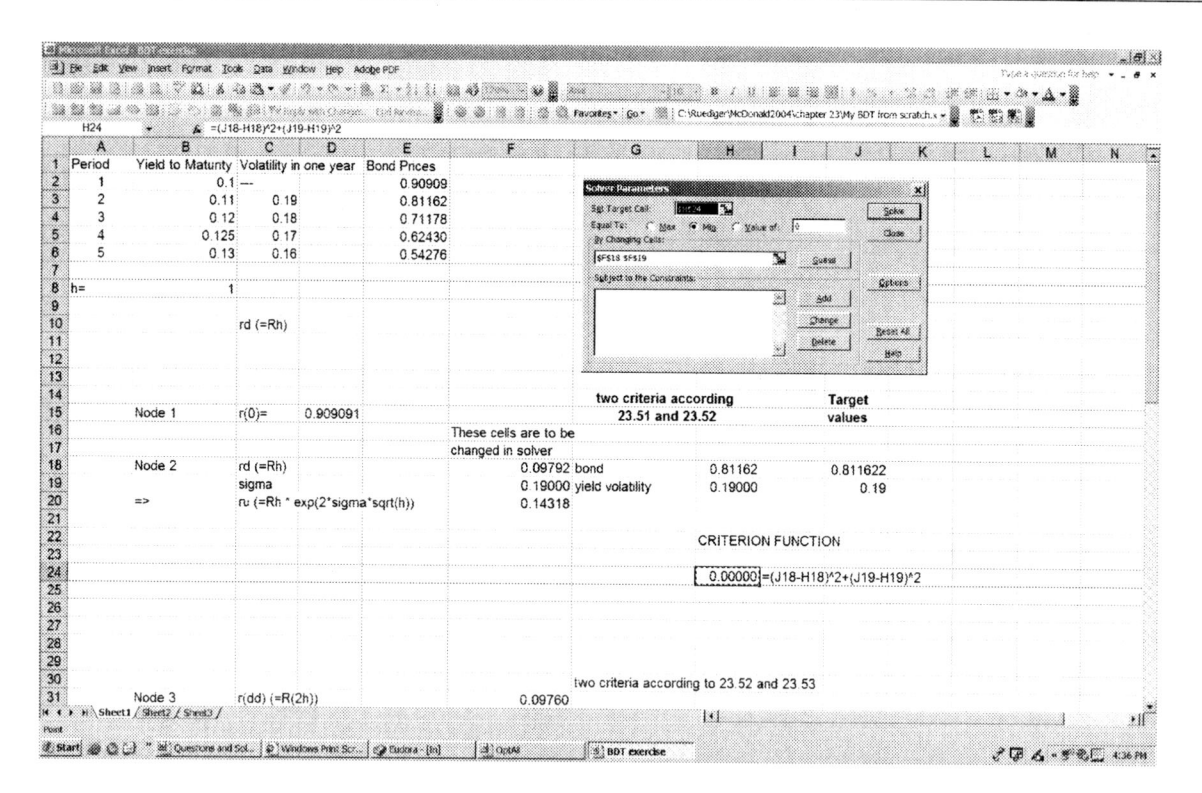

7. Let's start by writing down explicit formulas for $P(1, 4, r_u)$ and $P(1, 4, r_d)$. We need these two prices of a 3-year zero-coupon bond one year ahead from today in order to find the two inputs. By backward incursion, that is, by consecutively replacing the values of the previous node, and by factoring out twice the value of 0.5, we can write:

$$P(1,4,r_u) = \frac{0.25}{1+r_u} \times \left[\frac{1}{1+r_{uu}} \times \left\{ \frac{1}{1+R_{3h}e^{6\sigma_3}} + \frac{1}{1+R_{3h}e^{4\sigma_3}} \right\} + \frac{1}{1+r_{du}} \times \left\{ \frac{1}{1+R_{3h}e^{4\sigma_3}} + \frac{1}{1+R_{3h}e^{2\sigma_3}} \right\} \right]$$

$$P(1,4,r_d) = \frac{0.25}{1+r_d} \times \left[\frac{1}{1+r_{du}} \times \left\{ \frac{1}{1+R_{3h}e^{4\sigma_3}} + \frac{1}{1+R_{3h}e^{2\sigma_3}} \right\} + \frac{1}{1+r_{dd}} \times \left\{ \frac{1}{1+R_{3h}e^{2\sigma_3}} + \frac{1}{1+R_{3h}} \right\} \right]$$

Now, we can write our two main conditions as:

Bond price condition:

$$\text{4-year zero-coupon bond} = \frac{0.5}{1+r_0} \times [P(1,4,r_u) + P(1,4,r_d)]$$

Yield volatility condition:

$$\text{3-year yield} - \text{volatility}(1 \text{ year hence}) = 0.5 \times \{\ln[P(1,4,r_u)^{-1/3} - 1]/[P(1,4,r_d)^{-1/3} - 1]\}$$

Note that the power of $(-1/3)$ is required because we have to annualize the volatility, and the time horizon is three years.

8.

Node 4		Two Criteria According to Exercise 23.9			
r(ddd) (=R(3h))	0.087172369				target
sigma3	0.152682044	bond		0.624295	0.624295
r(ddu) (=r(ddd)*exp(2*sigma3*sqrt(h)))	0.11830	yield volatility		0.17	0.17
r(duu) (=r(ddd)*exp(4*sigma3*sqrt(h)))	0.160551633	p(1, 4, UP)		0.64568	
r(uuu) (=r(dd)*exp(6*sigma2*sqrt(h)))	0.217887675	P(1, 4, DOWN)		0.727769	

Create 4-year zero-coupon tree

Criterion Function
=(target − actual bond)^2 + (target − actual yield)^2

```
                                        100
                         82.10938
              70.456                    100
   64.56797807           86.16592
62.42951      77.1697                   100
   72.7769397           89.42118
              82.63617                  100
                         91.98173
                                        100
```

9. (a) The key to this question is to recognize that the coupon bond can be decomposed into three zero-coupon bonds. The first zero-coupon bond pays $10 after one year, the second zero-coupon bond pays $10 after two years, and the third zero-coupon bond pays $110 after three years.

We know that the one-year interest rate is 10%. Therefore, the one-year zero-coupon bond is worth $10/(1 + 10%) = $9.0909.

We have to evaluate three different payoff paths for the two-year zero-coupon. Interest rates could have gone (up, up), (down, up = up, down), or (down, down). In all paths, the zero-coupon bond pays $10. We can therefore proceed to value the zero coupon bond at t = 1 as either

$$\$10/(1+r_u) = \$10/(1+14.32\%) = \$8.747 \text{ or } \$10/(1+r_d) = \$10/(1+9.79\%) = \$9.108$$

In period t = 0, we can determine the value as usual as

$$P_0 = \frac{p \times P(1, 2, u) + (1-p) \times P(1, 2, d)}{(1+r_0)} = \frac{0.5 \times (\$8.747 + \$9.108)}{(1+10\%)} = \$8.116$$

For the three-year zero-coupon bond, we can use a similar strategy and value the bond recursively. We have:

$$P(2, 3, uu) = \$110/(1+r_{uu}) = \$110/(1+19.42\%) = \$92.112$$

$$P(2, 3, du) = \$110/(1+r_{du}) = \$110/(1+13.77\%) = \$96.686$$

$$P(2, 3, dd) = \$110/(1+r_{dd}) = \$110/(1+9.76\%) = \$100.219$$

178   McDonald • *Derivatives Markets*, Second Edition

From these values, we can easily calculate:

$$P(1, 3, u) = \frac{p \times P(2, 3, uu) + (1-p) \times P(2,3,du)}{(1+r_u)} = \frac{0.5 \times (\$92.112 + \$96.686)}{(1+14.32\%)} = \$82.574$$

$$P(1, 3, d) = \frac{p \times P(2, 3, du) + (1-p) \times P(2, 3, dd)}{(1+r_d)} = \frac{0.5 \times (\$96.686 + 100.22)}{(1+9.79\%)} = \$89.674$$

And finally, we have:

$$P_0 = \frac{p \times P(1, 3, u) + (1-p) \times P(1, 3, d)}{(1+r_0)} = \frac{0.5 \times (\$82.574 + \$89.674)}{(1+10\%)} = \$78.295$$

The coupon bond is worth $78.295 + $8.116 + $9.091 = $95.502
The tree is calculated by adding all three zero-coupon values at each node:

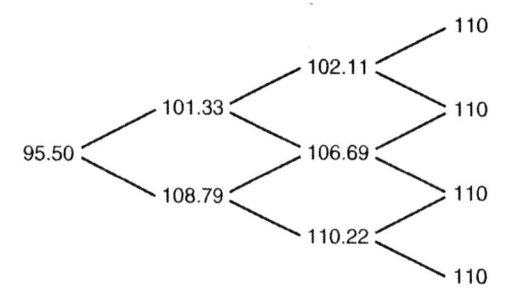

```
                          110
                 102.11 <
         101.33<         110
95.50 <         106.69 <
         108.79<         110
                 110.22<
                          110
```

(b) To calculate the ex-coupon tree, we have to deduct the coupon at each node a coupon is paid:

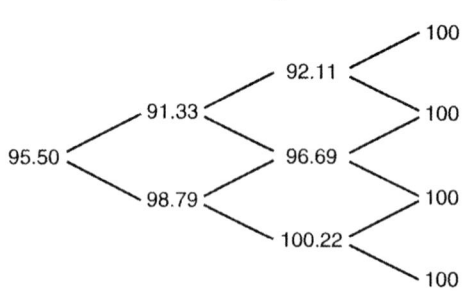

```
                          100
                  92.11 <
          91.33 <         100
95.50 <          96.69 <
          98.79 <         100
                 100.22 <
                          100
```

10. (a) We should use the tree without the coupon payments because we are not entitled to the coupon payments prior to possession of the underlying security.

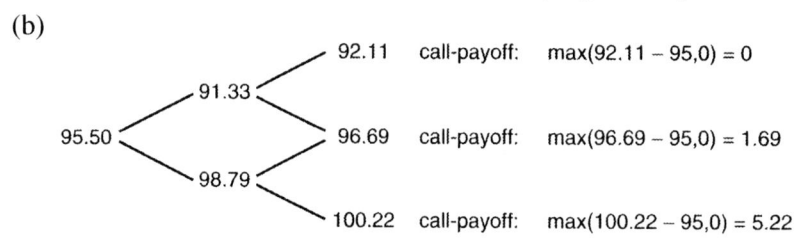

    (b)
```
                  92.11   call-payoff:   max(92.11 – 95,0) = 0
          91.33 <
95.50 <           96.69   call-payoff:   max(96.69 – 95,0) = 1.69
          98.79 <
                 100.22   call-payoff:   max(100.22 – 95,0) = 5.22
```

Therefore,

$$C(1, 2, u) = \frac{p \times C(2, 2, uu) + (1-p) \times C(2, 2, du)}{(1+r_u)} = \frac{0.5 \times (\$0 + \$1.69)}{(1+14.32\%)} = \$0.739$$

$$C(1, 2, d) = \frac{p \times C(2, 2, du) + (1-p) \times C(2, 2, dd)}{(1+r_d)} = \frac{0.5 \times (\$1.69 + \$5.22)}{(1+9.79\%)} = \$3.147$$

And finally, we have:

$$C_0 = \frac{0.5 \times (\$0.739 + \$3.147)}{(1+10\%)} = \$1.766$$

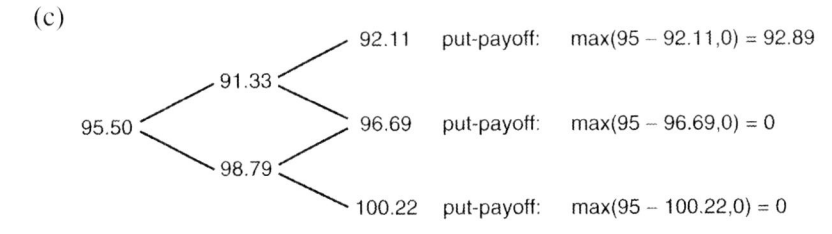

(c)

```
                   92.11    put-payoff:   max(95 - 92.11, 0) = 92.89
           91.33
95.50              96.69    put-payoff:   max(95 - 96.69, 0) = 0
           98.79
                  100.22    put-payoff:   max(95 - 100.22, 0) = 0
```

Therefore,

$$P(1, 2, u) = \frac{p \times P(2, 2, uu) + (1-p) \times P(2, 2, du)}{(1+r_u)} = \frac{0.5 \times (\$0 + \$2.89)}{(1+14.32\%)} = \$1.264$$

$$P(1, 2, d) = \frac{p \times P(2, 2, du) + (1-p) \times P(2, 2, dd)}{(1+r_d)} = \frac{0.5 \times (\$0 + \$0)}{(1+9.79\%)} = \$0$$

And finally, we have:

$$P_0 = \frac{0.5 \times (\$1.264 + \$0)}{(1+10\%)} = \$0.575$$

(d) We now have to analyze whether early exercise in period $t = 0$ and $t = 1$ is beneficial. For the call option, we have to compare the continuation value with the value of immediate exercise.

$C(1, 2, u) = \$0.739$. Value of immediate exercise: max $(91.33 - 95, 0) = 0$

$C(1, 2, d) = \$3.147$. Value of immediate exercise: max $(98.79 - 95, 0) = 3.79$

The value of immediate exercise in the down node is higher, and we would exercise early. This has the following consequence for the value in $t = 0$:

$$C(0, 2) = \frac{0.5 \times (\$0.739 + \$3.79)}{(1+10\%)} = \$2.059 \text{ . Value of immediate exercise:}$$

$$\max(95.51 - 95, 0) = 0.51$$

Therefore, the American call option is worth $2.059.

For the American put option, we compare:

$P(1, 2, u) = \$1.264$. Value of immediate exercise: max $(95 - 91.33, 0) = 3.67$

$P(1, 2, d) = \$0$. Value of immediate exercise: max $(95 - 98.79, 0) = 0$

We therefore early exercise the put option in the up node. This has the following consequence for the continuation value in t = 0:

$$P_0 = \frac{0.5 \times (\$3.67 + \$0)}{(1 + 10\%)} = \$1.668$$. Value of immediate exercise: max (95 − 98.51, 0) = 0

Therefore, the value of the American put option is equal to $1.668.

Chapter 24 Interest Rate Models

1. We can calculate that a 15% loss will occur if:

$$\$3m \times e^{(0.15 - 0.5 \times 0.3^2)\frac{1}{12} + 0.3\sqrt{\frac{1}{12}}Z} = 0.85 \times \$3m$$

or

$$Z = \frac{\ln(0.85) - (0.15 - 0.5 \times 0.3^2)\frac{1}{12}}{0.3\sqrt{\frac{1}{12}}} = -1.97764$$

The corresponding probability is: NormSDist(−1.97764) = 0.023984, or 2.40%

2. We can calculate the corresponding z-values by using the normsinv function of Excel. These are: $N^{-1}(0.1) = 1.28155$ and $N^{-1}(0.025) = 1.95996$

Using the values of the table, we can now calculate for the 90% VaR:

	Stock A	Stock B
VaR (1-day)	−0.07862	−0.13715
VaR (1-week)	−0.20037	−0.34785
VaR (1-month)	−0.3899	−0.67228

And for the 97.5% VaR:

	Stock A	Stock B
VaR (1-day)	−0.12038	−0.20913
VaR (1-week)	−0.30752	−0.52808
VaR (1-month)	−0.60157	−1.01400

3. (a) We first have to calculate the portfolio mean and standard deviation.

We calculate: $\alpha_P = \dfrac{W_1 \alpha_1 + W_2 \alpha_2}{W_1 + W_2} = \dfrac{2.5 \times 0.22 + 2.5 \times 0.219}{5} = 0.2195$

And

$$\sigma_P = \frac{\sqrt{W_1^2 \sigma_1^2 + W_2^2 \sigma_2^2 + 2 W_1 W_2 \sigma_1 \sigma_2 \rho}}{W_1 + W_2} = \frac{\sqrt{2.5 \times 0.42 + 2.5 \times 0.418 + 2 \times 2.5 \times 2.5 \times 0.42 \times 0.418 \times 1}}{5}$$

$$= 0.418$$

Now we can calculate, using Equation 24.7, that there is a 97.5% probability that in 1 week, the value of the portfolio will exceed:

$$\$5m \times \left[1 + 0.2195 \times \frac{1}{52} + (-1.95996) \times 0.418 \times \sqrt{\frac{1}{52}}\right] = 4.453114$$

The value at risk is therefore: $0.54689 million.

(b) The VaR we calculated in part (a) is close to the VaR we calculated in Question 24.2, part (b) for the same probability and time horizon (–0.52808m). If you thought they should be even closer, remember that we used the normal approximation in this question, while we calculated the value using the lognormal distribution in Question 24.2. You can recalculate the normal approximation for Question 24.2: It is –0.54962, which is very close to our calculations above.

4. The values from the inverted normal distribution are

$$N^{-1}(0.07) = 1.47579 \text{ and } N^{-1}(0.025) = 1.95996$$

1-week VaRs:

The annual mean and the annual standard deviation of the portfolio are 0.186667 and 0.314859. We have a value of the portfolio that is attained with 93% and 97.5% probability of $5.634913 million and $5.50807 million, respectively. Therefore, the 1-week, 93% VaR is –$0.36509 million, and the 1-week, 97.5% VaR is –$0.49193 million.

1-month VaRs:

The annual mean and standard deviation are as calculated above. We calculate a portfolio value that is achieved with 93% probability of $5.288509 million, and a portfolio value that is achieved with 97.5% probability of $5.024464 million. Therefore, the 93%, 1-month VaR is –$0.71149 million, and the 97.5%, 1-month VaR is –$0.97554 million.

5. First, we calculate the Black-Scholes price for the option, based on the above assumptions. Don't forget the dividend yield of 3%. We have a Black-Scholes price of $7.01338, and a corresponding delta of 0.79122. We invest $5 million in stock A, and stock A is worth $50, so we buy 100,000 shares. Since we sell 0.5 options for each share, we sell 50,000 options. Therefore, our initial portfolio value is:

$$W = \$5m - \$7.01338 \times 50,000 = \$4,649,330.868$$

Using Formulas 24.10 and 24.11, we can calculate the portfolio return and standard deviation to be: $R_p = 0.077997$ and $\sigma_p = 0.155995$. We know by now from the previous exercises that $N^{-1}(0.07) = 1.47579$ and $N^{-1}(0.025) = 1.95996$.

Using Equation 24.12, we can calculate for the 93% scenario:

$$\text{Value Portfolio} = \$4,649,330.868 \times (1 + 0.077997) \times \frac{1}{52} + 0.155995 \times \sqrt{\frac{1}{52}} \times (-1.4758)$$

$$= \$4,507,874.04$$

VaR = –$141,456.83

We have for the 97.5% scenario:

$$\text{Value Portfolio} = \$4{,}649{,}330.868 \times (1+0.077997) \times \frac{1}{52} + 0.155995 \times \sqrt{\frac{1}{52}} \times (-1.96)$$
$$= \$4{,}459{,}177.394$$

VaR = −$190,153.474

6. We can compute the exact value at risk by first determining the stock price that we will exceed with a 93% (or 97.5%) probability, and then computing the exact portfolio value at that price. We solve:

$$\$50 \times e^{(0.12-0.5\times 0.24^{\wedge}2)\frac{1}{52}+0.24\sqrt{1/52}\times(-1.4758)} = \$47.68703$$

and

$$\$50 \times e^{(0.12-0.5\times 0.24^{\wedge}2)\frac{1}{52}+0.24\sqrt{1/52}\times(-1.96)} = \$46.92475$$

For the 93% case, the option value has changed to $5.200775, and for the 97.5% case, the option value has changed to $4.673961. When calculating the new option values, don't forget that we are one week closer to expiration. The correct time to maturity is therefore 25/52, and NOT 26/52 = 0.5.

We can calculate for the 93% case a new portfolio value of $4,508,665, and a 1-week, 93% VaR of −$140,666. For the 97.5% case we calculate a new portfolio value of $4,458,777 and a 1-week, 97.5% VaR of −$190,554.

7. We have to use Formulas 24.10 and 24.11, and pay special attention to the cross-terms in 24.11—that is the tricky part.

For the mean, we calculate:

$$R_P = \frac{1}{W} \times [\alpha_1 \times S_1(\varpi_1 + N_1\Delta_1) + \alpha_2 \times S_2(\varpi_2 + N_2\Delta_2)]$$
$$= \frac{1}{7{,}045{,}440} \times [0.15 \times 100(30{,}000 - 25{,}000 \times 0.6003) + 0.18 \times 100(50{,}000 - 60{,}000 \times 0.4941)]$$
$$= 0.083918748$$

For the standard deviation, we calculate:

$$\sigma_P = \sqrt{\frac{1}{W^2} \times [2 \times S_1 \times S_2(\varpi_1 + N_1\Delta_1) \times (\varpi_2 + N_2\Delta_2)\sigma_1\sigma_2\rho + S_1^2(\varpi_1 + N_1\Delta_1)^2\sigma_1^2 + S_2^2(\varpi_2 + N_2\Delta_2)^2\sigma_2^2]}$$
$$= 0.166173026$$

We have indeed confirmed the values obtained in Exercise 24.5.

8. First, we have to calculate the option prices and deltas of the two options. We have:

	50-Strike	60-Strike
B-S Price	3.933228902	0.8621655
B-S Delta	0.582985049	0.1968702

From these values, we can calculate an initial portfolio value of W = $220,889.79. We calculate the portfolio return and standard deviation to be:

$$R_p = \frac{1}{W} \times [\alpha_1 \times S_1(N_1\Delta_1 + N_2\Delta_2)]$$

$$= \frac{1}{220,889.79} \times [0.12 \times 50(100,000 \times 0.5830 - 200,000 \times 0.1969)]$$

$$= 0.514043$$

$$\sigma_p = \sqrt{\frac{1}{W^2} \times [S_1^2(N_1\Delta_1 + N_2\Delta_2)^2 \sigma_1^2]}$$

$$= \sqrt{\frac{1}{220,889.79^2} \times [50^2(100,000 \times 0.5830 - 200,000 \times 0.1969)^2 0.24^2]}$$

$$= 1.028085973$$

Note that we have a leveraged position consisting only of options. Therefore, both mean and standard deviation are quite high.

We can now use our standard approach, and calculate the portfolio value that is exceeded at least 97.5% of the time, and calculate the difference as the VaR.

We have:

Portfolio Value	$161,349.75
VaR	−$59,540.04

It is not a good approximation because the payoff of the call ratio spread is highly non-linear. In particular, with increasing stock prices, we stand to incur unlimited losses. The delta approximation is likely to work poorly.

9. I simulated 10,000 draws. The natural cut-off is therefore the portfolio value after 250 observations, if sorted in ascending order. In my simulations, this was −$33,048.9959. Therefore, the VaR is −$253,938.746, considerably higher than what we calculated in Question 24.8. This confirms the suspicion about non-linearity we had in Question 24.8.

10. We can calculate the new variance to be:

$$\sigma^2 = (0.5797 \times 0.01 \times 10)^2 + (0.4203 \times 0.012 \times 15)^2 + (2 \times 0.4203 \times 0.5797 \times 0.01 \times 10 \times 0.012 \times 15)$$

$$= 0.017855$$

$$\Rightarrow \sigma = 0.133624$$

We can now calculate the 95%, one-week VaR as −$304,823.70.

Chapter 25 Value at Risk

1. Here are the results for all 14 sample years:

Name	DOW JONES	MICROSOFT	BOEING
12/25/1991	15.61%	35.59%	26.26%
12/30/1992	11.40%	32.76%	24.53%
12/29/1993	8.51%	25.66%	24.94%
12/28/1994	12.14%	24.98%	16.58%
12/27/1995	9.19%	31.35%	22.96%
12/25/1996	13.21%	24.05%	22.48%
12/31/1997	17.06%	36.55%	27.28%
12/30/1998	18.50%	41.17%	43.66%
12/29/1999	14.88%	37.71%	33.34%
12/27/2000	19.79%	61.74%	34.59%
12/26/2001	22.05%	44.90%	44.75%
12/25/2002	22.59%	30.91%	35.45%
12/31/2003	16.21%	27.32%	30.32%
12/29/2004	9.84%	16.81%	21.32%
Overall	**15.61%**	**35.03%**	**30.02%**

The result for the overall period is calculated as:

$$Volatility = \sqrt{\frac{14}{730} \times \frac{1}{729} \times \sum_{t=1}^{730} [\ln(S_t / S_{t-1})]^2}$$

Note that there is considerable time-series variation in volatility. Suppose you were to use the overall volatility, estimated over the last 14 years, as your best estimate for the future volatility. You can see that you are likely to use a bad estimate because there is volatility clustering, which you have averaged out by using too long of a time-series.

2.

Name	DOW JONES INDEX	MICROSOFT	BOEING
12/31/1991	14.35%	36.78%	27.46%
12/31/1992	10.14%	33.40%	22.72%
12/31/1993	8.64%	30.06%	21.55%
12/30/1994	10.81%	27.37%	18.70%
12/29/1995	8.83%	35.08%	24.78%
12/31/1996	11.81%	27.65%	22.85%
12/31/1997	18.71%	33.33%	33.33%
12/31/1998	19.57%	37.85%	42.76%
12/31/1999	15.79%	37.34%	33.92%
12/29/2000	20.33%	56.68%	41.09%
12/31/2001	20.91%	41.82%	42.90%
12/31/2002	25.41%	42.30%	38.74%
12/31/2003	15.97%	28.45%	28.44%
12/31/2004	10.60%	18.93%	20.06%
Overall	**16.20%**	**36.35%**	**31.53%**

The results of the daily volatility calculations are remarkably similar to the weekly volatility calculations.

3. Here is a figure of the time-series of volatility:

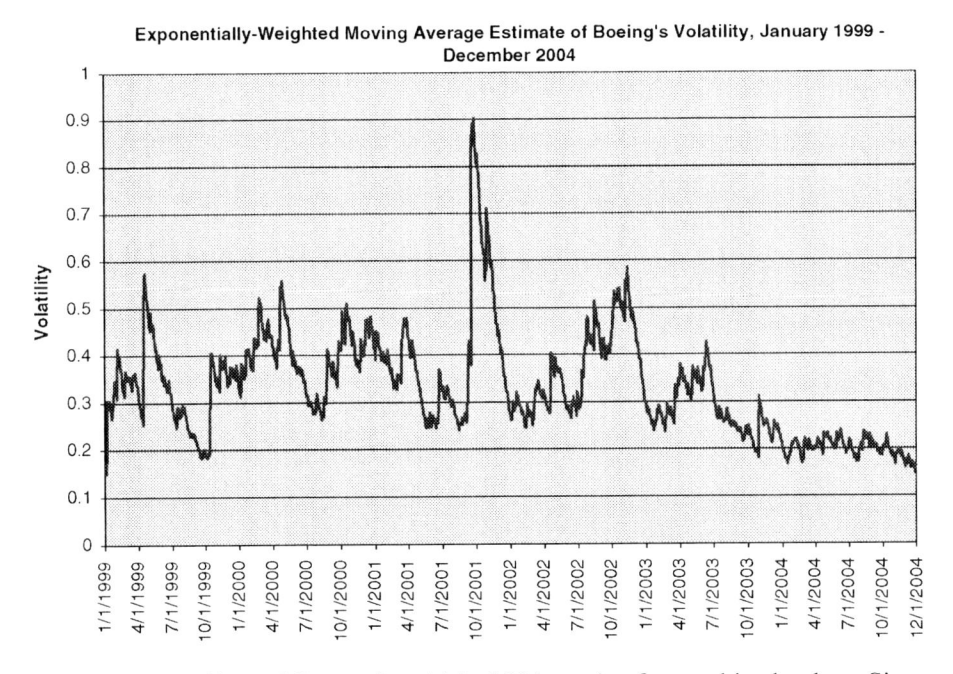

Exponentially-Weighted Moving Average Estimate of Boeing's Volatility, January 1999 - December 2004

Note how the effect of September 11th, 2001 carries forward in the data. Since we initially give a lot of weight to the observations that just happened (instead of equal-weighting as in the historical volatility calculations), the shock to returns on September 11th is felt well until January 2002 in the volatility estimates.

4. (a)

ret	Coef.	Std. Err.	z	P > |z|	[95% Conf.	Interval]
ARCH						
arch						
B2.	0.0726685	0.0059037	12.31	0.000	0.0610974	0.0842396
garch						
B3.	0.912731	0.0087233	104.63	0.000	0.8956336	0.9298284
B1	8.15e-06	2.12e-06	3.84	0.000	4.00e-06	0.0000123

(b) The unconditional volatility can be calculated as:

$$\sqrt{\frac{0.00000815}{1-0.0726685-0.912731} \times 252} = 0.3753$$

(c) We exclude September 17, 2001, and October 29, 2001. The first exclusion date is a particular problem for our time series. September 17, 2001 was the day stock markets opened again after the September 11 attacks. It is likely that a lot of stocks traded at considerable negative returns, although the shock for Boeing and more generally aviation/travel/insurance stocks have been especially severe.

ca). Now we have the following estimates:

ret	Coef.	Std. Err.	z	P > |z|	[95% Conf.	Interval]
ARCH						
arch						
B2.	0.0574573	0.0066211	8.68	0.000	0.0444801	0.0704344
garch						
B3.	0.929601	0.0082477	112.71	0.000	0.9134358	0.9457663
B1	6.00e-06	1.79e-06	3.35	0.001	2.49e-06	9.50e-06

We can calculate an unconditional variance of:

$$\sqrt{\frac{0.00000600}{1-0.0574573-0.929601} \times 252} = 0.3418$$

Interestingly, the effect on the unconditional variance estimate is relatively small compared to the big effect that excluding four days of IBM had on the volatility estimate that is described in the textbook.

5.

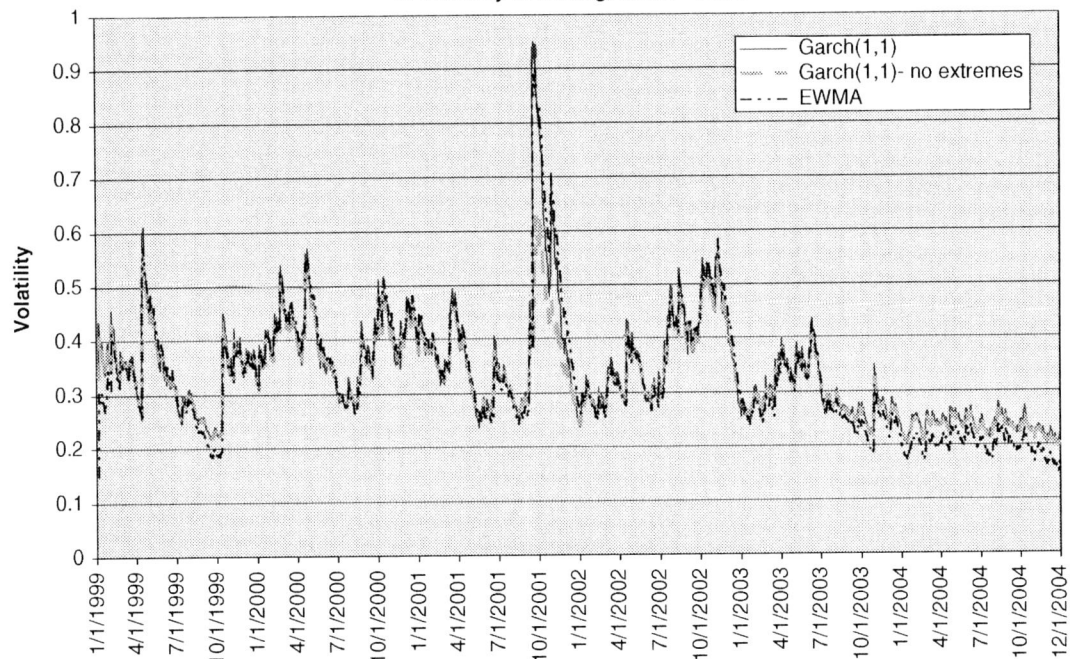

Comparison of Garch(1,1), Garch(1,1) without extreme absolute returns, and EWMA estimates of volatility of Boeing, Jan99 - Dec04

The three time-series of volatilities are quite close to each other, despite the different estimation techniques. The biggest difference is the behavior of the Garch(1,1)—no extremes line around September 17th and the following weeks. Since we have excluded the most extreme return, the volatility estimates from the Garch(1,1)—no extremes line is considerably below both other lines.

For the period January 2004 to December 2004, EWMA yields a volatility estimated below the estimates from both Garch models. The reason is that the parameter b that we chose (0.94) is higher than the parameter B3 we estimated for both Garch models. This means that the EWMA estimate puts more emphasis on the more recent observations, and you can see from the graph that Jan 2004 to December 2004 was a period of low volatility. This results in a lower line for EWMA.

6. We have:

S	100		$5-step
r	0.08	forward price	102.0201
sigma	0.3	K0	100
T	0.25	sum(put-term)	0.048748
delta	0	sum(call-term)	0.040555
		F(0,T) adjustment	0.001632
		Sigma2Vix	0.087671
		Sigma Vix	0.296093

7.

Implied volatilities for S&P 500 index options with expiry March 20, 2004

We can see a fairly typical picture for index-option implied volatilities: The out-of-the-money put options and in-the-money call options have a considerably higher implied volatility. Note that the implied volatilities estimated from bid prices for put options are unstable for small strike prices, an issue that was discussed in Problems 6-8 of the main text book.

8.

Implied volatilities for S&P 500 options with expiry of June 18, 2005 on January 12, 2004

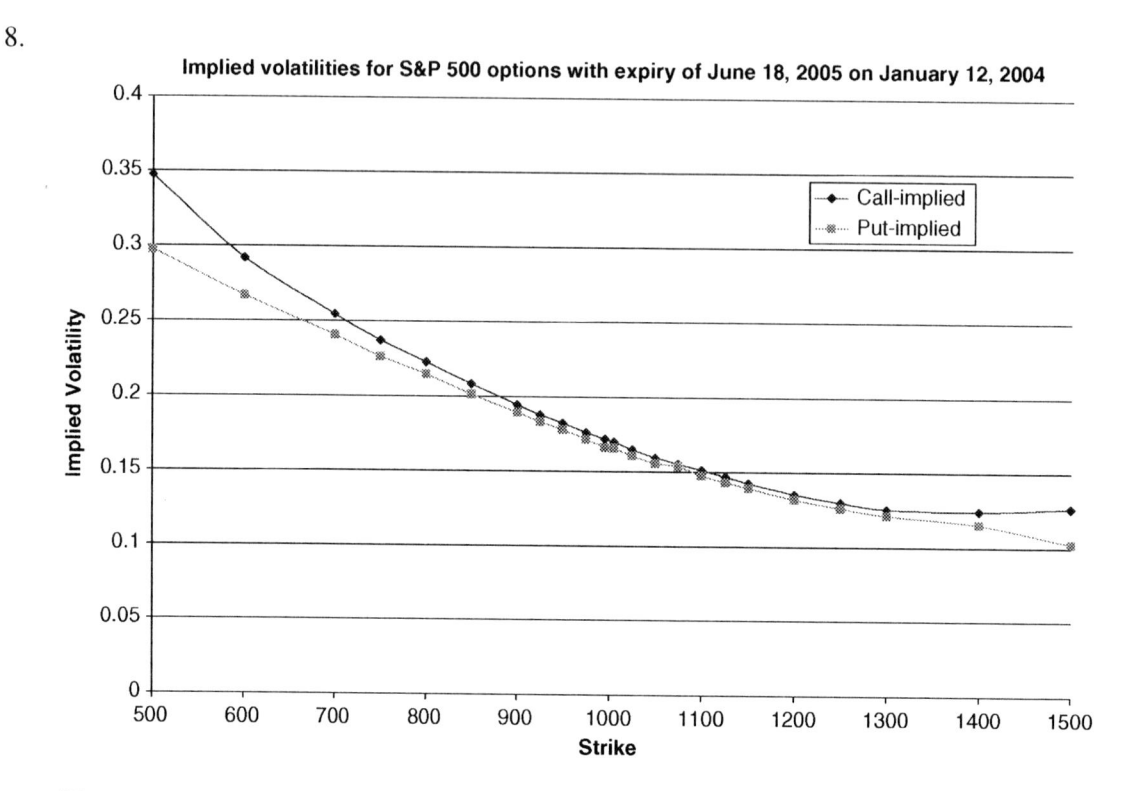

We see a typical volatility smirk. The series is very smooth, which is caused by the long time-to-maturity and our use of the average of ask and bid prices.

9. (a)–(c)

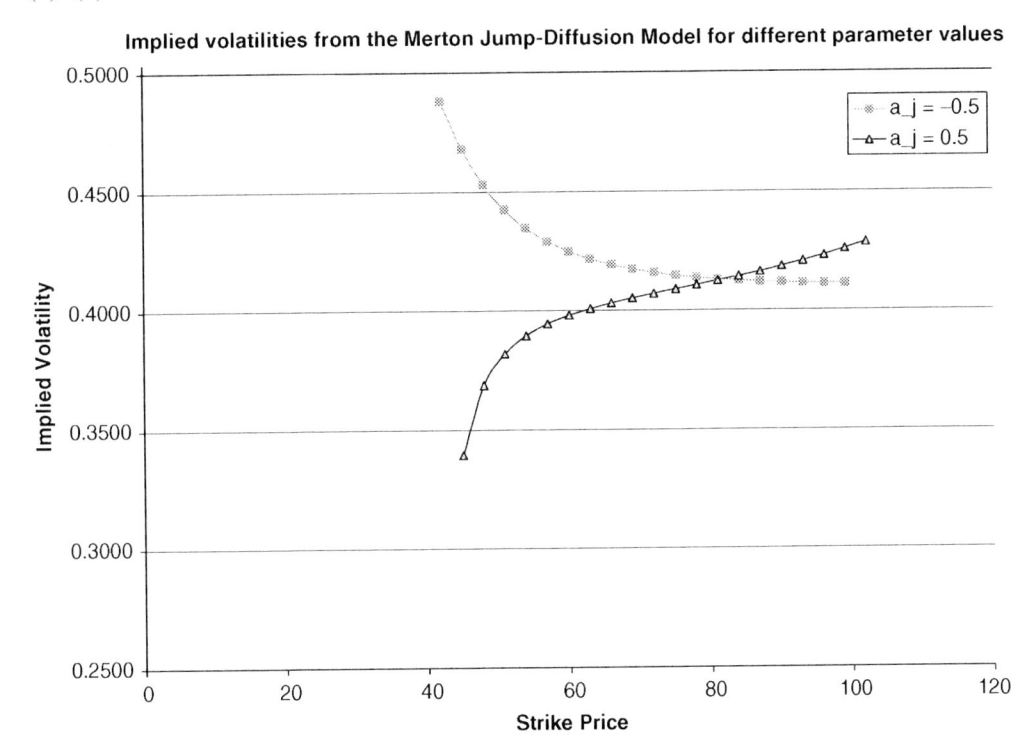

Implied volatilities from the Merton Jump-Diffusion Model for different parameter values

[Graph showing implied volatility vs strike price for $a_j = -0.5$ and $a_j = 0.5$]

The above graph shows that for a negative expected jump, the volatility is higher for in-the-money call options, and for a positive expected jump, the volatility is lower for deep-in-the-money call options. The jump-diffusion model can generate many different shapes of a volatility curve.

(d) You have demonstrated in part (c) that this statement is not correct. The statement holds if we condition on negative jumps in stock prices. However, if there are both positive and negative jumps of uncertain magnitude, we can generate many shapes for the implied volatility curve, and not all are consistent with the observed volatility smirk for index options, where in-the-money call options have higher implied volatilities.

10. These are the CEV prices:

	Beta = –4	Beta = –2	Beta = 0	Beta = 2	Beta = 4
45	37.71	36.42	34.54	32.80	32.83
48	35.25	33.95	32.12	30.12	30.23
51	32.81	31.51	29.76	27.51	27.76
54	30.37	29.12	27.47	24.99	25.44
57	27.97	26.78	25.26	22.58	23.30
60	25.59	24.49	23.13	20.29	21.33
63	23.25	22.27	21.09	18.14	19.53
66	20.96	20.12	19.15	16.13	17.90
69	18.72	18.06	17.31	14.28	16.44
72	16.56	16.08	15.57	12.58	15.12
75	14.48	14.21	13.93	11.04	13.93
78	12.50	12.44	12.41	9.64	12.87
81	10.63	10.79	10.99	8.39	11.92
84	8.90	9.26	9.68	7.28	11.06
87	7.31	7.86	8.48	6.29	10.29
90	5.88	6.59	7.38	5.42	9.60
93	4.62	5.45	6.39	4.66	8.98
96	3.53	4.44	5.50	3.99	8.42
99	2.62	3.57	4.71	3.41	7.91
102	1.88	2.82	4.00	2.91	7.45
105	1.29	2.19	3.38	2.48	7.04

These are the implied volatility curves:

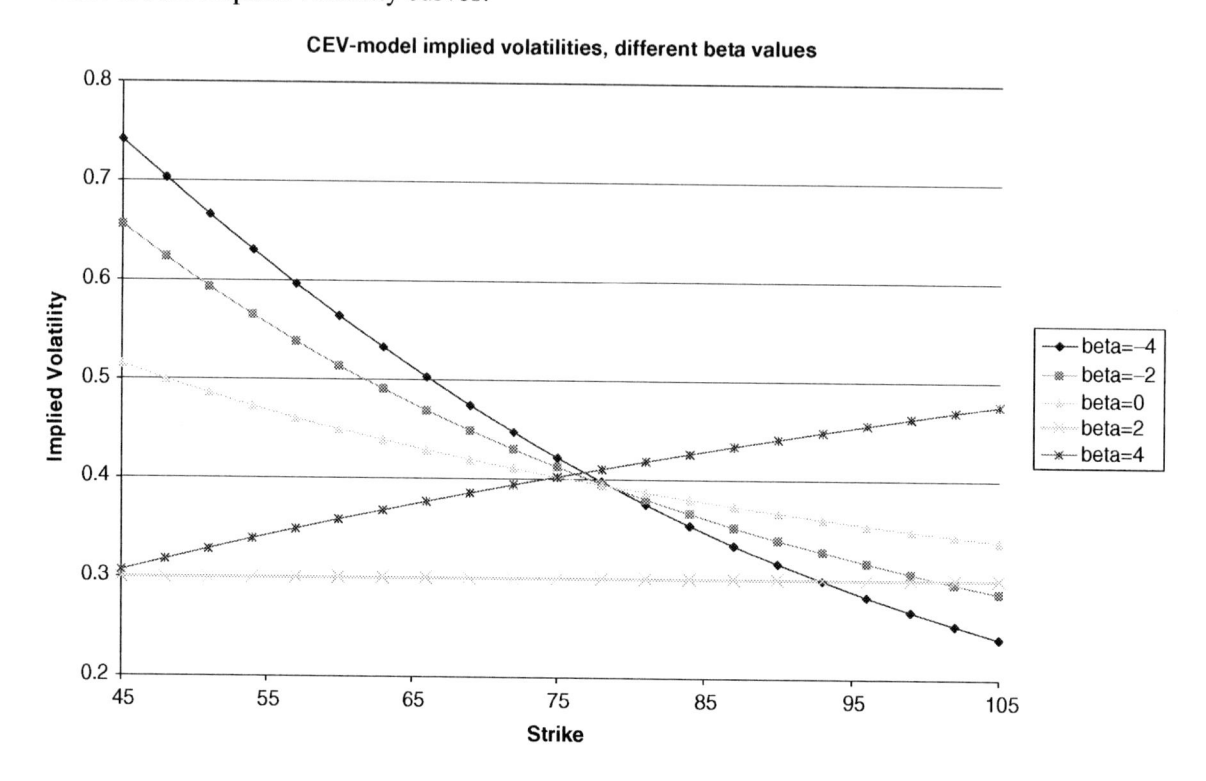

Chapter 26 Credit Risk

1. We need to use Formulas 26.115 and 26.117 of the main text book. We can calculate the true and risk-neutral probability of bankruptcy to be 0.3932 and 0.6412, respectively.

   To calculate the credit spread, we need to know the expected loss given default, which is one less the expected recovery rate. We can calculate for the risk-neutral probability measure an expected asset value conditional of default of 87.9695, and an expected recovery rate of 0.4398 (don't forget to divide by 200—the maturity value, and NOT by 100). Using the last formula to calculate the credit spread, we obtain a credit spread of 4.4496%. Of course, an alternative and probably easier way is to calculate the credit spread by subtracting the risk-free rate from the bond yield.

2. Using the formulas of the main text, we can calculate the following values for the yield, the probability of default, and the expected loss given default for all times to maturity:

Time to mat	1	2	5	10	100	500
Bond price	136.742	125.444	100.764	73.172	0.562	0.000
Yield	0.275	0.181	0.116	0.090	0.058	0.053
Prob default	0.710	0.660	0.620	0.605	0.646	0.771
Expected recovery	128.939	117.375	98.329	81.889	30.501	9.796
Expected loss given default	0.284	0.348	0.454	0.545	0.831	0.946

   The longer the time horizon, the less risky is the bond (the yield is going down). The upward drift of the assets makes it less likely that the bond defaults.

3. (a) Given the information in the text, we can calculate:

Mat val	300
Time to mat	2
Bond price	144.4920745
Yield	0.365278908
Prob default	0.925886944
Expected Recovery	148.4571336

   (b) The yield is very high because this is a risky bond—for us to be paid back in full, the assets of the company would have to double in value. This is unlikely, as you can see from the probability of default of 92.59%.

4. (a)

Mat val	100	100	100	100	100	100	100
Volatility	1%	5%	10%	20%	40%	60%	90%
Bond price	77.880	77.880	77.868	76.376	65.544	51.781	33.037
Yield	0.050	0.050	0.050	0.054	0.084	0.132	0.222
Prob default	0.000	0.000	0.002	0.107	0.388	0.572	0.752
Expected recovery	—	98.207	93.761	81.970	59.131	41.445	23.423
Expected loss given default	—	0.018	0.062	0.180	0.409	0.586	0.766

(b) For a maturity value of $200, we obtain:

Mat val	200	200	200	200	200	200	200
Volatility	1%	5%	10%	20%	40%	60%	90%
Bond price	149.935	145.682	139.079	125.736	100.050	76.771	48.038
Yield	0.058	0.063	0.073	0.093	0.139	0.191	0.285
Prob default	0.955	0.653	0.610	0.621	0.688	0.758	0.847
Expected recovery	192.169	180.177	164.908	137.910	95.982	66.142	36.756
Expected loss given default	0.039	0.099	0.175	0.310	0.520	0.669	0.816

(c) For a maturity value of $100, substantially below the current asset value of $150, an increase in volatility is bad for the bond holders because it increases the chances of a drastic reduction in asset value. However, even for a maturity value of $200, bond holders do not like an increase in volatility because the equity as a call option always increases in volatility, making the bond price lower and the yield higher.

5. We can calculate the following values for the bond prices, yields, and expected losses for the model with and without jump risk:

	Without Jump Risk	With Jump Risk
Mat val	175	175
Time to mat	10	10
Bond price	71.959	51.637
Yield	0.0889	0.1221

Incorporating jump risk makes the bond less valuable, and thus increases the yield.

6. The book provides a hint on how to price the issue when there is a bankruptcy trigger. Equity is then valued as a call option that knocks out if $A_t \leq \underline{A}$. Since debt is just the residual, we can calculate the debt value as Asset value at t = 0 minus the knock out option.

The value of the down-and-out call option with a barrier of $75 and a strike of $120 is equal to $49.501 so that the value of the debt with the bankruptcy trigger is equal to $100.499. Hence, we can calculate a yield of

$$\rho = \ln\left(\frac{175}{100.499}\right)\bigg/5 = 0.1109$$

The credit spread is equal to $\rho - r = 0.1109 - 0.05 = 0.0609$. To calculate the default probability, we have to think about when default can occur.

The firm can default if its assets fall below $75 during the next five years and if they are below $175 at expiration. This is a cash down-and-in put with barrier 75 and strike 75 and a cash down-and-out put with barrier 75 and strike 175. The second option needs to be a down-and-out put because once we default due to the bankruptcy clause, we cannot default anymore at maturity. We can convert these values to probabilities by multiplying by e^(r * t).

This yields an interim probability of default of 0.2079 and a terminal probability of default of 0.2295, or a total probability of default of 0.4373.

7. The easiest way to solve this question is to use matrix multiplication in Excel. You multiply the one-year transition matrix with itself to obtain the two-year transition matrix. In order to do so, enter into cells C5:E7 in Excel the probability matrix for the one-year transitions. Then, you should mark nine fields in Excel, say H5:J7, and press F2 on your keyboard. This allows you to enter a formula into the upper left cell. You should enter: = MMULT(C5:E7,C5:E7), and then press simultaneously shift + control + enter. The transition matrix for year two appears. To produce the transition matrix for year three, you should mark again nine fields, say fields H13 to J15, press F2 and enter = MMULT(H5:J7,C5:E7). This multiplies the two-year matrix with the one-year matrix to produce the three-year matrix. Repeat the step two more times, and you get the following result:

5-year matrix

	Good	Bad	Ugly
Good	0.675807	0.200773	0.123419
Bad	0.413493	0.363837	0.222669
Ugly	0.285886	0.300023	0.414091

8. (a) We can produce the table below by following the procedure outlined in the main textbook:

				Bond Payoff	
Number of Defaults	Proba	Total Payoff	Tranche1	Tranche2	Tranche3
0	0.512	3000	1500	800	700
1	0.384	2520	1500	800	220
2	0.096	2040	1500	540	0
3	0.008	1560	1500	60	0
Price			1426.844	731.6096	421.2805
Yield			0.05	0.089365	0.507781
Default probability			0.00	0.104	0.488
Average recovery rate			1	0.628846	0.247307

(b) The default probability for the senior tranche is zero. Even if all three bonds default, we can recover enough money from the three bonds to pay off the senior tranche in full.

9.

				Bond Payoff	
Number of Defaults	Proba	Total Payoff	Tranche1	Tranche2	Tranche3
0	0.8	3000	1500	800	700
1	0	2520	1500	800	220
2	0	2040	1500	540	0
3	0.2	1560	1500	60	0
Price			1426.844	620.2016	532.6885
Yield			0.05	0.254567	0.273144
Default probability			0.2	0.2	0.2
Average recovery rate			1	0.075	0

10. The difficult part of this exercise is to simulate correlated default events. Here is one possibility. Draw three correlated standard normal variables using the Cholesky decomposition that you learned in Chapter 19. Then, you can use the following if-clause in Excel to determine whether the default for any bond occurred:

=IF(NORMSDIST(Random standard normal variable)>=1 – default probability,1,0)

This results in a cell value of either 0 (no default event) or 1 (default event). Repeat this procedure for all bonds in your portfolio, and sum over all bonds. This gives you the number of defaults per draw. Then, you can define, for example, for the second-to-default bond the following:

= IF(sum of defaults <= 1, 1000 * EXP(-risk-free rate), 520 * EXP(–risk–free rate)).

This is either the present value of the full maturity value ($1000) or the present value of the recovery amount ($520). Here we specify that if there is less than one default, we are paid back the full amount, but for two (or more) defaults, we only get the recovery value back.

We can draw, say, 10,000 simulations and then take averages. This yields the Monte-Carlo price of the 2nd to default bond.

For a correlation coefficient of 0.4, we obtain the following results from the Monte-Carlo simulation:

	First-to-Default	Second-to Default	Third-to-Default
Expected payoff	854.6267	946.2626	988.2285
Price	812.946	900.1128	940.032
Yield	0.207091	0.105235	0.061841